Political Theory
and Modernity

Political Theory and Modernity

WILLIAM E. CONNOLLY

Basil Blackwell

British Library Cataloguing in Publication Data

Connolly, William E.
　　Political theory and modernity.
　　1. Political science — History
　　I. Title
　　320'.01　　JA83
　　ISBN 0–631–15805–7

Library of Congress Cataloging in Publication Data

Connolly, William E.
　　Political theory and modernity.

　　Bibliography: p.
　　Includes index.
　　1. Political science — History.　2. Modernism.
　　I. Title
　　JA83.C636 1987　　320'.01　　87–7151
　　ISBN 0–631–15805–7

Typeset in 10½ on 12 pt Ehrhardt
by Opus, Oxford
Printed in Great Britain by T.J. Press Ltd, Padstow

Contents

Preface

I teach political theory. Among the responsibilities of a political theorist in a Department of Political Science in America is teaching the 'foundational' course in the history of political thought. Because most theorists teach such a course, a small number of classic works in the west has become fashioned into a currency through which the exchange of theoretical ideas about politics occurs in America. To participate in this economy, one needs to acquire its currency. It enables a circulation of thought about circumstances and prospects of the age in which one lives. That is to say, it is a valuable currency.

Any valued currency is guarded by exchequers. In this instance the regulators guard texts, protecting their integrity and eliminating counterfeit readings. Too strict a protectionist policy, though, can depress thought. Perhaps we are witnessing today a modest, 'Keynesian' revolution in the economy of political thought, one that allows its currency to circulate more freely and its thought-folios to become more diversified.

I will not defend my stance to the reading of theoretical texts here. Partly because it is not offered as an exclusive approach, partly because it is best to let the orientation establish or defeat itself in actual readings of particular texts.

But some operative assumptions should be specified at the outset. I read and teach classic political thinkers as if they were interesting strangers who have moved in next door (or down the hall). One engages them, thinks about the conversation for a while, and then returns to continue it at a more refined level. Commentaries on the particular circumstances in which a thinker wrote or, more pertinently, the contexts which give specific meaning to the concepts deployed, are helpful to political thinking of this sort. But they are also insufficient to it. World historical thinkers need not be confined to the context of their thought because, first, thought is itself a creative response to particular conditions irreducible to its preconditions of existence, second, highly creative thinkers transcend and transfigure understandings of their own time, and, third, those in other times and places who use these texts as a prod to their own thought often come to them with questions, interests and anxieties divergent from those which governed the composition of the texts. Thinking is often advanced by lifting theories out of contexts in which they were created.

I seek to introduce a few classic theories to those who have not examined them previously, considering each in comparison to the others and all as visions of the modern way. This agenda means that certain dimensions of each theory must be pursued intensively, for example, the view each projects of the distinction between 'modern' and 'pre-modern' forms of life or the ideals of self and citizenship each deems to be most appropriate to the new world. It means that other dimensions become less salient, for example, the particular debates of the moment in which each thinker was entangled or the organizational details of the regime he endorsed. The objective is to think about unthought contours and assumptions in the present by thinking with and against a diverse set of modern political thinkers.

To pursue this object is to ponder some questions these thinkers posed more sharply than many do today, partly because the world they lived in had not yet buried them so deeply beneath a sediment of settled answers. To what extent, for example, is the free and responsible individual a creation of modern order or, alternatively, a universal which modern orders are distinctively designed to recognize? Is the idealization of the self as a subject (or agent or individual) tied more tightly to the claims of the self against the order or to the claims of the order against the self? What role does faith play in particular conceptions of reason, and what political constraints are required to keep the faith? What modes of being must be shuffled out of life to enable a particular set of modern achievements to be?

Finally, it is advisable to pose some questions to them, singly and in contrived pairings, which they may not have posed so acutely to themselves. How do probable and possible futures projected by each thinker appear when viewed from the perspective of contemporary actualities and possibilities? Are there undebated commonalities that frame debates and contests between these thinkers? In what ways might opposing assumptions between conflicting perspectives engender or complement each other? What do subversive elements in these theories reveal about how and why elements of life are subordinated in modern political discourse?

There is a fundamental respect in which Hobbes, Rousseau, Hegel and Nietzsche together enable thought about the contours of a contemporary world none anticipated fully. For each pushes thought into territory more modest thinkers avoid, and each reveals how thought is impoverished when it fails to think relentlessly, say, about the relations between a theory of knowledge and a mode of political reflection or the relation between an explicit theory of self and an implicit conception of nature.

One cannot, for instance, think very determinately about politics by subjecting a few familiar concepts to analysis. The analysis will either be very porous and general – thus susceptible to a variety of fillings – or it will, reluctantly perhaps, evolve into a new instance of theory in the classic tradition. For concepts move within theories, and to delineate a particular concept of freedom, or justice or power properly one is drawn eventually into elucidation of an entire theory. A political theory worth its salt draws an entire network of elements into its frame: it offers readings of divinity, nature, selfhood, language, gender, class, knowledge, the common good, the relations among past, present and future, and politics. Its categorizations may well exceed or scramble this list. But each articulation of a particular element, once it becomes stabilized, enables and confines the space in which other elements can be defined. The elements of a theory thus engender and delimit each other. And the greatest thinkers give food for thought by displaying new areas of thought to be digested if we seek to replicate, criticize or refine the thinking they make available. To study thinkers of the first rank is to learn how political thinking proceeds. There is no superior way.

It can never suffice to study one thinker alone. If one learns Hobbes or Marx alone, one learns nothing much about political thinking. For to think with and against Hobbes, one needs to engage other thinkers of similar stature, preferably living in other times or places, who pose questions and offer disparate findings at a similar level of profundity. These points of consonance and dissonance between disparate thinkers loosen the sediment in one's mind. But must one, then, study an indefinite number of thinkers from a wide diversity of eras in order to think deeply? Probably. But perhaps a compromise can be forged, at least temporarily. Perhaps thought about late-modernity can be advanced by considering a smaller number of thinkers commonly thought to be located at different ends of one or another spectrum of thought. Perhaps we can think critically about the way spectra are fixed today and how thought is distributed across them by studying what divides and unites the theories balanced on each edge. That is the strategy I pursue in this text. I try to foment thought about the character and prospects of late-modernity by examining four thinkers who articulate distinctive positions on these issues and by considering less thoroughly two others who provide counterpoints to them. I have selected Hobbes, Rousseau, Hegel and Nietzsche for primary attention, and Sade and Marx for secondary treatment, not because of any intrinsic ranking of the thinkers, but because, first, I have thought about these issues through the medium of these thinkers, and, second, they seem to me to provide a promising way to lift thought to the conditions and prospects of late-modernity.

It is probably true that the greatest political treatises contain critiques of their own themes. The richest thinkers subvert every attempt to fix their texts with a single reading. Does Rousseau not, for instance, express doubts in some places about the religious faith he endorses and defines as necessary to the general will in others? Yes. But if we rivet our attention, not on Rousseau the individual, but on the Rousseauian theory of the general will, these doubts and ambivalences become material for critical reflections concerning the theory itself. What is in the first context an appreciation of the richness and ambivalence of an individual thinker becomes in the second a critical reading of the structure and requirements of a theory. I will try to state the conditions of Hobbesian sovereignty, the Rousseauian general will, the Hegelian ideal of the realized state; I will explore the credibility of the assumptions and aspirations which sustain these theories; and I will then ask how critical examination of these ideals helps us to reconsider implicit assumptions and demands lodged in contemporary patterns of thought.

Finally, an apology. While I have profited from a variety of texts about the theories considered in this volume, I have not recorded such debts in the main body of this study nor responded directly to competing accounts of the classic texts examined. I find it impossible to pursue the first course without becoming entangled in the second. And the pursuit of both together would render this text too diffuse, drawing it too far away from its introductory mission and its critical engagement with the central texts to be examined. I have tried to compensate for the losses flowing from this decision by appending an annotated bibliography which specifies some of the debts and disagreements accumulated in this study.

This text has grown out of courses in which these themes were pursued. So my most pervasive debt is to graduate and undergraduate students at the University of Massachusetts and the Johns Hopkins University, respectively, who participated with me either in courses about these thinkers or in seminars in which contemporary texts about the structure of modernity were explored. In the latter seminars we studied Martin Heidegger, Michel Foucault, Hans Blumenberg, Charles Taylor and Tzvetan Todorov. Their influences are present in this study, even when they did not deal directly with the texts examined here. I would like to thank the Institute for Advanced Study, where I was a member during 1986–7, for providing me with time and support to finish this text and the National Endowment For the Humanities for funding my year at the Institute. I am thoroughly indebted to Jane Bennett, who read each of these chapters in its first draft, and to Richard Flathman, Steven Johnston, Thomas Eagles, Sanford Levinson, Bonnie Honig, Tracy Strong, Sheldon Wolin, Thomas Dumm, Sidney Maskit and Michael Shapiro for reading first drafts of selected chapters.

1

The Order of Modernity

The modern frame

Livy, the Roman historian, identified a dilemma plaguing his age: 'In our times we can neither endure our faults nor the means of correcting them.' And Hegel, as we shall see, located the dissipation of the Greek world in its inability to endure its own impulse to self-consciousness. Is late-modernity, then, the time when we can neither correct the modern drive to organize the world nor endure its consequences?

Or perhaps modernity is the epoch in which the destruction of the world followed the collective attempt to master it. That would make it unique at least, even if a few thinkers poised on the edge of other epochs thought the world itself was coming to an end. It might also call the modern project of mastery into question.

Even if modernity is not unique (it is too early to tell), it is at least distinctive. In its optimistic moments it defines itself by contrast to earlier periods which are darker, more superstitious, less free, less rational, less productive, less civilized, less comfortable, less democratic, less tolerant, less respectful of the individual, less scientific and less developed technically than it is at its best. Its opponents often endorse these differentiations while grading them differently. Modernity has lost a world of rich tradition, a secure place in the order of being, a well-grounded morality, a spiritual sensibility, an appreciation of hierarchy, an attunement to nature; and these vacated places have been filled by bureaucracy, nationalism, rampant subjectivism, an all-consuming state, a consumer culture, a commercialized world or, perhaps, a disciplinary society. If defenders and critics of modernity mimic people in other times and places in defining its own ways as special, the particular sets of items in the modern lexicon are different enough from those celebrated or decried in other cultures. The very persistence of these items and the contrasts they invoke reveal a distinctively modern mode of consciousness available for examination. This remains true even if the contrasts invoked falsify the alternative ways of life to which they refer.

Inside these different assessments of the modern condition are common understandings of its structural characteristics. Modernity is an epoch with no well-defined beginning or end; but once consolidated it gives modern articulations to persistent questions of meaning, the relation of human life to nature, the relation of the present to the past and the future, the form of a well-grounded order, and the relation of life to death.

It is not that there is a single set of modern answers to such questions. Far from it. Each particular response is under constant attack from alternative perspectives. It is more that modern debates have a distinctive character. They are well framed. If each element in modernity has been present, in some form or other, in other times and places, the ways in which they intersect establish a loosely bounded field upon which modern discourse proceeds. We might locate that field if we can grasp how certain debates grow upon it while other possibilities fail to take root. We might begin to understand it if we can see how certain adversaries sustain each other, how each keeps itself alive through its success in defining and maintaining its adversary.

In modernity, the insistence upon taking charge of the world comes into its own. Nature becomes a set of laws susceptible to human knowledge, a deposit of resources for potential use or a set of vistas for aesthetic appreciation. While each of these orientations jostles with the others for priority, they all tend to place nature at the disposal of humanity. Human and non-human nature become material to work on. The world loses its earlier property as a text upon which the will of God is inscribed and through which humans can come to a more profound understanding of their proper place in the order of things. But, ironically, in a world governed by the drive for mastery, any absence of control is experienced as unfreedom and imposition: the experiences of alienation, estrangement, repression, authoritarianism, depression, underdevelopment, intolerance, powerlessness and discrimination thereby become extended and intensified in modern life. The drive to mastery intensifies the subordination of many, and recurrent encounters with the limits to mastery make even masters feel constrained and confined. These experiences in turn accelerate drives to change, control, free, organize, produce, correct, order, empower, rationalize, liberate, improve and revolutionize selves and institutions.

Modern agencies form and reform, produce and reproduce, incorporate and reincorporate, industrialize and reindustrialize. In modernity, modernization is always under way. Even its latest self-critical fashions, such as 'post-modernism,' are rapidly refashioned into elements within it. The ambiguous legacy of the term 'modern' supports this perpetual process of self-critique and absorption. In its earlier meaning it meant that which is new or now, usually as a loss of the old; onto that was grafted the sense of that which differentiates an entire way of being from earlier, 'medieval' and 'ancient' ways life. Since modernity has lasted a few centuries some of the ways it initially differentiated itself from the past have now become rather old and stale. So what is at first beyond the pale of the old-modern typically becomes absorbed into the modern as part of its perpetual newness, its eternal coming into being. The aspiration to become post-modern is one of the paradigmatic ways to be modern.

If modernity strives to perfect agencies of change and progress, the locus, the ends and the means of agency become objects of debate. Is the self as subject (or person or individual) to be the privileged site of agency? Or is the state, the community, the class, the people to provide that site? Is the individual to be a bearer of rights and knowledge or to be assimilated to a larger agency through the medium of virtue, language, discipline or faith? Is knowledge of history and the self to be established in the same way as knowledge of nature or are these two distinct fields of knowledge? Is freedom to be understood negatively as the absence of restraints to behavior or positively as the provision of supports for self-realization? Is value to be defined by utility or rights? Is order to be based on techniques of discipline or contractual agreement between minimally defined selves or communicative modes of consensus?

Individualism and community, realism and idealism, the public interest and the common good, technocracy and humanism, positive and negative freedom, utility and rights, empiricism and rationalism, liberalism and collectivism, capitalism and socialism, democracy and totalitarianism – all grow up together within the confines of modernity. The fundamental importance of these differences must be comprehended in conjunction with an appreciation of how they establish and delimit each other upon the field of modern discourse.

Only to the extent we can map the terrain upon which these modern debates occur can we hope to open up possibilities of thought these very debates obscure. And to open up new possibilities of thought is to extend one essential dimension of freedom. If the quest for freedom as self-consciousness is among the defining characteristics of modernity, as Hegel and Marx think it is, the very idea of modernity expresses the aspiration to articulate the container into which its own discourse has been poured. The aspiration to delineate the frame of modernity is a paradigmatic idea of the modern age.

Modernity, then, is an epoch in which a set of contending understandings of self, responsibility, knowledge, rationality, nature, freedom and legitimacy have established sufficient presence to shuffle other possible perspectives out of active consideration. The room to maneuver allotted to each of the terms in this lexicon helps to demarcate the space within which the others may vary. Thus if one seeks to rethink radically dominant theories of the self, one is called into court for failing to live up to established theories of freedom or responsibility; if one seeks to rethink dominant understandings of nature, those thoughts are jeopardized by the effects they engender for established understandings of the modern self as a subject. Some modernists seek to discern the frame within which modernity is set, but many of its worried defenders condemn efforts to extend thought in this way as 'unthinkable,' 'self-contradictory,' 'self-defeating,' 'perverse' or 'mad.' These accusations may occasionally indicate the limits of the thinkable as such; but they may also disclose, darkly and imperfectly, boundaries within which modern discourse is contained.

To characterize this condition is not automatically to decry it. Maybe the modern frame, formed after experience with flaws in earlier frames, is the best available to humanity. Moreover, thought can go nowhere if it is undisciplined by some set of accepted constraints. And yet, in troubled times it may be imperative to try to push thought to the edge of those boundaries that give it its form. It may be important, however unlikely it is that the attempt will meet with complete success, to try to rethink the conceptions of self, truth, nature and freedom which bound modern discourse.

In our times we can neither endure our thoughts nor the task of rethinking them. We think restlessly within familiar frameworks to avoid thought about how our thinking is framed. Perhaps that is the ground of *modern* thoughtlessness. And perhaps that condition is linked to two others: in modern times the debate over how to master the world engulfed the one over whether to do so, while the dangers accompanying the project of mastery became most discernible just when the institutional structures of modernity became most tightly locked into this project.

The positions which occupy privileged sites within modern discourse cannot be presented on a list. They might, though, be apprehended indirectly and imperfectly through a comparison of divergent texts of the most profound quality which, in their very diversity, help to reveal the field upon which they stand together. It may be, as I think it is, that a few classical texts exhibit beautifully the small set of alternative patterns into which modern conceptions of self, freedom and order can be woven.

After this set has been iterated, compromise and reiteration set in, relieved no doubt by singularity of nuance and emphasis. It may be, as well, that within that set a smaller subset, selected because of the purity, reach and originality of each, can provide a series of markers by which to comprehend other theories on the field. These are the sorts of consideration that govern my selection of Hobbes, Rousseau, Hegel and Nietzsche as the primary theorists to be explored in this book. Each constitutes a type of theory to which others must appeal or strive to repeal if they are to participate in modern political discourse.

But how are we to interrogate such texts? If we sink each into its specific historical context, much of what is most important about it as an exemplar of modern discourse becomes submerged. If we treat these texts together as participants in a universal conversation in which each party provides different answers to the same timeless questions, we will miss distinctive features which might constitute the modern epoch. If we examine them, consciously or unconsciously, solely from the perspective of current debates and beliefs, we will surely end by congratulating ourselves for having advanced so far beyond them.

This problem of perspective assumes the appearance of a dilemma. If our debates are framed, how could we think outside that which enframes us? If we can think outside the frame, how could it be said that our debates are lodged within it? The dilemma would be complete if the metaphor of a frame were pursued relentlessly (probably issuing in a quest for the Great Framer), if it were not the case that modernity has emerged historically from other types of society which differed from it, and if modern conceptions lacked the historical porosity, density and ambiguity needed to stretch them beyond their established valences. But even in these less extreme circumstances the problem is severe enough. Perhaps we should focus initially on thinkers who were conscious of living on a boundary between ages and whose thought contained a series of stresses and tensions reflective of the attempt to think in such unsettled circumstances. If we concentrate on what Hobbes and Rousseau had to contain or overcome to bring their thinking into alignment with the modern world they partly lived in and partly anticipated, we may encounter elements in their thought which have tended to be occluded or domesticated by later political thought. Perhaps, in addition, we can approach the boundaries of modern thought by striving to apply an alien perspective to exactly those presuppositions and assumptions that adversaries in late-modern discourse tend to share.

To comprehend modernity, we need points of contrast and comparison of some generality. Surely 'medieval society' and 'the ancient world' are indispensable contrasts here. But what if we supplement these contrasts with those devised by a thinker to cope exactly with the dilemma of thinking outside the frame that enframes? What if we consult the thought of a thinker who posed the question of how 'to think around one's own corner'? Friedrich Nietzsche sought to interrogate modernity from the perspective of imaginary points in the future, and he developed a set of rhetorical strategies designed to loosen the aura of necessity and sanctity surrounding categories of the present. Nietzsche aspired to call modernity into question without either lapsing into nostalgia for one of the worlds it has lost or postulating a future utopia where we could finally reach a 'home in the world.'

It would be pernicious to examine classic modern texts without striving to engage each on its own terms. None would be allowed to challenge presuppositions and demands we cling to unconsciously. But this injunction identifies a corollary reason not to restrict oneself to an 'internal' reading of such texts. For these modern theorists cling too. We must therefore supplement internal readings of these texts with external interrogations if we hope to bring modern thought closer to the frame in which it is set.

Since Nietzsche is the thinker who strives insistently to disrupt the flow of modern thought, we will allow him to pose questions to the other texts they might not have posed so distinctly to themselves. That will not provide us with a neutral perspective from which to pursue the inquiry. None of the other orientations do that either. It might, though, enable us to discern affinities and commonalities among these divergent theories, alerting us to places in contemporary debates where assumptions and insistences quietly hold discourse together.

We will treat these four thinkers as if they were engaged in critical conversations with each other. And we will occasionally allow the latest thinker on the list to pose disturbing questions to the first three, focusing on those which his predecessors posed less starkly, or openly or persistently to themselves. This interrogative mode enables the texts to speak to our condition; it is guided by the thought of the thinkers investigated but not always by those aspirations and assumptions each insisted upon the most strenuously. Indeed, where insistence becomes most intense that is where appreciative exegesis must convert itself into skeptical interrogation.

None of these exemplary thinkers was gentle with opposing thinkers of note. For that matter, few contemporary advocates of contextualization, appreciative interpretation or immanent critique are generous with those who do not accept the universality of their favourite mode. This suggests that interrogation is one of the ways thinking proceeds when it seeks to unsettle settled patterns of thought.

A madman speaks

Aphorism 125 of *The Gay Science* presents a madman running into the marketplace crying 'I seek God! I seek God!' Those standing around, including unbelievers, are amused. They laugh and shout. 'Has he got lost...? Did he lose his way like a child? Has he gone on a voyage?'[1]

Nietzsche, who introduces the death of God as an interpretation of the modern condition and counsels us to affirm life in this new world without God or the vestigial beliefs through which he continues to haunt us, suggests that neither believers nor atheists quite understand what has happened. The 'pale' atheist finds the ravings of the madman to be amusing. He insists that God can drop out of the world without anything else changing fundamentally. The believer, on the other hand, glimpses something of the role God plays in life, but he does not yet discern how God's previous place in the world has been displaced.

It takes a marginal being, one not at home in the everyday world of education, leisure, business and culture, to announce this condition. A madman must make the announcement. And he is incited by this amusement and complacency.

'Whither is God?' he cried; 'I will tell you. *We have killed him – you and I.* All of us are his murderers... Who gave us the sponge to wipe away the entire horizon? What were we doing when we unchained the earth from its sun? Whither is it moving now?... Are we not plunging continually? Backward, sideward, forward, in all directions? Is there still any up or down?'[2]

The madman does not say that the proofs for God's existence have been disproven. He does not refute the 'ontological proof' of God's existence or the 'argument from design.' He says that God is dead. He no longer lives in the world. Indeed the minute that belief in God's existence turns on the possibility of human demonstration, he has already been killed. For would not the attempt of a finite being to prove the existence of an infinite one necessarily reduce the latter to the proportions of the former?

God lived in a culture in which assumptions about nature, knowledge, self, the past and language made room for him to be. Medieval culture, for instance, was not a monolith in which one global understanding of God and the world swamped all others. The nominalist movement, to be discussed later, reveals the extent of diversity in the philosophical culture of this period. But there was, nonetheless, ample room within its diversity for many to experience the world as enchanted, to discern,

darkly and obscurely, the will of God in the things, words, deeds and
events of the world. God lived in that world, not just in the sense that
people could have faith in a divine being, but in the sense that the will of
God shone through the ethics, politics, language and culture of the day.
As Paracelsus enunciated it late in the day, everything in the world is
bound up with everything else through chains of resemblance, and our
participation in this divinely inspired world of harmonies, correspond-
ences and resemblances is enhanced to the degree we come to
understand our place in them and to govern our conduct in accord with
resonances we receive from them:

The inner stars of man are, in their properties, kind, and nature, by their course
and position, like his outer stars, and different only in form and in material . . .
For the sun and the moon and all planets, as well as all the stars and the whole
chaos, are in man . . . Man consists of the four elements, not only – as some
hold – because he has four tempers, but also because he partakes of the nature,
essence, and properties of these elements. In him there lies the 'young heaven',
that is to say, all the planets are part of man's structure.[3]

God inscribed his will in this text and humans could read it. Thus, in
one common reading, knowledge consisted in bringing out the
harmonies residing in the world and in bringing human experience of the
world into alignment with God's Word as expressed in sacred texts from
the past. This sacred past obtained privilege over the present. And words
themselves bore a divine inscription: to glimpse their true meaning
through commentary on sacred texts was to move a little closer to God's
will and to the hope of salvation. Authority, then, resided in the text of
the world; on this field of discourse it was not feasible to treat words as
human instruments or to separate 'facts' from 'values.'

Medieval music and art attuned themselves to God's presence in the
world. They expressed and clarified the harmony of the world. Consider
an example from the twelfth century, drawn from Emile Male's text
Religious Art in France. In the 'Garden of Delights,' drawn in the twelfth
century, the will of God is revealed in the harmonies of his world. In one
of its miniatures the earth stands motionless with seven planets revolving
around it in concentric circles. Then an image of man is revealed 'in his
nakedness as he was created by the hands of God.'

Around him are representations of the four elements: fire and air, water and
earth. Man is formed of their harmonious union: his flesh of the nature of the
earth, his blood of the nature of water, his breath of the nature of air, his bodily
warmth of the nature of fire . . . Man is not only a summary of the world; he is
also its image. The round shape of his head recalls the world's sphere; its seven

openings, which are seven ways open to the senses, recall the seven planets which adorn the sky.[4]

Everything in the world is a sign, and the will to knowledge is the quest to read in each sign something of the larger pattern of harmonies, thereby moving a little closer to the will of the great Harmonizer. But this means that even monstrous things and events are signs. Natural catastrophes and human madness are among them. The madman falls away from man as the imperfect image of God on earth, but, as a created being, he also reveals something of the mystery surrounding the puny strands of understanding connecting humans to God. Madness becomes an inherently ambiguous phenomenon: a created monstrosity, an inarticulate profundity. The mad, as Shakespeare understood, revealed profound truths which could not be received clearly by other humans because they escaped the thin skin of human discourse. As Nietzsche says in a later aphorism, 'in an earlier time [experiences] shone differently because a God shone through them ... "Truth" was experienced differently, for the insane could be accepted formerly as its mouthpiece – which makes *us* shudder or laugh.'[5] To laugh at the madman is to verify that God no longer shines through the monstrosities of the world. Monstrosities are no longer signs of mystery.

It is no longer necessary or feasible for madness to bear truth ambiguously when Nietzsche's madman runs into the marketplace because the enchanted world of harmonies has now disappeared. Madness is now only a repository of unreason: a defect but not a sign. But this new orientation to the enunciations of madness becomes itself a sign of sorts when it is understood in relation to previous incarnations of madness. If God no longer shines through madness, it is because the divine light itself has been extinguished from the world. To laugh at the announcement of the madman is to reveal unwittingly the truth of his proclamation. God is dead. Not in the sense that it is impossible for individuals to have faith in God, but in the sense that a common faith anchored in a common set of experiences can no longer secure and protect itself from widespread revisionism, skepticism, doubt and unbelief. Modern madness is one of the signs of his death.

We killed God when we disenchanted the old world, when, for instance, we redefined the meaning and bearing of madness. And we displaced the old world because, as we shall see in the next chapter, it contained contradictions which could be borne no longer once they became apparent.

But what is lost if God is lost to the world? Well, first the hope of eternal salvation becomes even more precarious, though individuals can continue to cling to faith in an abstract God detached from the world of signs. Second, moral authority lodged in a divine will disappears: individuals and groups can ground their diverse moralities in faith, but God no longer serves as the unified center of a common morality. The old aspiration to ground a common ethic in the will of a shared God now fades into an empty yearning. But the death of God reaches still more deeply into the bowels of the world. The earth has become 'unchained . . . from its sun.' The word of the madman carries an ontological message.

If the world is not God's creation, truth is jeopardized. For, Nietzsche contends, the correspondence theory of truth, the theory that defines true statements to be those that 'correspond' to the way the world is in itself, is a thinly veiled theology. If the world is not designed by a creator, it is very unlikely that human capacities for cognition will correspond to the way the world is in itself or that the shape of the world will correspond to the human ability to know it. In an uncreated world the very possibility of co-respondence between a knowing self and a world to be known depends upon an improbable coincidence of human capacity with worldly structure. No pre-design of knowing self and known world ensures the coincidence sought. The will to knowledge is likely to encounter that which does not articulate smoothly with the categories imposed upon it. Once the import of the death of God becomes apparent to those who killed him, the 'will to truth' will appear as the will to impose human form upon the world and then to treat the imposition as if it were a discovery. The more tenacious that will is the more insistent it will have to be in making the world over to fit into its capacities for knowing and the more ruthless it will have to be with those people, actions and events deemed by it to be abnormal, irrational, perverse, unnatural or anomalous. In a world without a divine designer knowing is not a correspondence but an imposition of form upon the objects of knowledge. Or so Nietzsche says.

Other theories of truth now become problematic too. The 'coherence' and 'consensus' theories still impose the demand that truth be one, that a doctrine or theory not be treated as true unless it is the only one that meets the established standard of truth. They insist that the world must not be structured so that two or more readings in the same domain are equally able to render it intelligible to humanity. But if the world were not created, and if it did not mesh neatly with human capacities for cognition, why might not every human theory encounter slippage and undecidability in its structure? And where is the locus of truth if there is no God to bear it? It cannot be in the world itself, for these latter theories of truth shift the locus of truth from world to theory. They contest the correspondence theory, but they share its insistence that truth be one. Even the pragmatic theory strives to measure up to this standard. But the necessity of the standard stems from its residual connection to a creationist ontology; it becomes a mere yearning or demand once unchained from that ontology.

The death of God, by breaking the link between world and creation, unchains humanity from truth. The pale atheist, seeking stability and control in this life, perhaps to compensate for the loss of eternal life, inflates truth as he deflates God. But this inflation signifies a failure to explore the implications of the death he seeks to celebrate. The secularist retains faith in truth. It is a disguised faith. It is a 'bad-faith' of the sort that spawns the modern enterprises of critical theory and genealogy, games in which secular theories are unsettled by showing how their enunciations at one level presuppose a set of beliefs they purport to have outgrown at another.

This is the *modern* faith that Nietzsche hunts down, as it lodges itself silently inside theories of truth, individuality, morality, language, sovereignty, community and the common good. Its modernity resides in its ambiguous status as a demand for external guarantees inside a culture that has erased the ontological preconditions for them. Modernity is thus an epoch of secret insistence jeopardized by its own legacy of truthfulness and honesty: its bearers demand that every hidden faith be exposed, but faith is necessary to ground the superiority of modern life. Modernity thus spawns the critical theories and genealogies many of its defenders decry.

Think of the role that those modest metaphors 'up' and 'down' play in stabilizing modern discourse. 'Up' is positive, better, lighter, more intelligent, more spiritual. I'm up. He is in the upper class. This is a real upper. That is a high-level performance. She is a high authority. 'Down' is negative, depressed, animal, heavy, dumb. That was a low blow. I'm down today. She has bottomed out. Do these metaphors presuppose divinity, heaven and earth, higher spirituality and lower animality, closeness to and distance from God? If so, the death of God, once its implications are traced, could realign or decimate these directionalities. The death of God infects metaphor as well as reality, and, once one ponders carefully the issue of truth in relation to the metaphorical character of discourse, as Nietzsche certainly did, this infection in established metaphorical directionality spreads to everything else. It infects, for instance, the discursive distinction between the metaphorical and the real. 'Is there,' the madman asks, 'still any up or down?'

The implications of God's death, spread in all directions at once. The madman's announcement is made to those who live 'under' this cloud, but who have not yet looked 'up' to see what has happened. 'This tremendous event is still on its way, still wandering; it has not yet reached the ears of men . . . This deed is still more distant from them than the most distant stars – and yet they have done it themselves.'[6]

Only when 'they' work out the implications residing within modern culture, including its own demand to uncover every secret and to expose every lie, will they finally discern the clouds gathering above them.

Modernity and nihilism

Nietzsche is to modernity as the madman is to the marketplace. The messenger of nihilism, the one who gives the word that modern values devalue themselves, is treated by his audience either as mad or as the agent of an evil doctrine alien to them. Nietzsche would be the fool (or madman) of modernity, carrying a message that cuts against the grain of its insistence, calling upon it to affirm the earthiness of its earthly constructs, exposing it to the danger and destructiveness that reside within its highest ideals, counselling it to affirm them as human constructs and nothing less. But in the modern age the space for the fool has been squeezed out. The interlocutors of the messenger double as judges of normality. In modernity, dissent is often valued. But the fool courts insanity.

Nonetheless the messenger speaks, in a voice that strikes more responsive chords in readers living through the last decade of the twentieth century than it did for Nietzsche's contemporaries in the late nineteenth century. If the deed was once 'still distant' to those who had 'done it themselves,' it is now closer to us:

What I relate [in 1888] is the history of the next two centuries. I describe what is coming, what can no longer come differently: *the advent of nihilism* . . . This future speaks even now in a hundred signs . . . For some time now, our whole European culture has been moving as toward a catastrophe, with a tortured tension that is growing from decade to decade: restlessly, violently, headlong like a river that wants to reach the end, that no longer reflects, that is afraid to reflect.[7]

Why has the advent of nihilism become necessary? Because the history of western culture is driven by the insistence to found a world which fulfills our wish, either in this life or afterlife, to be at one with ourselves and the world, and because that insistence has spawned a second desire that the new world be grounded in a certain, external source: in God or (when that becomes incredible) in the dictates of universal reason, or the light of nature, or the contractual agreement of rational individuals, or the rational consensus of virtuous citizens, or the categories of a transcendental subject or the *telos* of history.

Nihilism – the will to ground value in the name of something higher – is the will to ground value in nothingness. When it becomes too difficult to deny this connection between transcendence and nothingness we have the 'advent' of nihilism. But the culture that eventually necessitates the advent of nihilism was established much earlier. Modern necessity is lodged in the earlier Christian demand to have a single, omnipotent God, in love with humanity, offering hope of salvation, and demanding universal obedience to his will. When that God is weakened, when the faith of individual believers must be intensified to compensate for the contraction of cultural space for a common faith, the advent of nihilism occurs. For now attempts to find a supplement or a substitute for the common faith run into grave difficulties while the insistence that such a substitute must be found remains intact. Each theory of substitution finds it all too possible to undermine the credibility of its competitors, but each also finds it all too difficult to sustain its own affirmations against the critiques of its opponents.

The efforts to fend off nihilism, to ward off its signs in the new world, spawn great violence and subjugation. The external signs are provided by the extension and intensification of new wars between states; the internal signs reside in the extension of standards of normality into new corners of the society and the individual. Madness, for instance, now becomes insanity. This is Nietzsche's reading, anyway: we 'move toward catastrophe, with a tortured tension . . . like a river that wants to reach the end.'

The advent of nihilism can be warded off once God is dead, but (to use an economic metaphor suited to the occasion) the price is high. Suppose, as Nietzsche invites us to, that the world contains no design, that the human animal requires social form to be while every particular social form enables it in some ways and disables it others, that the world is indifferent to human designs and resistant to our attempts to mold it to the heart's desire. In these circumstances the quest for a perfectly ordered self and a perfectly ordered world in harmony with each other can be maintained only by defining all conduct and events that differ from these forms as 'otherness.' They become dirt, matter out of place, irrationality, abnormality, waste, sickness, perversity, incapacity, disorder, madness, unfreedom. They become material in need of rationalization, normalization, moralization, correction, punishment, discipline, disposal, realization, etc. The modern quest to ward off the experience of nihilism becomes the drive to force everyone and everything into slots provided by a highly ordered system and to pretend the result is self-realization, the achievement of reason, the attainment of the common good. The advent of nihilism can be delayed by the formation of a highly disciplined self and society. This is Nietzsche's dystopia:

On that first road, which now can be completely surveyed, arise adaptation, leveling, Higher Chinadom, modesty in the instincts, satisfaction in the dwarfing of mankind – *a kind of stationary level of mankind.* Once we possess that common economic management of the earth that will soon be inevitable, mankind will be able to find its best meaning as a machine in the service of the economy – as a tremendous clockwork, composed of ever smaller, every more subtly 'adapted' gears . . . It is clear, what I combat is economic optimism: as if increasing the expenditure of everybody must necessarily involve the increased welfare of everybody.[8]

Modern denial of the advent of nihilism takes the form of organizing the self and the world to fit into a tightly demarcated order and treating everything that does not fit into it to be matter out of place in need of punishment, reform or destruction. We accept the form of a 'clockwork' to preserve the ideal of a natural unity. We accept the ideal of a natural unity to preserve the belief that a higher purpose governs life. The cleaner the ideal, the more dirt it discovers in need of cleansing; the more dirt eliminated, the more the things left behind shine with the glow of organization and discipline. This account exemplifies, then, how Nietzsche brings alien categories to familiar experience, inviting us to see, for instance, humanist advocates of self-realization as unwitting allies of technocratic agencies of social control.

But there are other responses too, responses which embody a certain recognition of nihilism accompanied by the yearning for another world, a world which meshes with the ideals we think it should exemplify. This is passive nihilism, a nihilism of despair and inaction. It is the nihilism of rage against the world because it is not what it would be if it were to give us a secure identity in a beautiful world.

The philosophical nihilist is convinced that all that happens is meaningless and in vain; and that there ought not be anything meaningless and in vain. But whence this: there ought not to be? From where does one get *this* 'meaning,' *this* 'standard'? At bottom, the nihilist thinks that the sight of such a bleak, useless existence makes a philosopher feel *dissatisfied*, bleak, desperate.[9]

The passive nihilist admits the inability to ground his highest values in a transcendent standard, but this admission leads him to devalue this world, to despise the world because it has deserted his ideals. He thought that the world was susceptible only to one interpretation, and now, finding out the defects in that one, he is unable to accept any interpretation as his own. He becomes passive, withdrawn, pessimistic. The passive nihilist thereby renders visible the demand inside the human urge to discover an 'aim,' a 'unity' a 'truth': 'he conceived such a whole *in order to be able to believe in his own value.*'[10]

To work through passive nihilism is to affirm the world and life *because* the modes of completion we experience are human creations. But that is another story. One that encourages us to ask Nietzsche, How can one who denies truth offer such confident formulations himself? What is the truth-status of these formulations about incorrigible dissonance between the world and human cognition? Is it possible to be a Nietzschean and to affirm a common set of standards to govern a way of life? How does or would one distinguish among them?

These are appropriate questions, and we will consider them in a preliminary way in the last chapter. But it is thoughless to demand answers to them too soon. For the very features of Nietzsche's thought which fuel the demand to crush it unless these questions are answered first are those which enable us to pose questions to ourselves which otherwise might slip away. Nietzsche fosters thinking, for those who do not ward him off before thought can proceed. Attentiveness to the Nietzschean mode of interrogation might enable us to identify patterns of insistence in the thought of Hobbes, Rousseau and Hegel; and those identifications might in turn teach us something about the problematic character of demands we automatically impose upon Nietzsche.

I intend to privilege a Nietzschean perspective in this text without endorsing each political pronouncement he made, or insisting that the basic perspective is ultimately beyond reconsideration or pretending that thought should rest here once and for all. For if the Nietzschean critique weakens the hold of these alternative theories, its own interrogation needs to come from a different direction. Perhaps Heidegger or Foucault rather than, say, Hegel or Marx or Habermas or Rawls will emerge as the most profound interrogators of Nietzsche after we have considered a Nietzschean interrogation of Hobbes, Rousseau and Hegel. For by considering the latter from the vantage point of Nietzsche's charges we might come to see how to revise some of the questions we would now pose to Nietzsche and to reconsider some of the standards we would now expect him to meet. And to modify the terms of interrogation is to move the boundaries of political thought.

It is time, then, to examine the case against the accused, or, as Nietzsche might state it: to listen to the nihilists speak.

2

Hobbes: The Politics of Divine Containment

The ontological context

There are many ways to set the background to a thinker of the stature of Hobbes. We could concentrate on the religious controversies, civil wars and struggles between parliament and the monarchy, showing how these events entered into Hobbes's concerns with peace and sovereignty and how they encouraged him to subordinate civil and religious bodies to the authority of the sovereign. That would situate Hobbes historically. But it would not explain his response to those circumstances. Numerous contemporaries of his living in the same circumstances reached quite different conclusions.

Perhaps we should pay close attention to interpretations of his thought offered by his own contemporaries, for they seem to be in an excellent position to understand him. But they disagreed with each other, and many of them accused him of atheistic beliefs he denied. There may be good independent reason to think that those accusations were themselves politically motivated, but we cannot judge whether these political motivations distorted or revealed the thought of Hobbes until we have examined the thought itself. At any rate we do have a warning from Hobbes, itself politically motivated, about the particular axes wielded by some of the critics of *De Cive*:

These things I found most bitterly excepted against. That I had made the civil powers too large; but this by ecclesiastical persons. That I had utterly taken away liberty of conscience; but this by sectaries. That I had set princes above the civil laws; but this by lawyers. Wherefore I was not much moved by these men's reprehensions, as who in doing this, did but do their own business; except it were to tie those knots somewhat faster.[1]

Perhaps we should examine his personal life. Although there is a paucity of documents available, we do know that his father was a rural clergyman, apparently a 'choleric drunkard' who left home after an altercation and difficulty with the law when Hobbes was very young; we also know that Hobbes remained single his entire life, that he lived a remarkably long life (1588–1679), that he had eccentric ideas about health some of which have now become more common (he exercised regularly, sang to keep his lungs healthy, and stopped eating red meat in middle age), that he was supported by a patron and was generally disliked by scholars in the universities, that he was excessively cautious about his physical welfare but courageous in the articulation of unpopular ideas. Some commentators might try to explain his apparent ambivalence toward religion and civil authority in terms of his probable ambivalence toward his father; but, even if he was in fact ambivalent toward his father, there are innumerable ways that orientation could find expression in life. A thinker might express consistent piety toward religious and secular authorities in print while showing hostility in other settings; or that pattern might be reversed; or both sides might find expression in the texts; or it might be outgrown; etc.

Perhaps it is useful to examine the way in which Hobbes's contemporaries and near contemporaries influenced his thought. It was a time of great intellectual ferment, when ideas received from an earlier period were undergoing radical reconstitution. René Descartes, Francis Bacon, Galileo and William Harvey are viable candidates here. But there were many more conventional thinkers of the day who did not stand in this relation to Hobbes – one would have to explain why orientations represented on this first list were selected by Hobbes rather than those on the second. And perhaps Hobbes was responding in his distinctive way to a larger set of developments that influenced other thinkers on the first list as well.

Each of these approaches could be pertinent to understanding the thought of Hobbes and none of them, singly or in combination, could suffice. For thought can be inspired, influenced, restrained by its circumstances, but not determined by them. There are too many ways in which a thinker, especially a thinker of the stature of Hobbes, can stretch the horizon of his times or creatively deploy the ambivalences in his life or redefine the constraints of contemporary debates. Thought has a moment of autonomy that makes it irreducible to the social and personal circumstances in which it arises, even if it cannot be understood well without taking its context of creation into account. Contexts inspire thought; great thinkers are inspired to reconstitute contexts.

In selecting a context through which to understand a great thinker we determine the level at which to approach his thought. None of those listed above reaches the level needed to understand Hobbes in relation to the frame of modernity. We will move closer if we try to understand the ontological setting in which Hobbes thought, a setting which inspired many of his most creative contemporaries as well.

In the last chapter we glanced at medieval and Renaissance interpretations of the world as a set of signs given by God, signs that allowed humans to discern darkly their place in the great chain of being. But this reading did not go unchallenged in the middle ages, and Hobbes, who set himself against Scholastic and Aristotelian modes of thought, profited from these earlier attacks on the dominant tradition. The nominalist tradition, crystallized around the thought of William of Ockham in the fourteenth century, established the challenge most pertinent to the Hobbesian agenda.

Early Christianity had staked itself upon the expectation of the imminent return of Christ to earth and the final resolution of earthly suffering for believers. But the delay of the second coming fomented crisis in its theology, or, perhaps, established the need for a theology that could explain why evil persisted in the world created by an omnipotent and beneficent God. The early Gnostics resolved this issue by positing God as a saviour who was not omnipotent, a saviour in constant struggle with an evil force in the world. But this dualistic solution sacrificed the idea of divine creation (God did not create the world and was thus not responsible for the evil in it) and concentrated Christian attention exclusively on the second coming. To maintain itself in the absence of a second coming Christianity needed to come to terms with this world and to relocate responsibility for evil within it.

The brilliance of Augustine is that he saved God as the omnipotent Creator by relocating responsibility for evil in the world he created. Responsibility for evil was bestowed upon humans, who through the gift of free will were worthy of being held responsible for their own sinfulness. Each sinner was counselled to probe his interior soul to purge it of inevitable temptations. In relocating responsibility for evil Augustine took the most significant step toward the conception of the self as an interiorized subject free and responsible for its own actions. And the relocation also enabled him to condemn Gnosticism as a heresy to be eliminated from Christianity.

But why could not God have created humans with freedom in a world free of evil? The dominant judgment was that this was an impossibility, even for an omnipotent and benevolent God: the perfection of free will for human beings required the existence of evil in the world. But if God had to allow evil to gain free will, does this necessity not reveal a certain limit to his creative powers?

The later medieval synthesis continues this process of coming to terms explicitly with the staying power of the mundane world by implicitly limiting God's power over it. In a world where the second coming was now delayed indefinitely the victory of the benign God realizing a design partially available to human knowledge over the God understood to be utterly mysterious to humans reassured believers about the significance of life and the prospects for salvation. But if the world realizes a set of essential harmonies imperfectly knowable to humans, these harmonies also represent the pinnacle and the limit of God's creative powers. The providential world of signs and harmonies becomes, from another angle, a world which sets restrictions to God's total power.

Nominalism adopts this alternative angle of vision. It emerges in the fourteenth century to save God's omnipotence even at the expense of enlarging the transcendental insecurity of Christian believers. God, the Creator, does not realize a pre-existing world design; for such a pre-design would also restrict his infinite power and knowledge. Nothing except the law of contradiction can be accepted as a limit to God's infinite power. The world God created is thus understood to be a set of contingencies which reflect only God's will; these contingencies could, if he were to will it, be transformed completely in any direction at any moment. God's omnipotence requires the radical contingency of the world.

But nominalism also makes the world of experience very fragile and uncertain; and it erases signs from the world that might give finite human beings clues about its design and God's intentions for them. If God is the pure Creator and the world humans inhabit is merely one contingent possibility among others, and if the organization of existing contingencies must, to save God's unlimited power to create and recreate at will, appear mysterious and arbitrary to finite minds lacking this infinite range of possibilities, then human experience and reason lose their power to glimpse the truth of the world. Words thus lose their expressive power: they become instruments useful for the mundane purpose of getting along in the world. And ethics loses its rational component: human morality becomes simply a response to the commands of God revealed in scripture. Human reason and security are sacrificed to save God's omnipotence.

Ockham's nominalism, called *via moderna* by his followers, is sometimes given an extreme formulation. If God commands us to hate him, we are obligated to obey his command, since we have no independent grounds for doing otherwise. And we cannot have confidence that the world corresponds even to our intuitive (perceptual) knowledge of it. 'Even if a thing has been destroyed the intuitive knowledge of it may be given to us (by God) and no intuitive knowledge is in itself and necessarily the knowledge that something necessarily exists: it may well be of something that does not exist.'[2]

To affirm the possibility of the percept's non-existence is to affirm God's omnipotence, but it is also to make the relation between human beings and the world upon which they stand uncertain and precarious.

Nominalism did point out tensions and contradictions in the medieval synthesis it challenged. It showed how one of its theses (the insistence on divine omnipotence) stood in tension with another (the world as a providential set of harmonies realized through creation and disclosed partially to humanity through signs implanted in it). But nominalism, heralding elements later to emerge in the Enlightenment, contained tensions of its own. Its point was to support unconditional submission to God, but it ran the risk of severing faith so completely from experience of the world that it would become impossible to determine what submission required. The faith that scripture revealed God's basic commands was potentially susceptible to the same corrosive analysis applied by nominalists to reason and perception. For scripture is God's word mediated through finite human believers.

Nominalism saves God's omnipotence by pushing him higher into the heavens, disconnecting him from the reason, experience, texts and signs that make up the mundane world. It thereby sets the table for later secularization: for the judgment that since nature does not contain divine signs there are no divine injunctions against the human quest to master it, for the corollary insistence that, since the world was not designed for human benefit, humans must assert more effective control over it to secure their material needs, for the attempt to shore up human power in this world through consolidation of human subjectivity, reason, technique, organization and civil society, for a devaluation of heaven and a revaluation of nature and human agency. There are some hints of this movement in Ockham's own theory of sovereignty. But in their larger compass these implications were neither intended by nominalists nor drawn by their admirers.

When Nietzsche's madman announces that we have killed God, he means that Christianity first begot an imperfect God implicated in the mundane world and then commanded it to withdraw to a remote outpost to redeem its infinite power. Christianity created an unstable God with self-destructive potentialities. The nominalist critique of the world of divine harmony discloses this instablility.

The light of reason

Hobbes is a nominalist who constructs a political theory. Hence he must attenuate the separation between the agent of infinite power and the powers of finite believers. He must qualify nominalism enough to give sovereignty solid ontological standing; but he must retain it enough first to give the sovereign free rein to define the common rules and second to undercut attempts by discontented subjects to appeal above the sovereign to a higher power. Hobbes walks a tightrope: to keep his balance he must overcome anarchic tendencies in nominalism and Protestantism without falling back into the net of Aristotelianism, Scholasticism, and 'Popism.'

Hobbes's nominalism is apparent enough. He treats words as human artifacts, fixed by definition. Knowledge does not reach to the essence of the world; it is created by humans and resides in a theory which meets the dictates of logic and strict definition. Knowledge of moral rules, like knowledge in mathematics, is a consequence of previous stipulations:

that five shall be the name of so many unities as are contained in two and three taken together . . . this assent shall be called knowledge . . . In like manner if we remember what it is that is called theft, and what injury; we shall understand by the words themselves, whether it be true that theft is an injury or not.[3]

Moreover, finite reason cannot bring us to a close knowledge of God. God is mysterious to finite beings:

No shape therefore must be assigned to God, for all shape is finite; nor must he be said to be conceived or comprehended by imagination, or any other faculty of our soul; for whatsoever we conceive is finite . . . For when we say that a thing is infinite we signify nothing really, but the impotency of our own mind.[4]

But human knowledge of God's will must be more extensive than pure nominalism allowed. There are two basic ways, Hobbes contends, that moderns can have access to God's will: through God's word revealed in scripture and through natural reason. Consider the link between the will of God and human reason:

it can further be asked how one can know what things God hath commanded. To this question it can be replied, God himself, because he hath made men rational, hath enjoined the following law on them, and hath inscribed it in all hearts: no one shall do unto another that which he should consider inequitable for the other to do to him.[5]

And again: '*Natural* is that which God hath declared to all men by his *eternal world* born with them, to wit, their *natural reason* . . .'[6]

Key interrelationships in Hobbesian theory among reason, sovereignty, the commands of God and the laws of nature can be extrapolated from these two formulations: a law is binding because it has been commanded by the right authority; civil laws are issued by sovereign command; the law of nature is issued by the command of God; and we 'can know what things God hath commanded' through 'natural reason' itself given to us by God.

Hobbes is a rationalist, but his rationalism is necessarily sustained by faith, faith that the 'light' of reason is 'given' by God, faith that the 'dictates' of right reason reveal God's commands to humanity.

Reason for Hobbes is hypothetical reason (if you want x then do y), and it is more than hypothetical reason: it is also the human window onto the will of God. We cannot know God in all his infinite power through finite reason, but we do know his commands for us through that instrumentality. Hobbes has faith in reason, and his rationalism is connected to the world and to God's will through faith.

But if this is correct, further questions arise. Why should we believe that the findings of reason and revelation actually reveal God's will? Why, as nominalists think possible and as Descartes pretends to test, might not an omnipotent being deceive us on essential points? And why should God's commands (however revealed) function as *laws* 'enjoined' on human beings?

We have faith that God 'hath made men rational' and that natural reason, carefully cultivated, uncovers God's basic commands and distinguishes them from the more numerous conventions that often parade as divine commands. But perhaps this faith is self-deluding. If Hobbes folded such a possibility into his political theory, his entire world would fall apart. If only hypothetical reason were left, the ground for civil peace would disappear from his theory. 'It is a common doctrine,' Hobbes concedes, 'that faith and holiness are not acquired by study and natural reason, but are always supernaturally inspired.'[7] Such direct inspiration would leave no principles of adjudication between opposing doctrines of eternal salvation; and inajudicable disagreements on the requirements for salvation would sow the seeds of frequent and destructive civil wars. For when the choice is between the risk of earthly death and the risk of eternal damnation, many will run the former to avoid the latter. We require faith in natural reason, then, to ensure that its dictates embody the will of God for human conduct; we need reason, so grounded, to still debates in which some disputants appeal to a higher and more subjective source of divine inspiration.

Hobbes's faith in natural reason is thus essential to his political theory. Hobbes sometimes seems to think that if we reason back far enough through the causal chain we will come to a first cause itself uncaused. But he also argued against Descartes, and in apparent conflict with this view, that there is no way to *demonstrate* that the world was created. Even if we accept, dubious as it is, the view that reason necessitates belief in a first cause, that only reveals that an austere God must exist *for reason*. It does not demonstrate that what is true for finite human reason must be true in itself; it teaches us nothing about the characteristics of the First Cause; and it does not teach us that the most fundamental findings of reason are also divine commands. But Hobbes needs to establish each of these points to ground his political theory. He needs assurance that a divine eye shines through the 'light' of reason.

In another context, exploring the elements of faith essential to salvation, Hobbes affirms a meta-faith that the scriptures given to us would not mislead us on the most 'essential points':

But for the deciding of questions of faith, that is to say concerning God, which transcends human capacity, we stand in need of a divine blessing (that we not be deceived in essential points), to be derived from Christ himself by the imposition of hands. For seeing to the end we may attain eternal salvation we are obliged to a supernatural doctine, and which therefore it is impossible for us to understand; to be left so destitute as that we can be deceived in necessary points is repugnant to equity.[8]

The corollary point for reason is this: we would not feel the obligatory power of the laws of nature unless they were the commands of God, and we could not know the substance of these laws unless God 'hath given us reason' to uncover his commands. It would be 'repugnant to equity' if God gave us natural reason and then 'deceived us in necessary points' by disconnecting the findings of this gift from divine injunctions. To do so would be to leave civil society 'destitute.' To have faith in reason as the key to the laws of nature is to have faith in God as the author of nature. And to have the first two faiths is to affirm a meta-faith in the equity of God. These three elements of faith are presupposed when Hobbes says, 'God himself, because he hath made men rational, hath enjoined the following law on them.'

Once we grasp the role that faith plays in the Hobbesian system we can see what turns on the central distinction Hobbes makes between knowledge and faith:

Lastly, between faith and knowledge; for this deliberately takes a proposition broken and chewed; that swallows it down whole and entire . . . for those things which exceed human capacity, and are propounded to be believed, are never more evident by explication, but on the contrary, more obscure and harder to be credited. And the same thing befalls a man who endeavours to demonstrate the mysteries of faith by natural reason, which happens to a sick man, who will needs chew before he will swallow his wholesome but bitter pills; whence it comes to pass that he brings them up again; which perhaps would otherwise, if he had taken them well down, have proved his remedy.[9]

The same thing befalls a man who endeavors to demonstrate faith in reason by further recourse to reason. Faith in reason is not a pill to be chewed and spat up again for further analysis. It must be taken down whole. It must operate as a pervasive assumption in the text not susceptible to further inspection by its own mode of operation. To try to prove the connection between reason and the laws of nature by rational means would be equivalent to validating a standard of knowledge by ascertaining whether it measures up to its own criterion. Such a circular route, by its small circumference and easy navigability, takes one nowhere fast.

So Hobbes repudiates the enchanted view of the world with its harmonies and signs. But he keeps a window open to the will of God. If God no longer shines through the pores of experience, his light has been simultaneously constricted and intensified. When Hobbes refers to the 'light' of reason or nature he is using a metaphor with significant scriptural weight. For instance, he quotes the Bible to the effect that 'the commandment of the Lord is pure, and giveth light to the eyes'; 'thy word is a lamp unto my paths'; and Christ is 'the true light, that lighteth every man that cometh in the world.'[10] The quotations remind us that seeing requires more than a seer and an object to be seen: it requires the light that enables an object to emerge into visibility. The source of light is thus a source of visibility.

Hobbes, in transferring the light metaphor to reason and nature, infuses them with God's authority. God shines through the light of reason; and reason makes his commands visible to us.

Reason tells us nothing about the mysterious attributes of God, but it tells us everything essential about God's will for us. The retreat of God to the heavens requires that reason be improved as an instrument through which his light is transmitted. God, after withdrawing from the mundane world of words and events, leaves the telescope of reason to enable human beings to discern his will for them from a distance.

It remains to ask, Why should we obey God's will revealed to us as the law of nature? Since we cannot comprehend the deeper purpose and meaning of God's will, what converts that will into an obligation for us? Hobbes responds to this question by referring to the logic of the Old

Testament, by reverting specifically to the Book of Job. The importance of Job for Hobbes's thought can be seen by recalling that two of his own texts are named after monsters introduced in it: Leviathan, the powerful ruler of the sea who 'beholdeth every thing that is high' and is 'king over all the sons of pride', and Behemoth, the monster of the land.

The Hebrew name Job means, equivocally, 'the hated, persecuted one' and 'where is the divine father?' The Book of Job deals with a good man who seeks God, but is nonetheless persecuted and injured by him. Job and his friends believe that God rewards goodness and punishes wickedness. But Job is subjected to repeated and horrible torments despite his goodness. And Job begins to think that God is simply indifferent to human concerns. Finally, God breaks his divine silence and speaks directly to Job, deploying in his speech ironic questions which open its meaning to more than one interpretation.

But Hobbes settles upon a single interpretation of this crucial text. 'And how bitterly,' Hobbes writes, 'did Job expostulate with God, that being just he should yet be afflicted with so many calamities! God himself with open voice resolved this difficulty in the case of Job and hath confirmed his right by arguments drawn not from Job's sin but by his own power.'[11]

God's right to demand obedience is 'drawn not from Job's sin but by his own power.' Hobbes resolves the problem of evil by appealing to a mysterious, omnipotent God whose power and purposes are simply beyond our finite powers of understanding. 'Where wast thou,' God asks Job, 'when I laid the foundation of the earth?'[12] And Hobbes makes that question the cornerstone of his doctrine of obedience.

We are bound to obey God's will, Hobbes insists, not because it is comprehensible to us, not because we have entered a covenant with him and not because it conforms to rules we would adopt ourselves were there no God. We are bound to God because he 'hath a right to rule and punish those who break his laws, from his sole *irresistible power*.'[13]

God, the mysterious Creator of the world, is master of the world he created. Where were we when he created it? Could any of us accomplish that feat? To say that God's power is irresistible is to say, first, that we properly fear a being so superior to us that it could create the entire world (and recreate it along entirely different lines if it wished); second, that while we cannot understand the point of everything created by God and every injunction he establishes to deal with the exigencies of common life between finite and prideful beings, we can have faith that there is a point to the rules established by such an all-powerful being; third, that since he will eventually have his way in any event, we might as well follow his word from the start; fourth, that we naturally stand in awe of such a being who is infinitely superior to us in every respect. To believe in such a being is to stand in a relation of fear, deference, humility and awe to it. God's 'irresistible power' cuts human powers down to size; its very irresistibility in the last instance converts this power into rules of responsible conduct in the first instance. Why did God create humans with so much pride and such an impressive capacity for self-deceit when their own interests or pride are involved? Why could we not have been created so that a lower dosage of pride generated the need for fewer injunctions of self-restriction? Where were you when God created the entire world from his will alone?

In *The Gay Science* Nietzsche asks, 'Where is the conscience that obligates one to obey one's conscience?' He means, Why do we accept the dictates of conscience as properly controlling over other impulses, desires, feelings and dispositions in the self? Can the conscience validate itself to be superior? Don't the other passions also insist upon their primacy when they surge up within one? What superior standard gives primacy to the one over the other? Prudence? But that would make prudence superior to conscience; it would reduce the laws of nature to calculations of private advantage; and there are many circumstances in the life of civil society where it would be most advantageous to pretend to obey the law while secretly eluding or evading it. Calculations of private advantage would often conflict with laws designed to support the public interest.

Hobbes answers his version of this question with prudence in the first instance and God in the last instance. God is the Commander-in-Chief who orders us to obey the dictates of reason over passion, unmediated conscience or private advantage.

Hobbes advances, then, a command theory of obligation with the chain of command originating in God and progressing through nature, reason, sovereignty and the self. If God were withdrawn from this system of command, each of the parts would crumble and the entire complex would fall apart.

Nature, madness and artifice

Hobbes is often held to believe that most human beings are self-interested most of the time and that a sovereign power must be devised that is able to contend with these self-interested beings. But this interpretation exaggerates and misleads. It exaggerates by treating human beings who are to become both self-interested and principled as if they were secure agents of self-interest prior to the education they receive in civil society, and it misleads by pretending that the self-interested individual is the problem when it comes closer to being the solution Hobbes offers for the problem he identifies.

'I deny not,' says Hobbes, 'that men desire to come together,' that most men are 'born in such a (dependent) position as to desire it.'[14] But to need society is not necessarily to be fit for it. And 'man is made fit for society not by nature but by education.'[15]

We tend by nature to be unruly, lustful, volatile, restless, passionate, unstable, moody and contradictory. We are creatures desiring social life but unsuitable 'in our pride' to its demand for stability of intention, reciprocity of expectation, reliability in transaction, circumspection in expression, quiescence in mood and rationality in the pursuit of self-interest. The problem of political rule is to convert this prideful, restless, moody and unstable being into a stable, calculable, cautious, reliable, self-interested individual. The Hobbesian 'individual' is, first, not a given but a formation out of material that is only partly susceptible to this form and, second, not merely an end in itself but more significantly a means to the end of a stable society. The Hobbesian individual is thus in part a product of the civil society which is to regulate it, and the Hobbesian problem is how to form it so that it will be able and willing to abide by the natural laws and contracts appropriate to civil society.

The way a theory defines and copes with otherness – with the things, actions, beings and events that fall outside the range of normality it accepts – illuminates its ideas about the character and stability of the normal individual. Hobbes thus speaks to the problem of the individual when he discusses madness, when he considers the causes and traits of a human being who falls below the threshold of rationality and self-interest. The mad are those who remain unsuited for civil society even if they live within its frame. They are not coherent or steady enough to be self-interested. 'But without steadiness, and direction to some end, a great fancy is one kind of madness; such as they have, that entering into so many, and so long digressions, and parentheses, that they utterly lose themselves.'[16]

Madness arises in those who have 'more vehement passions' than others, especially in those who experience an excess of pride, self-conceit or dejection of soul. When these traits become fixed or accentuated we call the sufferer mad, and the condition often goes together with the belief that one is God or with the profession of atheism. In either case the mad are disconnected from the commands of God; they are unchained from the foresight and self-restraint necessary to self-interest.

Madness is a condition to which some are particularly susceptible because of the 'evil constitution of organs of the body'; but it is one into which anyone could fall if the constraints of civil society were inoperative or if self-restraint of the most dangerous passions were relaxed. The potential for madness lurks in everyone. Indeed, madness haunts the interior life of every person.

'The secret thoughts of a man,' says Hobbes, 'run over all things, holy, profane, clean, obscene, grave and light, without shame, or blame.'[17] The specific madness lurking in each soul is likely to emerge during drunkenness, when some lapse into melancholy, others become surly, and others yet become aggressive braggarts. That is why drunkenness is a sin for Hobbes; it destroys the judgment and reason a self-restrained self needs. Madness, then, is a universal potential even if it is an extreme condition, and its overt presence in some reveals the degree of self-containment and social control needed in every normal self: 'For, I believe, the most sober men, when they walk alone without care and employment of the mind, would be unwilling the vanity and extravagance of their thoughts at that time should be publicly seen; which is a confession, that passions unguided are for the most part mere madness.'[18]

Civil society, properly formed, helps to protect each from the madness lurking in oneself and others. It converts a being dominated by unruly, lustful, unguided passions into the suspicious, calculating, prudent, sober, self-interested subject who is to populate the Hobbesian world. The Hobbesian ideal of the self-interested individual is not primarily the ideal of a self whose intrinsic nature is to be protected from the encroachments of society; it is first and foremost a self shaped into form suitable to civil society, a self whose guided passions protect society from the destructive effects of anarchic behavior. The Hobbesian individual is a domesticated human, an artifice made 'fit for society.'

But how is domestication to proceed and how are the domesticated ones to be convinced the product is worth the price for its production? When Hobbes discusses the state of nature he is talking to people already in civil society. He is not trying to convince them to move from a stateless condition to a state, from a condition in which the passions are wild to one in which they are domesticated. Rather, he is persuading imperfectly domesticated subjects that they, in their present state, should consent to remain there and should commit themselves more fully to the habits and principles that ensure the stability of their condition, even though that condition does and must carry many 'inconveniences.' It is, then, no argument against Hobbes that the participants in the state of nature could never have agreed, because of rational mistrust, to a contract that would enable them to escape that condition. That is evident: war and madness prevail in the Hobbesian state of nature. The state of nature is a construct that tells us what it would be like to live amongst others in a condition where civil power has been removed.

The state of nature is shock therapy. It helps subjects to get their priorities straight by teaching them what life would be like without sovereignty. It domesticates by eliciting the vicarious fear of violent death in those who have not had to confront it directly. And when one confronts the fear of early and violent death, one becomes willing to regulate oneself and to accept external regulations that will secure life against its dangers. The fear of death pulls the self together. It induces subjects to accept civil society and it becomes an instrumentality of sovereign control in a civil society already installed. So, while Hobbes seeks to dampen the unruly and lustful passions, he seeks to elicit and accentuate this one. It is a useful passion, useful to an ordering of the self and to peace and quiet in the social order.

When we examine the fear of death we understand it to be both a controlling disposition in the stabilized self and a disposition it is obligated to cultivate. 'A law of nature is a precept or general rule, found out by reason, by which a man is forbidden to do that which is destructive of his life . . . or taketh away the means of preserving the same.'[19] One is forbidden to do that which is destructive of one's life. Suicide is a sin. The subjects to whom Hobbes speaks find that they are already disposed to fear death and they are further told that they are obligated to seek to preserve their lives even if they become inclined to do otherwise.

But to protect one's life is also to contain one's most dangerous passions. To live so as to avoid the risk of death, to cultivate the disposition to live a long, secure life, is to convert oneself into the self-contained self demanded by civil society. For the self-interested individual is a highly organized self. It is a self that must regulate its utterances by the effects they might have on others, must convert its desires and impulses into interests, must govern its passions by reference to dangers or disadvantages they might generate. The paradox of the self-interested individual is that in its very individuality it must be oriented closely to the attitudes of others and the prospects of the future; it must internalize a set of social norms while pretending only to think of itself in doing so; and it must regulate its most individual impulses to regularize its external appearance. For even the most sober individual would be 'unwilling the vanity and extravagance' of his thoughts be 'publicly seen.'

The self-interested self is an artifice, an artifice celebrated by Hobbes as the one most conducive to a well-ordered society. Most of the rules of prudence and morality and most of the maxims followed by the sovereign are designed by Hobbes to produce and maintain this artifice. Because it is artificial, it must be formed; because it is a human artifice containing internal resistance, its form must be maintained by the vigilant application of rules and policies; because its creation is essential to individual security, the individual participates in the creation and protection of its own self; because its form is crucial to social order, the sovereign power attends to its maintenance. Every element in the Hobbesian order functions in its way to pull the self together.

Rhetorics of nature and sovereignty

In such a condition there is no place for industry; because the fruit thereof is uncertain: and consequently no culture of the earth; no navigation, nor use of commodities that may be imported by sea; no commodious building, no instruments of moving and removing . . . no knowledge of the face of the earth; no account of time; no arts; no letters; no society; and which is worst of all, continual fear and danger of violent death; and the life of man, solitary, poor, nasty, brutish and short.[20]

Two things may be noted about this famous characterization of the state of nature. First, the grammatical structure of the text itself expresses the slide from the complexity and convenience of civil society to the simplicity and starkness of a world without it. The formulations become progressively more austere, until even the verbs are dropped from the last clauses: 'no arts; no letters; no society' – no complexity; no connections; no verbs. And life in that state is stripped so completely of cultural and prudential support that only single words can signify its utter barrenness: 'and the life of man, solitary, poor, nasty, brutish and short.'

Second, the grammatical structure combines with other rhetorical elements to elicit in the reader something of the loss of continuity, the emptiness, the fear that would govern life were there no common power to bring order to it. The grammatical and rhetorical structure of this sentence does not merely give a concise description of a stateless condition; it instills a response and elicits a conviction in the reader: the inconveniences accompanying the self-restrictions, indignities, and insults to one's pride in civil society are infinitely preferable to the danger and emptiness brought on by its absence; a rational person would accept many inconveniences to avoid this state.

Hobbes generally derides writers and speakers for deploying a passional 'eloquence' that activates explosive human passions and induces irresponsible action by those inflamed:

Now the nature of eloquence is to make *good* and *evil, profitable* and *unprofitable, honest* and *dishonest* appear to be more or less than indeed they are . . . Nor is this the fault in the *man*, but in the nature itself of *eloquence*, whose end, as all masters of rhetoric teach us, is not truth (except by chance), but victory; and whose property is not to inform, but to allure.[21]

Those who study society should use a cool, reasoned language which speaks to the mind rather than to the passions.

But Hobbes, the master rhetorician, exempts himself from this critique because his own eloquence cools the passions and subdues volatile desires. It is the eloquence of reason itself that calms unruly and dangerous passions. And so Hobbes introduces an ambivalence into modern discourse which has now become all too familiar. He judges the words of others to be too rhetorical while endorsing his own rhetoric in the name of truth and order. 'So also reason and eloquence, though not perhaps in the natural sciences, yet in the moral, may stand very well together.'[22] Hobbesian eloquence excites fear and instills faith. Since both are essential to the world of Hobbesian reason and order, the eloquence which instills them is necessary and that which jeopardizes them is intolerable.

The Hobbesian account of the state of nature encourages those already in civil society to treat the laws of nature as injunctions of the self. For they tell how to avoid that awful state. The first law of nature is to preserve one's life, thereby to 'seek peace and follow it.'[23] The second law calls upon each to 'lay down his right to all things; and to be contented with so much liberty against other men, as he would allow other men against himself.'[24] The other laws develop implications of these first two. Most of them impose obligations of self-restraint upon the individual, such as, crucially, the performance of covenants, the obligation to mutual accommodation, the injunction against revenge, the injunction against 'countenance' or declarations of hatred or contempt for another, the obligation to restrain pride, and the command to control arrogance.

The fifth law of nature is particularly pertinent to a reading of Hobbes that interprets the individual to be an artifice formed by rubbing off irregular features that do not 'fit' neatly into the form of civil society. Complaisance is the obligation to 'accommodate himself to the rest.' We come to society as diverse 'stones,' each of which must be sculpted to fit into the edifice under construction.

For as that stone which by asperity and irregularity of figure, takes more room from others, than itself fills; and for the hardness, cannot easily be made plain . . . is by the builders cast away as unprofitable, and troublesome: so also, a man that by asperity of nature, will strive to retain those things which to himself are superfluous and to others necessary; and for the stubbornness of his passions, cannot be corrected, is to be left, or cast out of society, as cumbersome, thereunto.[25]

The law of nature obligates each to participate in that process by which he becomes an individual who fits into the mold of civil society. To become a Hobbesian individual one must give up much of one's own individuality. Those too stubborn to accept correction or refinement are on warning: they will be 'cast out of society, as cumbersome, thereunto.'

The law of nature is recognizable in the state of nature. But none is operative until there is a common power to fear and each can be assured that his own submission will not place him at a double disadvantage with others; otherwise he will suffer both the burden of regulating himself to obey the laws of nature and the intrusions of others who refuse to abide by them.

If the laws of nature are not operative in the state of nature, is the only motive to obey them fear of penalty from the sovereign? I think not. There are in fact three motives, all of which must be in place before the laws are secure. The laws are obeyed, first, because they are commands of God relayed to humans through natural reason; second, because they enable individuals, once each has been formed into a stable self, to preserve life and enjoy the benefits of civil society; and, third, because an effective sovereign will punish anyone who breaks them.

These are not narrow rules of earthly prudence resting upon stable and universal dispositions. Each motive for obedience needs the support of the others. Even when the sovereign power is installed, individual considerations of earthly interests alone would often counsel the individual to dissemble whenever an advantage might be gained by appearing to abide by the rules while secretly evading, eluding or conspiring to subvert them. So the command of God is as important as prudential deference to an earthly sovereign. But mere obedience to the commands of God is not sufficient either. First of all, these commands are very abstract and general in character; they must be filled out by specific decrees from the sovereign. And, second, given human dispositions to pride and self-deception, each is tempted to claim that God commands whatever supports his own glory or advantage in particular situations, and the resulting contest over the dictates of the reason 'God hath given us' would sow civil disorder unless a sovereign retained final control over the official content of the laws. At different points Hobbes builds protections against each of these dangers: the sanctity of the laws of nature requires the support of God, prudential appreciation of the benefits of civil society, and a sovereign power able to enforce the laws of nature through a variety of instruments.

Strategies of sovereignty

The laws of nature command us to accept a contract in which sovereignty will be securely installed. Hobbes insists that the sovereign power itself not be a party to this contract because that would introduce an element of reciprocity into the relations between sovereign and subjects, compromising the integrity of sovereign power. Since, as we have suggested, it is unlikely that beings in a state of nature could actually agree to such a contract to escape it, the real point of these imaginary legal maneuvers is to convince subjects that, benefiting from sovereignty and perceiving now the effects of life without it, they should obey the sovereign power even when it inconveniences them.

There is more advice to the subjects of sovereign power in the Hobbesian texts. But once the contract has been signed a subtle shift occurs. Hobbes now offers more of his advice to the sovereign, including how to maintain authority once the subjects are installed in civil society. The sovereign's task is to maintain the individual as an obedient subject.

There are two types of strategy available to the sovereign. The sovereign can foster obedience through the threat of punishment to offenders. Those who have cultivated self-interest will be responsive to that threat, and the very visibility of the threat, by exciting the fear of death, encourages the individual to organize itself into a self-interested subject susceptible to these controls. But more affirmative tactics are also appropriate here. The self-contained self requires a form of public discourse that keeps its lustful, aggressive and prideful passions under wraps. The sovereign must cleanse the public environment of debates and texts that inflame the passions:

For when equal orators do combat with contrary opinions and speeches, the conquered hates the conquerer and all those that were of his side, as holding his council and wisdom in scorn, and studies all means to make the advice of his adversaries prejudicial to the state; for by thus he hopes to see the glory taken from him, and restored to himself.[26]

The sovereign must prohibit inflammatory rhetoric and must foster a public discourse that cools the passions, concentrates the mind upon the laws of nature, discourages feelings of pride, hatred and revenge, opposes the 'promiscuous use of women,' links disobedience to the prospect of death, and in general encourages the subject to contain unruly characteristics. Hobbes prefers monarchy to democracy partly because the mass in democracy is like a 'great many coals, though but warm asunder, being put together inflame one another.' And every Hobbesian recommendation about public discourse is designed to use rhetoric in the service of peace, quiet, regularity and obedience. While Hobbes protects a private sphere outside the glare of public life, the public world itself is to be an austere, antiseptic place. Understanding that 'in the well governing of opinions consisteth the well governing of men's actions,' and that in the well governing of action consisteth the well governing of the self, the public rhetoric of Hobbesian society is designed to quell the explosive potentialities residing in the interior of each self and in the social relations between prideful selves.

There is an internal connection between Hobbes's analytic method of political inquiry and his commendation of precise, cool discourse in public life. The author, in the Hobbesian method, first announces the definitions of key terms and then reaches conclusions by drawing out the implications of those terms. The reader of a text by Hobbes will thus find page after page of definition: one is first drawn into a definitional web and then squeezed into a Hobbesian universe of rules and implications. By controlling the definitions Hobbes controls the implications to which the reader consents. In this sense he is a textual bureaucrat. His texts anticipate the rule-bound character of bureaucratic society and the experience people have of increasing the weight of power bearing down on them as they enlarge the sphere of consent.

Similarly, the sovereign, in the Hobbesian political system, first controls the definition of public terms and then draws out the implications of those definitions for the laws of the land.

Each strategy works best if it is received as the cool, detached presentation of reason itself at work, disconnected from the pride or advantage of the underlaborer presenting it. Each, that is, works best if it is legitimized by its sibling. When the Hobbesian method is set in this light it is best understood as part of a political strategy of regulation and control. In the hands of the analyst and the sovereign it constitutes an apparatus of order and regularity; it operates to delegitimize irregularity, disruptive thoughts, and actions flowing outside the channel of Hobbesian reason.

A mode of discourse does not merely describe a world that exists independently of it; it helps to constitute the character of the social world it delineates. Hobbes knew this. He was quite overt in talking about it and in pondering the connection between his method of inquiry and the power of his sovereign. He was even overt, as we have seen, in condemning rhetorics which disturb the artifices he favored while himself adopting an alternative rhetoric designed to hold these formations together. In Hobbes's thought we discern overt connections that later become more unconscious in the thought of others. The rhetoric of method in political thought belongs with the rhetoric of peace and quiet in public life. Each supports its sibling, and the disciplines of one instill those required by the other.

The sovereign must 'be judge of what doctrines are fit to be taught' in order to 'prevent discord and civil war.'[27] Equally important, the sovereign must monitor the structure of public discourse to prevent discord within the very selves upon which order is grounded. Hobbes, the author, must in turn present his strategy of sovereignty as the findings of reason itself. Hobbes, the opponent of rhetoric and eloquence, is the eloquent rhetorician of reason, method and order. For in the new world, where words have lost their close connection to divinity and where the order of things seems more fragile, somebody must take charge of definition.

Reason, faith and power

The Hobbesian sovereign sits firmly in the saddle, but he does not weigh heavily upon the people. This at least is the aspiration Hobbes seeks to realize. The laws must be clearly defined and rigorously enforced, but they are to be few in number. The state cannot succeed if it penetrates too deeply into daily life. It contains passions; it regulates public conduct; it sets limits. But it does not determine life.

But because all the motions and actions of subjects are never circumscribed by laws, nor can be, by reason of their variety; it is necessary that there be infinite cases which are neither commanded nor prohibited, but every man may either do or not do them as he lists himself.

But what if the sovereign power overreaches itself and tries capriciously to govern too many areas of life? First, Hobbes thinks that a sovereign power which overreaches itself will fail eventually. For the laws will become too many and too complicated, and many will be unenforceable. But, second, the sovereign, though created by an earthly pact, is accountable to God in the last instance. This is a central reason Hobbes prefers monarchy to either democracy or aristocratic rule. While the monarch does not sin against his subjects in acting capriciously or ruthlessly, he sins against God if he breaks a law of nature. This unity between the will of the sovereign and the will of the individual is not operative in other forms of rule; its presence in this case makes it possible to hold the monarch responsible as an individual when sinning against God in his capacity as sovereign: 'But in a monarchy, if the monarch makes any decree against the laws of nature, he sins himself; because in him the civil will and the natural are all one.'[29]

Religion now emerges as the linchpin of the Hobbesian system. It is necessary to the conviction that reason uncovers the laws of nature and its God; it is necessary to secure obedience to the 'laws' of nature; and it is necessary to rein in a monarch who holds absolute power over his subjects. What is the ground of religion in the Hobbesian system? What is the relation of reason to faith in Hobbesian religion?

Hobbes does and must argue militantly against the idea that the scripture is plain and clear to every person in a Christian Commonwealth, and he must oppose the idea that salvation requires obedience to everything in the sacred text. For these convictions foster endless dispute over the meaning of scripture, and, since the disputants often believe that immortality hangs in the balance, some might be willing to disobey the sovereign or fight each other to the death over such details of interpretation. The only answer is to insist that the elements of faith essential to salvation are few and simple, and that disputes over other points are inessential. This solution enables the sovereign to control the terms of public worship without compromising the salvation of those whose inner beliefs deviate from his on certain details; it makes it immoral for subjects to convert doctrinal disputes with each other into civil war; and it provides a common core of religious doctrine to be professed by all in public.

In a Christian Commonwealth – the sort of Commonwealth brought into history after Christ was born and sovereigns became Christian – a few simple elements of faith are necessary. It is necessary to believe only that 'Jesus is the Christ' and that Christ is the Savior who promises a second coming of the Kingdom of God. Now this faith, indemonstrable by natural reason alone, shows that Hobbes places some confidence in the truth of scripture. Scripture must not be tossed into a trash bin, even though the word of scripture is tainted by the limited powers and fanciful imagination of its human recorders, transmitters and recipients. But how can faith in the core Christian truths be extracted from scripture without pulling some dangerous and extraneous material along with it, especially since the scripture does not neatly divide itself into these two components?

Hobbes invokes the authority of natural reason to guide scriptural interpretation:

Nevertheless, we are not to renounce our senses, and experience: nor, that which is the undoubted word of God, our natural reason. For they are talents which he hath put into our hands to negotiate, till the coming again of our blessed Saviour; and therefore not to be folded up in the napkin of an implicit faith, but employed in the purchase of justice, peace, and true religion. For though there be many things in God's word above reason: that is to say, which cannot by natural reason be either demonstrated or confused; yet there is nothing contrary to it.[30]

Everything in scripture which appears to be at odds with our natural reason must either be brought into alignment with it or treated as a transcendent mystery beyond human understanding. Reason, as the 'undoubted word of God' appears here to transcend faith and scripture alike. But does Hobbes not fold reason up in a napkin of implicit faith when he defines it as the human window onto the will of God? There is no way Hobbes can prove by means of reason itself that it was given by God to humanity to discern his will for them or that he intended it to be the judge of scripture. Hobbes enunciates that principle, then, as an act of faith: we must have faith that reason is the undoubted word of God, endowed by him with so much primacy over any other instrumentality given to us that there can be 'nothing contrary to it.' If religion is the linchpin of the Hobbesian system, reason is the linchpin of religion; and if reason is the linchpin of religion, faith is the linchpin that links reason to 'true religion.' If Hobbes rationalizes Christianity, he also Christianizes rationality: faith is the chain which draws reason, justice, peace, sovereignty and true religion together into one system.

Natural reason tells us that God exists, that he is omnipotent, that he has 'care of the actions of mankind,' that he governs the world, that he gave us laws of nature to guide our conduct, that we are to obey those laws as his commands. Faith assures us that these dictates of natural reason are elements in any true religion and precepts in any well-governed Commonwealth. It then informs us further that 'Jesus is the Christ' and that Christianity, once it squares itself with the dictates of natural reason, is the highest religion.

Hobbes must inflate the importance of reason to fill the space opened by the retreat of divine signs from the old world. But there is systematic instability in any theory which insists upon the primacy of human reason in disclosing laws commanded by God. It introduces an infinite God to invest reason and its laws with absolute, uncontestable authority; but it can only establish the link between finite reason and the infinite being through an act of faith which becomes contestable and vulnerable as soon as it is identified. Perhaps Christ is the son of a God whose teachings, properly interpreted, instruct humanity to give primacy to scripture whenever it conflicts with the dictates of natural reason. Perhaps Christ is not the son of God but a self-deluded megalomaniac who fosters intolerance of other theisms and a-theisms. Perhaps God created the world and had no interest in giving commands to the creatures in it. Maybe God's putative 'care of the actions of mankind' is a human invention, jeopardizing the concept of an omnipotent God by investing it with a need to receive love and obedience from human subjects. Maybe God's limited ability to care for mankind belies human belief in divine omnipotence. Maybe a God did not create the world, hence it contains no divine commandments and reason provides no window onto divine dictates. Maybe God created the world and endowed those of extreme pride with special grace. Or maybe not.

In the *Dialogues Concerning Natural Religion,* written by David Hume a century later, one of the participants deploys Hobbesian considerations to sever completely the link between reason and God which Hobbes had sought merely to attenuate:

> let us become thoroughly sensible of the weakness, blindness, and narrow limits of human reason; let us duly consider its uncertainty and endless contrarities, even in the subjects of common life and practice; let the errors and deceits of our very senses be set before us; the insuperable difficulties which attend first principles in all systems . . . when these topics are displayed in their full light . . . who can retain such confidence in this frail faculty of reason as to pay any regard to its determinations in points so sublime, so abstruse, so remote from common life and experience.[31]

Hobbes needs faith to ground reason, God and sovereignty, but he makes it all too easy for many to doubt, oppose or modify the faith he swallows. He needs reason to ground the laws of nature in God, but its own internal limitations make it all too easy to lose faith that Hobbesian reason discloses the laws of a being 'so abstruse, so remote from common life and experience.' It is not that faith is impossible in a Hobbesian world. It is both very possible and inherently susceptible to variation. No *common core* of faith about the equity and commands of God can be assured once the finitude of human reason and its essential role in interpreting scripture and the dictates of nature have been recognized. Once the corrosion begins in this common faith it can only be stilled by a yet higher act of common faith, but there is no new instrumentality above reason which can ensure that all or most will now swallow the *same* pill. Hobbes needs faith to ground reason, but he requires something else unavailable to him to ground faith. It cannot be the sovereign: sovereign authority itself depends upon this core faith in reason. A core faith enforced only by habit and coercion lacks exactly the property required by Hobbesian faith in natural reason: it must be felt inwardly if it is to do its work in the Hobbesian world; it must be able to put a stop to fundamental doubt whenever established habits or sovereign authority come into question.

After the Hobbesian attempt to ground authority in the new world falters, those with Hobbesian instincts face an impasse. They can either pretend that Hobbesian reason is sustainable without recourse to a common faith or they can accept the dissipation of a common faith and insist upon extending Hobbesian principles of control more deeply into the fabric of society. The first strategy faces serious obstacles, several of which are now visible in the aftermath of Hegel's critique of the Enlightenment and Nietzsche's exposé of the element of faith in secular reason.

What about the second? How would a Hobbesian system look if faith were dropped out of its self-understanding? Its principle of sovereignty would be shattered. Order would be based upon command, but sovereign commands would lack the intrinsic, obligatory status Hobbes invested in them. Obedience would rest upon prudence narrowly construed, and each would be wary of the possibility that others would take advantage of him behind his back. Either all hell would break loose or the space vacated by faith would be filled with civil power.

If order were maintained, power would touch everyone and everything. Once the soul was closed to the eye of God, new mechanisms of surveillance would be needed to keep a close watch on every aspect of conduct that might jeopardize the integrity of the order. Many areas of life Hobbes took for granted would provide potential hotbeds of dissidence, rebellion, corruption and evasion. Coercive power would penetrate more deeply into the body politic; public space would be defined more broadly; words and conduct would be regulated more extensively; the self would be subjected to more detailed regulations to help it maintain its self-control. Power would become more pervasive, corrupt and fragile: pervasive because it must replace the eye of God with the earthly eye of power; corrupt because each new regulation or rule would present new occasions for conspiracies of evasion between authorities and selected subjects; fragile because the omnipresence of power would convert many laboring under it into secret enemies waiting for the chance to disrupt, destroy or replace it.

It is impossible to maintain a command theory of political obligation without a Commander-in-Chief who assumes responsibility in the last instance. This, I think, was clear enough to Hobbes. It is perhaps one of the reasons that democracy acquires a progressively better name as secularization advances. For it replaces faith in a common God with common faith in the civilizing power of citizenship. This point, though, is less clear to later thinkers who seek to defend a secularized version of Hobbesian theory.

3

Rousseau: Docility Through Citizenship

The eloquence of nature

Hobbes emigrated from the old world to a new continent of thought, bringing considerable baggage from the world left behind; Rousseau explores adjacent territory on the same continent. If we heed both the differences and the affinities between them, we may come closer to assumptions, alternative possibilities and defining anxieties which mark early modernity. Upon this field we may discern how one who criticizes self-control through self-interest is pressed to affirm it through the cultivation of virtue; how one who denies that the state of nature is war is impelled to conclude that the natural course of social development breeds conflict and corruption; how one who withdraws authority from scripture is drawn to see more of God's word inscribed in the light of nature; and how one who denies sovereignty to a ruler governing self-interested individuals is encouraged to give it to citizens ruling themselves as virtuous subjects.

Rousseau knows that the issues of the well-defined self and the well-defined order acquire new weight in the modern age. He knows that the modern world intensifies the demand for order partly because it reduces the individual's inclination to accept it:

I observe that in the modern age men no longer have a hold on one another except by force or self-interest; the ancients, by contrast, acted much more by persuasion and by the affections of the soul because they did not neglect the language of signs . . . The face of the earth was the book in which their archives were preserved.[1]

The disappearance of the world of divine signs and the accentuation of self-interest go together. When the self is not enclosed in a cosmic world of divine meanings it tends to invest more significance in the microcosmic world of the self. And if the self then confines its love to itself, the demands of order intensify while the means of attaining it are reduced to force and the manipulation of self-interest. Force may become less spectacular than it was in 'the ancient world,' but it enters into more areas of life. Self-interest flourishes, but it provides more energy for collusion and corruption than it does for a well-ordered society.

Rousseau's modernity resides in accepting the demise of the world of miracles, divine texts and sacred signs inscribed in custom, welcoming possibilities the new world opens up, clarifying dangers it embodies, and seeking substitutes for those losses which appear too threatening. Rousseau knows the old world he idealizes cannot be recaptured, but he seeks to duplicate its eloquence with a new language which exerts a new hold on people by its distinctive powers of 'persuasion and the affections of the soul.'

Cold, hypothetical reason cannot be adequate to this task. It 'can determine our opinions but not our actions.' Reason must be infused with a rhetoric which, reaching below custom, expresses the claims of nature and inserts appropriate sentiments into the soul. Nature speaks to humanity through reason and sentiment, but its voice is so subdued by the clamorous life of civil society that a great rhetorician is needed to bring it to life.

Make the language of the mind pass through the heart, so that it may make itself understood . . . I shall, so to speak, call all of nature as a witness to our conversations. I shall bring the Eternal Being, who is the Author of nature, to testify to the truth of my speech.[2]

These words are addressed to the reader as Rousseau explains how he will finally acquaint Emile with the pitfalls and virtues of sexual passion, how the tutor will enable his pupil to sublimate desire into love and love into a stable union. But the words convey as well how Rousseau proceeds when he teaches his readers elsewhere about the constitution of a well-ordered self and a well-ordered state.

To instill the highest sentiments in the reader Rousseau must dramatize simultaneously dangers and possibilities residing in the new condition. If 'what the ancients accomplished with eloquence was prodigious'[3] because they lived in a world of divine signs, Rousseau must accomplish at least as much in a more austere setting.

Consider how this new eloquence speaks through Rousseau:

Man is born free and everywhere he is in chains. One who believes himself the master of others is nonetheless a greater slave than they. How did this change occur? I do not know. What can make it legitimate? I believe I can answer this question.[4]

The statement 'man is born free' refers first to the human condition prior to society. But it also heralds a new world in which the very withdrawal of divine signs allows humanity to think through the thick accretions of custom to the natural human condition. 'Man is born free' thus announces that we are released from enclosure in a set of divinely ordained customs. We are on our own more than before; we are now in a better position to acknowledge that we are free in this world to become what we are potentially. This freedom also makes the world more threatening. When custom, texts, words and events no longer glow with divine light, the world of lived experience feels less providential. Custom looks more alien. And nature – the self and its world as they appear when custom is peeled away – is found to be a set of simple inclinations stretched and distorted by the play of culture.

Thus '. . . and everywhere he is in chains.' The new exposure to natural freedom alters the experience of established custom. These are now conventions that surround us and obscure nature. Neither given by God nor established by free will, this dense network of historical accretions is now experienced as a set of chains. The new possibility of freedom exacerbates the experience of unfreedom; the enhanced sense of the conventional character of established rules, customs, laws and commands accentuates the sense that they are constraints. So to be free by nature is to be chained by arbitrary convention.

This is a modern thought expressed through new eloquence: it emerges in a world where the old ground is unsteady, where the experience of convention is more intense, where conventions are suspect until rendered legitimate by consent and where, thereby, the issue of legitimacy becomes more prominent and less tractable.

'Man is born free and everywhere he is in chains.' Rousseau announces in a phrase new promise and new dangers. And the formulation sheds light upon the experience of those who receive it: the modern age is the time when the quest for freedom and the experience of alienation grow together. The Rousseauian rhetoric of natural freedom first articulates the lived experience of alienation and then promises to reveal how it might be transcended. 'What can make it legitimate? I believe I can answer this question.' The reader is seduced by a promise to eliminate chains he may never have felt bound by so tightly before encountering this text. The reader has felt 'the language of the mind pass through the heart.'

But the ground of legitimacy must be as new as the ideal of freedom. It cannot be located in scripture, for the withdrawal of the world of divine signs has also cast doubt on the reliability of the sublime text:

No one is more filled than I with love and respect for the most sublime of all books . . . But I maintain that, if the scripture itself gave us some of idea of God unworthy of Him, we will have to reject it on that point, just as you reject in geometry the demonstrations that lead to absurd conclusions. For, of whatever authenticity the sacred text may be, it is still more believable that the Bible was altered than that God is unjust or malevolent.[5]

Legitimacy can no longer be grounded in scripture, for scripture may falsify the word of God; it cannot reside in the longevity of tradition, for tradition too may falsify that word. It cannot reside in simple self-interest, for, as we shall see later, Rousseau believes that self-interest alone divides and corrupts an order rather than drawing it together. It must reach a light from God that is unclouded by custom or scripture, a place that sheds divine light upon convention and scripture alike. Rousseau is drawn by these considerations to the idea of a state of nature; he is drawn to a state existing beneath the artifice of convention and the historicity of tradition, to a state where, even though human life is incomplete there, the divine light shines brilliantly into the sentiments. To succeed in this venture he must enable nature to speak to the heart of civilized beings; he must articulate a rhetoric of divinized nature to replace the rhetorics of divine revelation, custom and clerical interpretation.

The first task is to show how God, withdrawn from the world of sacred signs and texts, remains in nature and finds expression, for those who will consult him, in human sentiments. The insistent faith that guides this quest is that 'it is still more believable that the Bible was altered than that God is unjust or malevolent.' The scripture may misrepresent God; custom may not embody his signs; priests may lie in his name; but there is still a place on earth where God lives. The Rousseauian skepticism must stop at the point where the light of God shines into nature, revealing him to be a just being, who loves humanity and who gives it enough understanding to discover how it might achieve happiness on earth. Even though natural man cannot yet see God in nature, civilized man must come to see him there. This faith is necessary if blunt skepticism in the other areas is not to lead Rousseau to despair about everything. The ice upon which Rousseau walks is getting thinner, but he encourages us to join him on it nonetheless.

To understand Rousseau's faith and the rhetoric it spawns we might listen to the profession of faith of the Savoyard Vicar, a simple country priest introduced by Rousseau in Emile just when Emile confronts desire and must learn the difference between mere goodness and the virtue that maintains itself against contrary pressure from the passions. At the point Emile encounters inner turmoil God is introduced to help resolve this struggle in the right direction.

The vicar's faith is simple: 'be just and you will be happy.' He avoids profound questions about the nature of God or detailed questions about rites of worship which could not be important to God himself. For the former transcend human powers of reasoning and the latter could only be answered by reference to a sacred text which was written by men and which offers contradictory answers. Thus, God may have created the world or he may exercise his power on a world that exists independently of him. 'The idea of creation confuses me and is out of reach.'[6]

God speaks through nature, though his voice is not always heard:

But it is not enough that this guide exists; one must know how to recognize it and to follow it. If it speaks to all hearts, then why are there so few . . . who hear it? Well, this is because it speaks to us in nature's language, which everything has made us forget. Conscience is timid . . . The world and noise scare it; the prejudices . . . are its cruelest enemies. It flees or keeps quiet before them.[7]

Rousseau, too, must speak to us in nature's language, even as he takes us from the state of nature to civil society, even as he deploys human words to record the unvocalized themes of nature and even as he envelops nature's language in a more complex vocabulary appropriate to social beings.

Reason, given to us by God and guaranteed by him as a route to divine truths necessary to human life, provides the medium for human understanding of nature. 'The greatest ideas of the divinity come to use from reason alone. View the spectacle of nature; hear the inner voice. Has God not told everything to our eyes, to our conscience, to our judgment? What more will men tell us? Their revelations have only the effect of degrading God by giving Him human passions.'[8]

The 'light of reason' reveals basic human sentiments 'as nature first showed them to us,' and we are then able to build upon this base a kind of being and a way of life which develop harmoniously together in the right direction.[9]

We cannot prove that there is a God because that would be to prove that reason, which tells us that God exists, is given to us by God. Such a proof is internally impossible. Belief in the God of natural religion is ultimately based on faith. The crucial faith is that God would not have given us reason unless its findings correspond to his will for us, faith that 'he did not endow me with understanding in order to forbid me its use.'[10] Once this initial faith is secure, faith itself becomes self-sustaining. We then observe the world and consult our sentiments, discerning the equilibrium toward which they tend if only we will participate in enabling it.

My son, keep your soul in a condition where it always desires that there be a God, and you shall never doubt it. What is more . . . bear in mind . . . that in every country and every sect the sum of the law is to love God above everything and one's neighbor as oneself . . ; that nothing is truly essential other than these duties . . : and that without faith no true virtue exists.[11]

These statements are attributed to a vicar and not to Rousseau himself, and it is likely that the faith Rousseau endorses for civil society varies in some ways from this account. But Rousseau himself endorses the view that 'without faith no true virtue exists.' Faith, in Rousseau's hands, shifts its locus from scripture to nature because the world is no longer hospitable to the primacy of scripture in defining a common God. And reason, as the medium through which nature must now be understood, assumes priority over any alternative medium which contradicts it. Rousseau is no longer required, as Hobbes had been, to go through a tortured analysis to show that the findings of reason square with an austere reading of scripture. Faith in reason requires faith in God, and that in turn requires faith that God gave us reason to discern his will in nature. Rousseau now speaks in his own voice:

When a man cannot believe what he finds absurd, it is not his fault; it is that of his reason. And how should I conceive that God could punish him for not having made for himself an understanding contrary to the one he received from him?[12]

To legitimize reason Rousseau naturalizes religion; to naturalize religion he introduces a simple state of nature where everything is simple and peaceful; to enable the state of nature to speak to civilized beings he transcribes 'nature's language' into human discourse; and to redeem us from the degeneration which haunts life once it moves away from that simple state he offers a doctrine of moral regeneration. Each step in this doctrine implies the credibility of the others, but also, each step expresses an attempt to replace those elements of revelation and eloquence lost to modern politics with a new eloquence which draws the reader into this yearning for political redemption.

The first sentence of *Emile* reads, 'Everything is good as it leaves the hands of the Author of things; everything degenerates in the hands of man.'[13] That sentence could also serve to open the *Discourse on the Origin and Foundations of Inequality,* for it explains why Rousseau insists on making the state of nature so simple, pure and gentle.

The simplicity of nature

Let us therefore begin by setting all the facts aside, for they do not affect the question. The researches which can be undertaken concerning this subject must not be taken for historical truths, but only for hypothetical and conditional reasonings better suited to clarify the nature of things than to show their true origin.[14]

Hobbes and Locke tried to reach the state of nature, but they did not get close to it. They depended too much upon observation of how human beings feel, think and act in civil society, especially the civil society of seventeenth-century England. Speaking of 'need, avarice, oppression, desire and pride,' they 'spoke about savage man and they described civil man.'[15] The first reason to set the facts aside, then, is that the observable facts mix traits of natural man with those acquired in society. Empiricism is unsuited to the question.

The second reason is that the construct of a state of nature reveals human beings not merely as they might have been prior to the influence of society, but as they must have been when they left 'the hands of the Author of things.' The natural condition must be a condition of simplicity, innocence and perfection. And its perfection must degenerate only through action in which human beings themselves are implicated. The state of nature is Rousseau's transposition of the Garden of Eden from scripture to nature; his hypothetical reasonings are guided by faith, by the insistence that everything God does is good and that all evil comes from human action. It is a testimony of faith, an early modernization of the Christian answer to the problem of evil.

Humans in this state have very simple desires for food, shelter, sex. And they also feel simple compassion for others suffering pain. There is no resentment, vanity, pride, love, virtue, friendship, hatred, revenge or fear of death. For these states and relations require the emergence of reason, language and social life; and these conditions are absent in the state of nature. 'I see an animal . . . satisfying his hunger under an oak, quenching his thirst at the first stream, finding his bed at the foot of the same tree that furnished his meal; and therewith his needs are satisfied.'[16]

Life in this condition is simple and sentiments are pure. There is no war, because desires are too simple, the means too meager and the rewards too slight. Natural 'man' (as Rousseau describes humanity) is pure; each individual is self-sufficient; life is peaceful. Things would have stayed this way if man were not endowed with two additional capacities.

First, the capacity for freedom is instilled in human nature, differentiating humans from beasts.

Nature commands every animal and the beast obeys. Man feels the same impetus, but he realizes that he is free to acquiesce or resist; and it is above all in the consciousness of this freedom that the spirituality of his soul is shown.[17]

Second, God endowed natural man with the faculty of perfectibility. Humans have the capacity to realize a higher essence, partly through free actions they themselves take. These two capacities make it possible for humanity to elevate itself to a higher state; they make it impossible for humanity to remain in the natural state indefinitely; and they engender the evils which befall humanity while it seeks its perfection. These ingredients in the human condition spawn good and evil. Before following Rousseau along the path of human development and deterioration we should examine more closely why complex passions and desires are impossible in a state where reason and language have not emerged. 'For one can desire or fear things,' Rousseau asserts, 'only through the ideas one can have of them or by the simple impulsion of nature; and savage man, deprived of every kind of enlightenment, feels only this last kind.'[18]

Consider the feeling of resentment. To resent the action of another I must believe that the other is an agent capable of acting intentionally and worthy of being held responsible for the actions undertaken. We do not resent trees when we bump into them; or when we do, we can be brought to see that the feeling is misplaced. To resent a specific individual who meets this threshold condition, I must additionally believe that he injured me purposely or negligently and that the injury is not deserved by something I did previously. Resentment, then, is a complex reactive attitude, drawing upon a whole reservoir of understandings, assumptions and judgments about self and others in a setting where the parties share principles of judgment.

We are unable to discriminate resentment from anger, hate, jealousy, fear, rage, annoyance, indignation, anxiety or disgust merely by noting differences in internal sensations or observable physical states. They form a complex web of negative reactive attitudes in which each helps to constitute by contrast and comparison the characteristics of the others; they are differentiated primarily by the different ideas and judgments which enter into each. These complex attitudes thus presuppose a complex self, modes of reasoning, language and a common morality; they presuppose exactly those achievements that Rousseau excludes from the state of nature.

A couple of implications follow from this analysis. First, if complex reactive attitudes must be absent from the state of nature, war, corruption, evil and vice must be absent too. There is no capacity or need for these states if there is none for the reactive attitudes which enter into them. Second, the kind of analytic method Hobbes recommends, whereby one divides a social complex into its most elementary particles and examines the characteristics of each in isolation, cannot work either. Each of the elements of social life is internally connected with others: the complexity of ideas helps to constitute the complexity of emotions; the complexity of emotions expresses a socially established density of self; the density of the self presupposes the development of language and reason; the development of reason and language in turn reflects social relations, a dense self and complex emotional attitudes. Rousseau cannot adopt the analytic method favored (but not always followed) by Hobbes because he adopts a social holism in which each element presupposes and helps to constitute the others. He thus does not face the problems confronting Hobbesian theory, in which the complexity of the concept of society adopted outstrips the method espoused for studying it.

Rousseau, though, faces another problem. For it is not clear in such a theory of holist interdependency how the first move out of a state of nature could occur, how one of these elements could develop sufficiently on its own to supur a corollary movement of the others. Rousseau's holism predisposes his theory against the idea of a state of nature while his faith makes such a state both attractive and necessarily susceptible to a dialectic of transformation.

Rousseau opts for a gradual, interminable process whereby long, cold winters draw people together into primitive interdependency. Language, social relations, the foresight that grows with reason, primitive methods of agriculture and metallurgy, the introduction of private property whereby each begins to recognize the difference between thine and mine, the development of individual skills and a social division of labor – these forms initially unfold slowly and disjointedly and then acquire a common momentum which hastens the pace of change. Together they begin to shape the modern person who seeks freedom, experiences the pleasures and miseries of sociality, suffers under the experience of dependency and inequality, and manifests the complex and socially induced traits of vanity, violence, corruption and deceit.

Rousseau is at his best in delineating the character and effects of these traits, at his worst in showing how they could and must have evolved out of the simple state which preceded them.

When the process of evolution has reached an intermediate point circumstances combine with the individual's capacity for freedom and perfectibility to engender the sorts of contrast and comparison from which complex emotions and attitudes emerge.

People grew accustomed to assembling in front of huts . . . song and dance . . . became the amusement or rather the occupation of idle and assembled men and women. Each one began to look at others and to want to be looked at himself, public esteem had a value. The one who sang or danced the best, the handsomest, the strongest, the most adroit or most eloquent became the most highly considered . . . From these first preferences were born on one hand vanity and contempt, on the other shame and envy; and the fermentation caused by these new leavens eventually produced compounds fatal to happiness and innocence.[19]

Vanity, contempt, shame and envy grow up in circumstances where people share standards of achievements, skill, beauty, well-being and virtue and find themselves with different abilities or dispositions to measure up to them. These reactive attitudes naturally accompany the emergence of social life, but they insidiously negate its potential to realize justice and virtue. For these are self-defeating and infectious passions. To be vain, for example, is to demand constant deference and praise from those who are necessarily thought to be inferior. Since one's vanity is satisfied by a being whose judgment is unworthy of appreciation, the desired feeling of self-glorification is never quite achieved. Vanity and contempt are destructive passions that become insatiable through inability to satisfy the impulse that drives them. And shame and envy are the counterpoint reactions of those treated with contempt because they do not excel in a setting where the very idea of excellence requires some to fall below the standard. These new leavens produce 'compounds fatal to happiness and innocence.'

Even the highest emotions and attitudes engendered in society are essentially ambiguous in character. Take love. 'Let us begin by distinguishing the moral and the physical in the sentiment of love.'[20] The physical is that feeling of lust which inclines one sex to copulate with another. The moral is that 'artificial sentiment' of exclusive and durable connection 'extolled with much skill and care by women.'[21]

But while the first is indispensable to the second and while the harmony of both is indispensable to the stability and virtue of society, the combination is also unstable and combustible. The force and variability of the first threatens to unravel the stability of the second.

What's more, love contains further ambiguous characteristics. Since love must be exclusive to be special, it creates perfect preconditions for jealousy, envy and revenge. While love is 'tender and gentle,' it becomes an 'impetuous fury' at the least obstacle. If one shifts commitments to another, 'jealousy awakens . . ; discord triumphs, and the gentlest of the passions receives sacrifices of human blood.'[22] Moreover, though Rousseau does not put it in exactly these terms, even the non-sexual element in love is ambiguous. To love another is to care for the welfare of the other as one cares for oneself and to need the other to care similarly for you. But in circumstances of conflict, where, for instance, the beloved is drawn to a new, more suitable mate or where the beloved's advancement creates trouble for one's own welfare, these two components of love move in different directions. Jealousy is likely to be covered by dissimulation and self-deceit whereby one pretends to take only the welfare of the lover into account while campaigning vigorously on behalf of one's own need.

Love is essentially ambiguous, then. It elevates individuals and contributes to the bonds of social life while it sows seeds of individual suffering and social destruction. Its very formation creates room for jealousy, envy, violence, dissimulation and self-deception. And a similar analysis could be made of the fear of death, pride, beauty, self-respect, ambition and love of God. Rousseau's solution to the problem of a virtuous order must establish ways to curtail relations and traits that are simply destructive. It must also face the more subtle task of enabling affirmative emotions and dispositions to develop while containing the unruly and destructive elements inherent within them.

But that story must wait, for at the stage we are describing the participants are experienced enough to feel the benefits of the new ways and too innocent to discern the dangers residing within them. By the time they are in a position to figure it all out it will be too late for them to do much about it. If God is not responsible for the evils we innocently create, then Rousseau's theory resolves the problem of evil; but if human innocence precludes human responsibility for evils flowing from it, then Rousseau's theory of transition from nature to society embodies its own problem of evil.

Once Rousseau has finessed the move from a simple state of nature to the next, more complicated stage of comparison and interdependence, his dialectic of social development and the intensification of inequality, vice and exploitation proceeds very smoothly. The logic is simple: 'the vices that make social institutions necessary are the same ones that make their abuse inevitable.'[23] And as the vices intensify, the evils accompanying their correction do too. As the division of labor becomes more developed and less escapable, people find it advantageous to appear to be more worthy, deserving or meritorious than they are; and since well-being is now dependent more upon others' judgment of worth than upon one's own self-subsistent labor, appearances become everything. Those who refuse to participate in the game of appearances suffer a double disadvantage. They receive less than they deserve, and they contribute more than others merit. Everyone becomes incorporated into the game of ambition and dissimulation until a state of society is finally reached reminiscent of the one Hobbes had reserved for the state of nature.

Consuming ambition, the fervor to raise one's relative fortune less out of true need than in order to place oneself above others, inspires in all men a base inclination to harm each other, a secret jealousy all the more dangerous because in order to strike its blow in greater safety, it often assumes the mark of benevolence.[24]

We are now at the stage where a parody of the Lockeian contract becomes necessary. The rich are insecure and the poor feel cheated. A great swindle is pulled off by the rich and powerful who have the most to gain from a civil contract, promising to benefit all through an act of common benevolence. They say, 'let us protect the weak from oppression, restrain the ambitious, and secure for everyone the possession of what belongs to him.'[25] But they establish a civil contract in which inequalities already established by hook or by crook are treated as natural entitlements to be protected by the new civil authority. Everyone runs to meet his chains, for 'although they had reason enough to feel the advantages of a political establishment, they did not have enough experience to foresee its dangers.'[26]

The new political contract legitimizes injustice. And the system which emerges establishes a set of relations and reactive attitudes which make many hate the condition they are in and most act in ways which maintain them: 'citizens let themselves be oppressed only insofar as they are carried away by blind ambition; and looking more below than above them, domination becomes dearer to them than independence, and they consent to wear chains in order to give them to others in turn.'[27]

Inequality becomes self-perpetuating, on Rousseau's view, once it has been institutionalized. Its tendency to self-perpetuation flows from the dissatisfactions and resentments it spawns. For the system of stratification first excites destructive passions of vanity and contempt, envy and resentment, and then channels them into outlets which reinforce the system. The psycho-logic of the channeling process reveals why those in the middle levels of a stratification system are likely to vent resentment against those below them rather than against those whose privileges, attitudes and treatment activated it in the first place. The marginal members of the middle class suppress the real source of resentment to identify vicariously with those above them whom they wish to join and who are too powerful to oppose successfully; they then discharge their accumulated rancor against those whose suffering is too close for comfort and whose very powerlessness makes them a more promising target of vilification. Their weakness against the tyranny of the powerful is concealed through the petty power they exercise over the weak. In a word, 'they consent to wear chains in order to give them to others in turn.' Since their reactions help to maintain the system which incited them, the system remains intact to incite them again. Resentment thus maintains the order which engenders it. Here, in embryo, we have a critique of Hobbesian and Lockeian theories of consent, an explanation of why middle classes tend historically to oppose those below them, and why movements to reverse unjust inequality constantly run up against opposition from within the ranks of those victimized by it.

Human powers of reasoning and sociability have been perfected through evolution from the state of nature, but the species has deteriorated in other respects. If everything is good as it leves the hand of God, it tends to degenerate in the hands of human beings. But does perfection in some respects require degeneration in others? And are humans responsible for this degeneration? If they are not, is God then responsible for the fall?

Rousseau, I think, responds to these issues by pointing to a *possible* world in which human reason and freedom are perfected and degeneration does not occur. If the fall can in principle be avoided, then its occurrence rests upon human action for which God is not responsible. The ambiguous picture of a state of nature touched by a divine hand and yet susceptible to deterioration now spawns a vision of an ideal order attainable at least in principle.

The paradox of politics

In some circles of contemporary political thought the problem of evil has been reduced to the problem of the free rider. A Rousseauian theory of virtue, it is thought, fails to confront the issue of the free rider; hence it cannot understand political evil or how to redress it. But this is quite wrong.

While Rousseau did not think the free rider exhausted the problem of evil in politics, he was very aware of its existence. His critique of a politics founded merely upon the realism of self-interested individuals was grounded in the conviction that it offers a utopian solution to the problem of the free rider. If Hobbes, as Rousseau sometimes intimated, had actually grounded order on the calculative reasoning of self-interested beings governed by a wise sovereign, Rousseau's critique would provide the definitive argument against him. We shall treat the critique here, however, as further evidence that Hobbesian theory does not rest upon such a utopian basis. It is a critique in advance of theories which do.

The free rider is the person or corporation that benefits from a common practice promoting the public good while evading conformity to the practice producing it. Once a few free riders emerge in a few areas of life, other citizens are driven to join them. For compliers now lose both by abiding by the practice and by losing benefits which come only with widespread compliance. The question is, How is the free rider to be drawn into the fold of the public good? The realist answer is to devise ways, either by building artificial incentives into the market or by increasing legal penalties for infractions, to make it in the self-interest of each agent to promote the public interest. Rousseau finds this solution to be utopian.

In *The Geneva Manuscript*, written as the first draft of *The Social Contract*, Rousseau imagines an 'independent Man' of reason listening to a 'wise man' advise him to consent to the laws because it is in his self-interest to do so. The independent man responds:

I am aware that I bring horror and confusion to the human species, but either I must be unhappy or I must cause others to be so, and no one is dearer to me than myself. I would try in vain to reconcile my interest with that of another man. Everything you tell me about the advantages of the social law would be fine if while I were scrupulously observing it toward others, I were sure that all of them would observe it toward me. But what assurance of this can you give me, and could there be a worse situation for me than to be exposed to all the ills that stronger men would want to cause me without my daring to make up for it against the weak? Furthermore it will be my business to get the strong on my side, sharing with them the spoils from the weak. This would be better than justice for my own advantage and my security.[28]

In a society without civic virtue either agents of regulation must penetrate into all corners of life or the free rider finds plenty of room to roam. Moreover, even in the first case the free rider would eventually corrupt the administrative system itself. Self-interest, while one precondition of a good society, is radically insufficient to it. Any society built on it alone will become corrupt and repressive. Even an order in which self-interested subjects consent only to obey the letter of the law will become corrupt. This is Rousseau's charge.

Three elements combine to produce this result. First, in a society without civil virtue, lacking a common set of ends which citizens have interiorized as purposes and goals of their own, people can always find space to evade, escape, contest, delay and creatively interpret laws governing the common life. This is because the letter of a law never covers perfectly or completely every instance to which it is meant to apply. No rule, however carefully written, can extend to each unforeseen instance in which it might apply, nor will it anticipate all the strategic uses to which it might be put by independent agents of self-interest.

Second, the self-interested agent will have every reason to look for such gaps and holes in the letter of the law, and since by definition such an agent has no commitment to the spirit of the law, nothing will constrain this search for loopholes. Thus, 'prudence is never as quick to imagine new precautions as knavery is to elude them.'[29]

Third, once a few profit by this means, they will see the advantage of banding together to exploit the weak; and many others will discern the double disadvantage of being placed in this vulnerable position, suffering both from abiding by the law when others escape the burdens it imposes and from the deleterious effects on the common good of widespread evasion. Each will think it essential to 'get the strong on his side' to avoid increasing his vulnerability even further; everyone will seek to avoid becoming the weak against which others unite for the purpose of 'sharing the spoils.'

Everyone will want to appear to abide by the law while cultivating ruses and alliances which shift the real burden to the weak. As new laws are enacted to patch up discernible holes, new openings will be discerned in the new regulations. The people will be highly regulated; disaffection and corruption will grow; and the public interest will decay. And as this process occurs the politics of resentment described earlier will enter into it, exacerbating the double dialectic of social discipline and moral dissolution. In an inegalitarian society where self-interest smothers virtue, 'laws are powerless against the treasures of the rich and the indigency of the poor; the first eludes them, the second escapes them; one breaks the net and the other slips through.'[30]

Rousseau, then, not only has a conception of society in which 'everyone would like to benefit without being obligated to cultivate the bonds it requires,'[31] he insists that a society consisting of self-interested selves cannot resolve this problem. Theories which pretend to do so within these terms are utopian: they project onto the world possibilities incapable of realization, and they fail to confront the intimate relationship between protection of the common good and cultivation of civic virtue among citizens.

Once the indispensability of civil virtue has been established, a deeper issue of political evil is brought to light. It is the issue theories based upon the notion of the self-interested self seek to avoid by pretending that self-interest can provide the adequate base of a healthy order. All societies evolve innocently: they introduce changes and reforms before experiencing all the effects implicit within then. The normal course of innocent evolution tends, as we have seen, to introduce exploitation and corruption into the order. And once dissimulation and corruption have sunk their roots deeply into an order, the cultivation of civic virtue becomes impossible. There is, then, a paradox insinuated into the very center of politics.

In order for an emerging people to appreciate the healthy maxims of politics, and follow the fundamental rules of statecraft, the effect would have to become cause; the social spirit, which should be the result of the institution, would have to preside over the founding of the institution itself; and men would have to be prior to the laws what they ought to become by means of laws.[32]

For virtue to flourish just laws are needed to enable citizens to cultivate affirmative dispositions while containing the negative passions which accompany them. But just laws can only be willed and followed by a virtuous people, and the normal course of social evolution does not produce such a people. Thus effect must become cause, but it does not do so; cause must become effect, but it lacks the appropriate antecedent.

This is the paradox of politics which, if Rousseau is right, haunts every civil society. Realist theories of the free rider seek to ward it off when they insistently define self-interest to be cause and solution to the problem they formulate. But this insistence exacerbates the phenomenon it seeks to regulate. Detailed regulation of self-interested individuals makes it all the more necessary for them to become more aggressively and creatively self-interested; they therefore become less governable even while following the letter of the law. Realism is a utopian doctrine of politics.

Rousseau discerns no clear, historical solution to the paradox of politics. He does contend that once we are in a position to recognize the paradox we are also in a position to theorize its solution. The theory of the general will, while providing the answer, is unlikely to be translated into historical actuality. For its truth can be recognized only by a people who have evolved well beyond the innocence of nature, and by that time the order within which they reside is likely to be too corrupt to be able to assimilate its wisdom. Rousseauian theory provides hints to actual politics about how to avoid worse evils or to improve things modestly. But unless a people with a uniquely fortunate history happens to fall into the hands of an impossibly wise Legislator, the ideal itself remains humanly possible and historically unattainable. That is, its form is available in principle to beings constituted as humans are, but it is not available to any people whose innocent course of evolution deviates from the strict preconditions of social structure, personal sentiment and initial leadership needed for its actualization. To formulate the ideal is to deepen understanding of the perils of politics and to complete the glorification of the Author of nature by revealing how social life too could be good if only it escaped corruption by human hands. Even if the ideal is unavailable histoically, its possibility in principle places responsibility for evil in the hands of humanity.

The politics of virtue

The self-interested individual is not the only form the self can assume. It might become virtuous. It might sublimate self-love into attachment to the common good, extending its love of self to reach the social whole while containing socially disruptive passions attached to self-love. The virtuous self, living in a society which fosters the common good, internalizes norms and laws established by society as principles and goals of its self. The laws become the self's own premises of conduct, and it becomes as free as one can be in civil society.

A person is free when he is the author of the principles he follows. For then the constraints he faces are self-imposed and his purposes are self-defined. But to be free in this sense, one must first domesticate those elements in onself – one's particular will – which inhibit one from recognizing and willing the laws applicable to everyone, and one must then suppress doubts one might have that the common principles actually reflect the general will. The virtuous self must do a job on itself while keeping faith that the common good in which it participates makes the internal victory worthwhile.

Rousseau, then, shifts strife and conflict from civil society to a site within the individual itself. Demanding more from the self than Hobbes did, he must intensify the struggle within it which Hobbes identified, and he must seek a more complete victory for the interior voice of virtue. Because of the essential ambiguity of the highest passions, because of the destructive character of the lowest passions, because a social form activates all these potentialities as it realizes some, and because the virtuous self is essential to a well-ordered state, the self becomes the locus of strife between the forces of good and evil. Politics becomes interiorized. Everything in society must be devised so that the self can wage this quiet battle successfully, and the very stringency of the external organization Rousseau commends reveals the intensity of the internal battle and the fragility of any momentary victory for the forces of virtue and goodness.

Rousseau withdraws politics from the general will and relocates it quietly inside the selves which will these general laws. From the vantage point of social order, the best policing is self-policing. All of Rousseau's rhetorical powers are thus deployed to make the internal struggle appear softer than it must be and to establish an equivalence between the self-policing of the self, freedom, and a well ordered polity. Here is an example of Rousseauian eloquence on behalf of one party in this internal struggle:

What man loses by the social contract is his natural freedom and an unlimited right to everything that tempts him and that he can get; what he gains is civil freedom . . . For the impulse of appetite alone is slavery and obedience to the law one has prescribed for oneself is freedom.[33]

What is lost is lowly and trivial, while the gain elevates and ennobles one. The virtuous self discovers 'his ideas broadened'; his very 'feelings ennobled,' his 'whole soul elevated'; he transcends 'appetite' and attains, as 'master of himself,' true 'moral freedom.' Self-control through social internalization becomes freedom; acting on one's natural inclinations becomes slavery. Though Rousseau always acknowledges losses accompanying virtue, he also compensates the self for them through metaphors which promise to lift, elevate, perfect, purify and realize the self. Is the self brought closer to God through these rites of self-purification? Is that the promise of promises? The metaphors suggest it without insisting upon it.

It is now notorious that in Rousseau's theory man is citizen and woman is not; he the formal authority of the family and she the informal inspiration of private virtue; she the bearer of intuitive judgment and he the agent of reason; he immoral if he commits infidelity and she doubly so if she does the same. These differences, while imposing a double load of self-denial and self-restraint on women, must not erase important affinities and complementaries between virtuous males and females in a Rousseauian universe. Both male and female are docile, though in different domains; in both cases a strict sexual virtue is crucial to the formation of civic virtue; and each polices any inclinations and passions within the self in discord with those prized in common.

It is doubtful whether one could execute a critique of Rousseau's sexual politics without revising fundamentally his theory of the general will and all theories of civic virtue and community indebted to him. For the point of Rousseauian 'complementarity' within the family is to eliminate politics within it so that the will brought to the public forum is unadulterated. It is a notable (or acutely revealing) part of a more general quest for purity and singularity of purpose in public life. If one defines woman to be the double victim of Rousseauian virtue, then man becomes by definition at least a victim. The losers differ in the degree to which they lose, but *if* there are losers in this Rousseauian world there can be no winners. The moment the ideal of purity and virtue begins to smell badly in one place the odor will spread everywhere. One's view of Rousseau on women thus crystallizes one's view of everything else in the theory: to oppose him vehemently here is to project an ideal of selfhood and citizenship at odds with those located at the center of his theory; it is to evaluate Rousseauian commendations of chastity, docility and self-containment against a more robust standard of self-assertion and a more assertive standard of politics.

The general will is simultaneously the product of a community of virtuous selves, the rationale for each restraint the self is to impose upon itself, and the reward for the self's cultivation of itself into an agent of virtue. The goal is to 'find a form of association that defends and protects the person and the goods of each associate with the common force and by which each one, being united with all, only obeys himself and remains as free as before.'[34] And the means is to establish harmony between the self and the law-making authority so that each obeys as a subject only the laws he wills as a citizen, so that each is subjected only to himself in obeying the laws of the land.

While everyone gives everything in principle to the general will, it only enacts laws that apply to everyone or anyone equally; it is called into play only where there is a serious evil to be remedied; and it does not establish the basic traditions governing the order but presides over a fortunate people whose basic traditions already dispose them to it. These three characteristics of the general will curtail severely its role as a determinant of life. It is difficult to cite examples of laws which meet the first two conditions and have not already been resolved by the third precondition. And there is no sense in trying to install the general will in a society where the right traditions are not already installed. The small size of the state, its geographic insulation from other states, a family life with a male head of household, chastity of male and female, the cultivation of civic virtue, an economy consisting of self-subsistent farms, a rough equality among each of the homesteads, the minimalization of commercial life, a simple and common civil religion, the avoidance of extensive foreign relations, a citizen militia built around defense – these are conditions for the formation of a general will rather than creations of it.

One of the ways the Rousseauian politics of the general will protects its purity is by presiding over a social form in which there is seldom need for it to be brought into play. If Rousseau is a communitarian, it is a community in which public politics is minimized, tradition controls much of life, and citizens subject themselves to self-control in preparation for the occasional call to validate through formal action principles already implicit in the common life.

If this reading is correct, the mystery of the general will dissolves into its institutional and dispositional preconditions of existence. When they are all intact, assembled citizens, following their sense of the public good and ignoring those private interests that would give some a particular advantage, concur on a finding that expresses conditions, virtues and traditions already intact. The general will works when will is enclosed in a circle of prior determinations expressing Rousseau's prior sense of the good life; it unites subjective will and objective truth if and because its prior determinations do. It is the capstone of an idealized practice rather than the determinant of a social form. We can clarify this reading further by considering the relations between the general will and two of its determining elements.

The natural sequence of events tends, as we have seen, to foster inequality, but in a state such as Corsica where fortune has not yet introduced inequality, the laws of the land should work to mitigate the natural sequence. Equality, meaning roughly that no one is so rich that he can buy another or so poor that he can be bought, contributes in three ways to the general will.

First, if the conditions of existence among citizens is roughly equal, each will be in a good position to know what resources and needs the others have. Equality makes the order more transparent to its participants. It is harder for some to exaggerate their own suffering, and it is difficult for others to follow their private inclination in discounting the extent of suffering that exists. Each citizen, in extrapolating from his own condition to that of others, is in a better position to discern when they appear to be more than they are and to admit when he is inclined to make them appear less than they are.

Second, in an egalitarian society I have some interests in common with others. If each of us tries, we can think of laws which will benefit all without placing any under a special hardship. And since class divisions are not highly developed, the pressures to unite against others to enact the interest which is more dear to some of us do not become so powerful. We can discern the common interest more clearly and resist the particular interest more readily in a society that is already egalitarian.

Third, in an egalitarian society the passions of vanity and contempt, which grip the rich, and those of resentment and envy, which invade the poor, do not take root so easily. Even when they do emerge, it is easier for those seeking to be virtuous to subject them to self-restraint. For in an egalitarian society each can look into the eyes of the other with self-respect and civic regard. Trust, friendship and dignity grow in circumstances where contempt and resentment are not inscribed in the social order; and the sense of justice, as Rousseau understands it, flourishes in a world where these civic dispositions gain hegemony over the negative passions in the internal life of citizens.

Equality, then, encourages the knowledge, interests and virtue which prompt citizens to will laws that treat everyone and anyone equally. Equality helps to set the stage for the general will and the enactment of the general will treats those subjected to it equally. Each presupposes and engenders the other.

Faith, generality and will

If equality stands in a relation of condition and criterion to the general will, the relation the latter bears to civil religion is even more fundamental.

Every good society must be founded on a civil religion. Otherwise the state will be rent by two competing powers, each treating itself as sovereign – as the authority of finality when the chips are down. Rousseau recognizes Hobbes to be the theorist who perceived the real importance of this point:

Of all Christian authors, the philosopher Hobbes is the only one who correctly saw the evil and the remedy, who dared to propose the reunification of the two heads of the eagle and the complete return to political unity, without which no state or government will ever be well constituted.[35]

But Hobbes then vitiated his own insight by failing to see how thoroughly 'the spirit of Christianity' is incompatible with a true civil religion. If 'everything that destroys social unity is worthless,' the priests are paradigmatic examples of worthlessness; for their religion seeks to give church priority over state and too often disjoins preparation for the afterlife from the dictates of civic virtue in this life. Rousseau opposes to the Hobbesian doctrine of sovereign control over the details of public worship a civil religion in which all share one simple and basic conception of God while treating differences in the details of worship and ritual to be unimportant to salvation or the life of the polity.

The dogmas of the civil religion ought to be simple, few in number, stated with precision, without explanation or commentaries. The existence of a powerful, intelligent, beneficent, foresighted, and providential divinity; the afterlife, the happiness of the just, the punishment of the wicked; the sanctity of the social contract and the laws.'[36]

The very brevity of this formulation signifies at once its centrality to the theory and the refusal of its author to pursue refinements of faith into the dark corners of theology. For the God who reveals himself to all through nature also limits his presence to a few clear and distinct ideas. Any further exploration by finite human minds merely obscures the original message: it sows doubt and conflict among the faithful. Rousseau is intolerant of theological doctrine because it corrodes the common faith, and the unity of the general will dissolves along with it.

Rousseau is tolerant of religious difference as long as all members endorse the core set of beliefs. This rules agnostics and atheists out of Rousseauian politics. They are enemies of civic virtue because they are adversaries of faith. Rousseau's position on those Christians who insist on the primacy of the Bible, and the necessity of commentary presided over by trained priests and ministers, is less easy to define. But, clearly, they would be at odds with the civil religion if their text and commentaries contradicted any of its basic tenets. His civil religion is to displace the Christianity of revelation through a sacred text because the possibility of stable and universal readings of the text has been swept away by ontological developments which inaugurated the modern age.

It is easy to see how the civil religion supports virtue and the general will with its authority: it promises an afterlife to the just, identifying justice with the findings of the general will; and it promises punishment for the wicked, identifying wickedness with acts which oppose virtue. Civil religion provides transcendental motivation to become virtuous.

But Rousseauian faith does not simply support the general will. It also enters into its very constitution. The general will redeems the purity lost through the original fall from the innocence of nature. It is the condition where reason, sociality and complex emotions develop in harmony with virtue, where we are finally at one with ourselves and at home in the civil society in which we reside. It establishes at a higher level the purity lost when humanity fell out of the state of nature; it brings human beings closer to God by purging them of corruptions innocently created by their own hands.

The general will contains two dimensions which must coordinate perfectly in the Rousseauian vision of the good life. The first consists of citizens banding together to will proposals that could apply to everyone generally. The second consists of citizens discovering through deliberation, in circumstances of individual purity and pursuit of collective unity, a single, objective conclusion, bestowing legitimacy on the result because it is true. These two dimensions are brought into perfect coordination through Rousseauian insistence that citizens, properly motivated, must uncover a single, true will when they gather together to consider general issues. The insistence that generality and singularity be coordinated is grounded in Rousseau's natural religion.

The Rousseauian concept of the virtuous citizen smuggles the second idea through the back door while our attention is fastened on the discussion of how citizens exercise their will. For the definition of what counts as virtue flows from a prior conception of the good virtuous citizens are to will in common. Virtue is constancy and purity. Those who exercise virtue in common seek singleness of purpose, each purging his civic will of everything which detracts from the possibility of achieving a single, common will. Once the definition of virtue is fixed, virtuous citizens willing together must converge upon a single, true result governing all.

We can discern the separate elements at work in the theory as Rousseau worries about the impurity of the common will when it is an expression of citizens who have lost their virtue. 'Does it follow from this that the general will is annihilated or corrupted? No, it it always constant, unalterable and pure.' [37] It is 'constant, unalterable and pure,' even when it is not willed. Add docility, and we have the definition of the virtuous woman promulgated in *Emile*.

The defining traits of the general will, once will is subtracted from them, correspond to Rousseau's definition of the virtuous self. But this seems to whirl us around inside a very small circle. The will defines virtue and virtue defines what is to be willed. How do we know what is virtuous or that it must be constant, unalterable and pure? Does a general will define virtue or does virtue constitute the general will? Neither. The natural religion hovers in the background, orchestrating both and saving the theory from vicious circularity.

Rousseau insists that everything is pure as it leaves the hands of God, and that it must become simple and pure again when humans lift themselves to the condition he intended for them. This insistence is not only designed to save human beings in God's eyes; it is designed to save God in Rousseau's eyes. For this is the only God he can accept. The only God who can stand in Rousseau's good grace is one who guarantees 'the happiness of the just, the punishment of the wicked; the sanctity of the social contract and the laws.'

The truth of the general will is not simply willed; it is recognized through willing under the right conditions of virtue and religious belief.

This idea emerges openly when Rousseau considers the virtuous citizen whose will deviates from the collective result. For when citizens vote on the general will, they are not asked to 'approve or reject this proposal, but whether it does or does not conform to the general will which is theirs ... Therefore when the opinion contrary to mine prevails, that proves nothing except that I was mistaken; and what I thought to be the general will was not.'[38] Why could one not conclude that the general will might have issued in two wills here, each of which conforms to its criteria of existence? Because the Rousseauian general will does not aim merely at generating several outcomes in each issue area each conforming to its criteria of generality; it demands a single, true will applicable to all. If virtue aims at generality and singularity, the agent with the contrary view is imperfectly virtuous until he corrects his own will. If a minority can be mistaken in its will despite the best will in the world, perhaps the general will is more than a will: perhaps it is the discovery of a higher will which shines through ours when we purify ourselves. God's will, which shines through nature, also shines through the general will when it is properly formed. And if God's will is to shine through the will of citizens, they must convert themselves into instruments of that will; they must purify themselves of extraneous desires and impulses, until they are able and willing to establish singularity of purpose together. The dictates of Rousseauian faith determine both how the state of nature must be in its purity and how the general will must coordinate generality and singularity of will perfectly.

If Rousseauian faith were subtracted from the interior life of the Social Contract, one set of supports for virtue and the general will would disappear. But, more fundamentally, it would then become highly contestable whether the politics of virtue requires the organization of each self so that it converges with all selves on a single general will and whether the result of willing in common must be considered imperfect or false unless it generates a single, true conclusion. The necessary nexus between virtuous citizens and singularity of common purpose would be questioned or broken.

In social thought, a set of presuppositions functions as a set of demands the theorist imposes upon theory. In life, faith operates as a set of hopes and demands the living impose upon the world. Rousseau is insistent and demanding. He demands unity and purity and seeks guarantees for its truth in his faith; he insists that an entire people evaluate their actual existence by that faith too, even though none is likely ever to achieve fully the purity sought, even though they are likely to evaluate themselves negatively and critically by comparison with the standards of purity they are called upon to endorse. Rousseauian insistence engenders alienation in life; his faith, from the vantage point of those who refuse it, becomes the demand to enclose life in an artificial mold weighted down by ontological armor. That insistence fosters alienation within the ideal society among those struggling to bring their souls and bodies into alignment with Rousseauian purity; it fosters a perpetual yearning for unity and singularity of purpose in other societies where the Rousseauian ideal of politics merely haunts the souls of the members. It is, from the vantage point of a theory which eschews the faith it offers, a nihilistic theory.

Consider a civil society in which citizens do not insist in advance that their wills be coordinated perfectly in public discourse, in which they expect citizens of good will to reach opposing conclusions on many general issues, in which they think twice about imposing a common rule because of the legitimacy of a diverse set of wills, and in which they realize that sometimes an authoritative, general policy is needed even if a single will is not realized. Pornography becomes an issue. Some conclude that it degrades those depicted, encourages violence and, therefore, that it must be prohibited. It speaks to distorted desires which must be contained or eliminated; it uses the cover of freedom of expression to assault the dignity and integrity of those it depicts. Others, giving less weight to these points, conclude that any prohibition in this area might confine aesthetic sensibility in any area and constrict human creativity in all areas of life. Pornography, while dangerous, also calls attention to aspects of human life which do not fit neatly into this or that container of virtue. It emerges, they say, whenever virtue is too tightly defined; it operates as a protest against it. The demands of virtue must be relaxed.

Without prior insistence that their wills, when each is pure, must converge, it is very likely they never will. Only a practice or theory which inclined its prior definition of virtue and the good life in one of these directions would permit convergence here. Each position outlined above gives priority to a standard that carries repugnant implications to the other. One equates life with exploration, danger, creativity and minimal restraint on the exploratory sensibility, even if it assaults the all too vulnerable self-image of others. The other equates life with decency and the protection of dignity, even if the free attainment of the former sets severe limits on 'exploratory' sensibilities. Their discursive engagement clarifies and crystallizes these differences rather than dissolves them. And this might remain the case even after each bracketed out those interests that were most immediately advantageous to him or her in the case before them.

One point of this example is to suggest that faith in the possibility and desirability of unity actually devalues the political dimension of life.

Politics emerges when a general policy is needed, but the issue to be resolved resists the attempt to dissolve it into a single will. Creativity is then called into play. Perhaps a compromise is reached. Perhaps the need for a common decision is reconsidered after the depth of the disagreement is revealed. Perhaps one side attains a victory but dissent by other parties keeps the contestability of the issue alive. Perhaps one side wins and refuses to concede space to the defeated parties. But even here the defeat is at least acknowledged to be such; the issue is not dissolved into a moral unity in which the losers now know themselves to be mistaken or lacking in virtue.

Rousseau seeks to dissolve politics into unity and to ground unity in the faith of a religion inscribed in the fabric of civil society. From the vantage point of his faith, that looks like a beautiful possibility to yearn for even while admitting we are unlikely to achieve it. From the vantage point of these who see that faith as a form of childlike insistence, the yearning fosters alienation from life; it constitutes a devaluation of politics; it reflects a refusal to affirm fundamental dimensions of the human condition.

To expose the element of faith in Rousseau's theory is to go a long way toward defeating his ideal of community and toward calling into question contemporary ideals which bury this faith even more deeply in their categories. For the same considerations Rousseau brought against the universality of traditional Christianity can be brought against the universality of his natural religion and its incorporation into civil society. If many today cannot locate those few simple dogmas in nature, the civil religion could only be enforced through coercion, and if the Social Contract requires a large dose of coercion to maintain itself, it cannot, on Rousseau's assumptions, hope to foster virtuous citizens seeking to realize a common will.

When the universality of Rousseauian faith is withdrawn, the ideal it holds together falls into pieces. When the ideal falls apart, the starting points of Rousseau's theory begin to look highly contestable. It is no longer necessary to believe that nature is good in itself or that the general will must be able in principle to re-establish that perfection at a higher level. Some may continue to keep the faith, but their attempt to universalize a political vision expressive of it would now require manipulative controls and coercive regulations to sustain itself against those who would resist or evade its strictures. The Rousseauian vision collapses, not because it is impossible for some to have faith in it, but because its faith is not generalizable in the modern age in which it is offered. Its eloquence can speak only to some; its vision is a nightmare to many. That defect is fatal to a vision which eschews the use of force to achieve singularity in the general will.

The collapse of the Rousseauian vision does not break every insight in the theory. Its parts teach even if the whole cannot marshal enough faith to pull itself together. To crystallize his vision, Rousseau revealed much about perplexities facing the new world which called these reflections into being, about the complexities of freedom and citizenship, about the ways in which moral psychology and social structure are interwoven, about the destructive effects of inequality, about the internal defects of a politics founded merely on the self-interest of its citizens, about the paradoxes of political life. Perhaps he even teaches us something about the human urge to find a home in the world, about the inventiveness of that urge in locating new paths to fulfill itself, and about dangers involved in pursuing this path to its end.

First Interlude:
Hobbes, Rousseau and the Marquis de Sade

The holy alliance

Rousseau, it is correct to say, is the critic of Hobbes. Better, each is a critic of the other. We are expected to judge between these theories. And if we find the options to be too starkly defined, we are invited to work out a compromise, drawing on Locke, or Mill or Tocqueville to guide the mediation process. But what if we avoid choice or compromise this time because each path is so well-worn, because the insights it provides to thought are correspondingly worn down? Perhaps thought about the modern condition advances further, first, by pulling each theory to its extreme pole and, then, by striving to identify those complementarities which locate the poles on the same plane. It may be possible to approach boundaries of early modern thought by identifying commonalities between opponents. And maybe these commonalities can then be brought to sharper definition through engagement with a dissident text designed to subvert the commonalities of its own day.

Consider some differences between Hobbes and Rousseau. Hobbes thinks the state of nature is a condition of war, while Rousseau finds it to be a state of simple bliss; the first treats the subject to be a self-interested being, while the second finds the virtuous self to be a precondition of the good life and a just order; the former prefers the sovereign to be a monarch, because one ruler is less likely to become inflamed than many rubbing together, while the latter invests sovereignty in the general will, because only it can unite freedom and legitimacy in one will; this one seeks freedom in those areas of life which sovereignty can afford to leave alone, that one in harmony between the will of the self and the general will; one gives the sovereign authority to define the details of religious practice, the other thinks the sovereign can ignore those details; one celebrates commercial life and the other thinks it breeds civic corruption;

this one accepts inequality and that one finds equality to be an essential condition of the good life; one thinks that his principles can be applied everywhere, the other doubts his can be applied anywhere; each would judge his competitor to be utopian, finding unrealistic hopes or assumptions lodged at crucial places in the thought of the other.

But affinities and complementries abound between these two theories as well. Both Rousseau and Hobbes repudiate pre-modern doctrines which invest God's will in custom. Both are wary of the Bible and the clergy as interpreters of God's will. Both seek a new site for God to shed illumination on human affairs. Both locate nature as a place where the light of God is reflected. Both identify reason as a medium of that light, insisting that God would not endow humanity with such a faculty and then fill it with conclusions that misrepresent his will for them. Both are disturbed by disruptive human passions, seeking ways to temper some and sublimate others. Each celebrates a form of self-restraint to give the self coherence, make it predictable and render it suitable for order: one by converting an impulsive being into a self-interested subject who accepts moral restraints on self-interest, the other by converting a passionate being governed by self-love into a virtuous self who internalizes the standards of a just community. Each supports political order with the dictates of an official religion supported by the sovereign power, unamenable to public criticism by an independent church or by non-believers. Both theorists give primacy to order in the soul and the polity, thinking about the self first and foremost in terms of its susceptibility to the dictates of a well-designed order. Each tends to moralize the order he endorses and to define that which differs from these endorsements as foolish, mad, vicious or irrational. Difference – that which deviates from the mold of the order or the model of the self but still finds expression in the world – is enclosed in a moral code and treated as defect, excess, vice or irrationality to be corrected, improved, punished, excluded or instilled with faith. Each hopes that the sovereign power will be able to confine itself to a few simple laws, letting self-interest in commercial life or virtue in community life unite with faith to stabilize a just peace. Finally, as a result of the interior organization of the self, the moralization of difference, the closure of religious belief, the quest for univocality in the voice of the sovereign, and the minimilization of sovereign action, neither leaves much space for politics in the common life, fearing that volatile and destructive passions will overflow self-interest or virtue if public debate, uncensored texts or erotic passions seep into the common life.

We have here two theories of peace and quiet, peace in the self and quiet in the common life. Each does pursue its own vision in ways that distinguish it from the other, but these competing visions also complement each other when they compete within the actual life of a state. Each vision dramatizes how it does or would contribute to freedom, and debates between them deflect attention from ways in which they can function together as agents of social domestication and discipline.

In modern life appeals to virtue (to normality, common expectations, tradition, models of identification, patriotism) can sometimes foster self-restraint in support of the public good and self-mobilization in pursuit of common purposes. And when these appeals begin to cut against the grain of the self, counter-appeals are invoked to self-interested components of the individual, appeals to think about one's own priorities first, to react suspiciously to the invocation of ideals, to act independently on one's own behalf in this world. The self-interested individual does secure a moment of independence, but its full status is highly ambiguous on that score. For the self-interested agent is also an organized self. It too requires social discipline and self-regulation to maintain itself; and, once it becomes stabilized and predictable, it also renders itself responsive to the dictates of the order through its susceptibility to promises, incentive systems and coercive threats. If we think of the modern self as a site both for the blandishments of virtue and the manipulation of self-interest, we can see more clearly how these competing ideals of the ordered self can insinuate themselves into the complexity of the modern individual; and we can discern ambiguities in the relation of the individual to itself and the order concealed by the dominant terms of debate between the two ideals. The politics of the debate between them tends to obliterate a more general question: How much of the self must be drawn into the orbit of social discipline through interest and virtue for a modern order to maintain itself? What are the effects on the self and the world of this intensive organization of self?

The modern self is more complex and diverse than either of these models implies. Nor is it reducible to a combination of the two. Nor do the two in conjunction reveal the modern self to be colonized completely by the dictates of order. There is much about the modern self which escapes both these alternative models and the diverse strategies of social discipline to which it is subjected. Nonetheless, when we remember how Hobbes and Rousseau each theorized the self first and foremost from the vantage point of its compatibility with a dream of order, and when we acknowledge that modern orders depend on intensive and extensive organization of the self to maintain themselves, we are in a better position to see how these opposing ideals of self can function as complementary strategies of discipline within the confines of modern life. Humanism and technocracy, individual interest and social utility, rights and virtue, therapy and punishment, and rehabilitation and deterrence – the fixed poisitions in these debates are not simply to be shuffled into a duality which gives primacy to the individual on one side and the order on the other. Each possesses the potential to be deployed on behalf of a politics of order; the rhetorical and organizational resources of one become available for use when those of the other fall short of the mark.

But how could two alternative modes of discipline be applied to the same self if Hobbes and Rousseau each applied his model to a single self, each uncongenial, as we have seen, to the structure of the other? For the two modes of social discipline to function in a complementary way a more complex self must be brought into being, incorporating elements from both of these models. The theory of the unconscious is undeveloped when Hobbes and Rousseau are writing, but the model of selfhood and order each endorses accentuates the need for regulation by the self of its self. Considered in relation to each other, these two political theories of self prefigure the modern theory of the stratified subject, a complex formation containing mechanisms for pursuing interests and exercising virtues, and containing that in the human animal which would overwhelm or undermine them. The stratified subject contains a superego, providing a new site for the old virtuous self; an ego, containing the old self-interested and rational self; and the it (or id), housing passions, desires, impulses which do not fit neatly into either of the first two slots. By attending to these early modern dreams of harmony between the form of the self and the structure of order we can thus translate the psychological theory of the stratified subject into a political theory of the modern self. This political theory of the self provides access to an interconnected set of sites in the self upon which a variety of engagements occur between the dictates of order and that which accepts, resists, evades, endorses and subverts them.

The modern theory of the stratified subject, with its levels of unconscious, preconscious, conscious and self-conscious activity, and its convoluted relays among passions, interests, wishes, responsibility and guilt, locates within the self conflicts which Hobbes and Rousseau distributed across regimes. This places the two theorists together in an ambiguous position with respect to contemporary questions about the relation of the self to the order in which it is formed. For if neither developed a theory of the unconscious or a corollary theory of self-consciousness – there was not yet need for either – both have a more overt understanding than most contemporary thinkers of the political relation between a form of self and the order in which it acquires form. Each thinks overtly about what has to be contained or developed, mobilized or immobilized, for the self to fit the order he idealizes. They understand as part of a political debate, then issues about the self in its relation to order that in contemporary life have tended to be couched in psychological, social and philosophical vocabularies. They thus encourage us to listen today to political issues muffled by the unpolitical vocabularies into which they have been sunk.

The blindness of nature

If Hobbes and Rousseau seek to domesticate desire by channeling it into interest and virtue, the Marquis de Sade deploys the same vocabulary of passion, nature, God reason and light to hammer down these constructions. By bringing the light of philosophy into the bedroom he exposes the element of cruelty in desire and attacks the self-violence inherent in these dreams of self and order. He uses the rhetoric of nature to extinguish the light Hobbes and Rousseau had seen reflected in it, thereby alerting us to the political bearing of rhetorical devices. He is the other of Enlightenment, using its own devices against it, perhaps bringing out implications it had left in the dark, certainly requiring those who would walk in the footsteps of Hobbes and Rousseau either to change the basis of their thought or to acknowledge the element of violence lodged in their designs.

Philosophy in the Bedroom, published in 1795 after the reign of terror accompanying the French Revolution, presents itself in its title as a text suspended in ambiguity. Sade will bring the light of philosophy to a place Hobbes and Rousseau kept shrouded. 'Everything must be seen,' says the libertine Madame de Saint Ange, when she brings her young protégée to the room of brilliant lights and mirrors: 'no part of the body can remain hidden.'[1] Here, where artificial light replaces the light of nature, is where the play of passion and desire can be observed and experienced most closely. But here, too, discourse is less likely to seek a truth as it exists separate from desire. Bedroom talk is designed to excite passion, spur desire, overwhelm modesty; it brings, as Sade says, theory and practice as close together as they can be, but it does so in pursuit of seduction rather than truth.

So, one is often uncertain in reading this text when its philosophy is to be translated into public action or when its point is to use language to excite passions in the bedroom. This ambiguity is signaled overtly after we have been treated to a fifty-page disquisition on republican government inserted into the middle of the text. Le Chevalier, a participant in the induction of young Eugénie into the pleasures of libertinage, argues against allowing cruelty and violence in this 'republican' state, and Dolmance, the tutor in this series of lessons, responds that his comrade's reasoning has faltered: 'we are constantly led astray by false definitions when we wish to reason logically.' A more lucid set of definitions, illuminated by the light in this very room, will restore the original argument in favor of cruelty. Eugénie, the object of this debate, responds:

'You triumph, Dolmance, the laurel belongs to you! The Chevalier's harangue did but barely brush my spirit, yours seduces and entirely wins it over. Ah, Chevalier, take my advice: speak rather to the passions than to the virtues when you wish to persuade a woman.'[2]

Reason is an instrument of persuasion. It can speak to the passions, the interests or the virtues, but not to itself. When seduction is its goal, it will speak to the first. Sade would seduce us away from modesty and virtue in the bedroom; he would incite that which Hobbes and Rousseau contain. But while bedroom talk flows freely into every conceivable topic, the effects it is to engender outside that room remain suspended in uncertainty. Are its principles to be translated directly into public life? Are they to be confined strictly to this room? Is, perhaps, the course to be altered as these currents flow into other arenas of life?

We cannot answer these questions with assurance. We can, though, treat Sade as a dissident thinker whose positive formulations are designed to crack the foundation upon which the theories of Hobbes and Rousseau rest. If nature can allow these things, it cannot provide the altar at which Hobbes and Rousseau pray.

Philosophy in the Bedroom has a simple organization. There are brief scenes of initiation in which one woman and two, sometimes three, men instruct Eugénie by example, followed by lengthy discussions of the moral, social and political implications of these exercises. Each rite of initiation is carefully organized by Dolmance. Often each participant is both penetrater and penetrated, assaulter and assaulted, in the same scene; each is connected to all, consenting to receive the pleasure and cruelty he or she bestows on others. A theory of self and sociality may be represented in these geometrical gymnastics. The self, formed through intensive social organization, becomes overwhelmed by an ocean of feeling, revealing aspects of the human animal which reach beyond the official form of the self. But this transgression is itself carefully orchestrated, confirming that the self requires organization even to transcend itself. Each moment of submergence in the organized system of sexual exchange is followed by a renewal of the discursive attack on conventional manners and morality, an assault in particular on the natural status custom bestows on its own artifices of self and convention.

Clearly, one point of each ritual is to show through representation how we are moved by thoughts and fantasies that inflict cruelty on others and ourselves. Each might be repelled by some of these rites, bored by many, incited by a few, and suspended in ambivalence by yet others. But each experiences somewhere in these Sadeian exercises the relation of cruelty to desire. To eliminate all cruelty, say, to eliminate even the pleasures that gossip bestows as we spread cruel rumors about those with whom we are engaged, would be to put desire itself on ice. We must lie to ourselves to deny these experiential truths. Since virtue counsels honesty, the virtuous ones should be the most willing to acknowledge these truths. But virtue also pretends that desire can be dissociated from cruelty, if only life is ordered correctly. So the virtuous ones must be the last to admit these things and the first to condemn honesty about them. They mask gossip, for instance, in a show of concern for the objects of their malice. Men and women of virtue are thus inveterate agents of deceit. Their tyranny over others and themselves colludes with the deceits they cultivate so carefully.

Dolmance is an enemy of the modest, simple, chaste, transparent woman of virtue Rousseau celebrates in Emile, mostly because these traits make her too docile, too dead, too obedient to the rule of a single virtuous male and too responsive to the dictates of an unnatural order. He insists that much of the pleasure of debauchery resides in shocking the simple sensibilities of this artificial woman of virtue. It is not that he would replace her with an independent woman because, at least in the text before us, he insists that each woman must accept sexual advances from any man even though she is not to become the permanent property of any single one. The woman as libertine is freed from the restraint of virtue to be shackled by another set, but Dolmance paints a very unattractive picture of the virtues left behind.

Ah, Eugénie, have done with virtues! Among the sacrifices that can be made to these counterfeit divinities is there one worth an instant of the pleasures one tastes in outraging them? Come, my sweet, virtue is but a chimera whose worship consists exclusively in perpetual immolations, in unnumbered rebellions against the temperament's inspirations. Can such impulses be natural? Does Nature recommend what offends her? . . . Theirs are not . . . the same passions as ours; but they hearken to others, and often more contemptible . . . There is ambition, there pride, there you find self-seeking.[3]

Eugénie becomes the double of the Rousseauian woman of virtue. Each calls the other into being; neither could be without the opposition of the other. The very character of Eugénie's pleasures and desires are defined against the restrictions her virtuous mother would impose upon her. Rebellion is sweet, particularly when it unleashes passions that press so urgently against the body. It combines release and revenge in one act. Equally, her mother's chastity and humility could not be virtues were it not for women such as her daughter to condemn and avoid.

They create each other, these two. And they stand to each other as Sade stands to all thinkers who try to deify nature. Here, too, each opponent defines the space in which the other can be, and each uses the power at his disposal to establish hegemony for those standards he would endorse. It is just that, outside of the Sadeian text, the power of the contestants inclines sharply to one side of the duality in which the contest occurs.

To see the light of God in nature one must, for instance, assert that cruelty goes against the law of nature. Sade's opponents thus give him a fund of deceits and subdued passion to work upon in seducing thinkers away from these timid prescriptions for life. But the established dualities of enlightened discourse (virtue/vice, modesty/indecency, natural/ unnatural, reason/unreason) set a trap for anyone who would try to expose the standard authorizing them. Sade, through his attack on nature as the ground of morality, becomes defined officially as the voice of that which is unnatural, monstrous, mad. He is not allowed to show his opponents how their own standard of nature authorizes the most heinous acts, perhaps because the eloquence of nature is not understood to include room for ironic discourse. The authorities simply apply the standard to the texts he deploys to subvert it. He thus brings upon himself censorship, imprisonment and detention in an asylum. The Secretary at Charenton, an asylum for lunatics where Sade is housed during his later years, concludes that he 'is suffering from the most dangerous of mental disorders,' that his writings 'are no less bereft of reason than his speech and actions,' that 'the greatest care' must be taken 'to forbid him the use of pencils, ink, pens and paper,' that though he is not in a state of 'complete lunacy,' he is 'suffering from a special kind of madness which does not permit his continued freedom in society.'[4] Those whose 'evil constitution of the organs of the body,' as Hobbes put it, blind them to the light of nature must be confined and silenced so that they will not distort the organs through which others perceive its truth. Even nature, it seems, makes mistakes.

In the *Discourse on the Origin of Inequality* Rousseau reached a critical juncture where his thought might have followed either of two directions. After showing the social contract to be a great swindle, he could either have constructed a model of republican anarchy, where legal regulation is minimal so that political tyranny can be avoided, or pursued the ideal of republican community, where virtuous selves seek to concur unanimously on the laws governing everyone. Rousseau, with some reservations and doubt, followed the second path. It seemed to be implied by his faith that everything was good as it left the hands of God and could approach perfection again if only a virtuous people could be found. Sade, through the voice of the anonymous author of 'Yet Another Effort, Frenchmen, If You Would Become Republicans,' placed in *Philosophy in the Bedroom*, pursues a perverse version of the path Rousseau forsook. His critique of the tacit contract 'Frenchmen' previously had been expected to endorse sounds very much like Rousseau:

Well, I ask you now whether that law is truly just which orders the man who has nothing to respect another who has everything? What are the elements of the social contract? Does it not consist in one's yielding a little of his freedom and wealth in order to assure and sustain the preservation of each?[5]

There is an alternative contract worth signing. It avoids entangling the individual very firmly in the tentacles of the law by accepting the risk that others will harm one out of envy, or revenge or desire. First, the state should abrogate all laws 'comprehended under the indefinite names of impiety, sacrilege, blasphemy, atheism, etc.'[6] because they assert specious commands from a God who is 'plainly an idea without object.'[7] If God existed, if he were benevolent and if his word were of utmost significance to human beings, surely he would not make it so difficult to decipher that word, and certainly those who consult nature to hear it would not come away with such radically diverse interpretations.

Sade here replicates and mimics arguments Hobbes and Rousseau had brought already against the ability of humans to give precise and universal interpretations of scripture and against the moral authority of priests; he merely applies them now to the terrain they themselves have invested with divine light. There is no rational necessity that nature provide the place in which the light of a God is reflected:

it is far less essential to inquire into the workings of Nature than to enjoy her . . . ; it is but necessary to interrogate the heart to discern its impulse. If they wish absolutely that you speak to them of a creator, answer that things always having been what now they are, never having a beginning and never going to have an end, it thus becomes as useless as impossible for man to . . . trace things back to an imaginary origin which would explain nothing and do not a jot of good.[8]

Religion is the 'cradle of despotism' because it always creates a privileged set of priests to interpret God's will in their own spirit and to threaten worldly or afterwordly sanctions against those who do not abide by it. A republican state will disconnect its laws completely from religion.

Second, when deciding which thoughts and actions to limit, it is proper to consult nature, even though it does not reflect the light of God. When one consults this de-deified nature, one finds that it equips humans with a vast diversity of propensities, passions, desires and inclinations and that it is far better to allow this diversity to find expression than to try to model each self after some specious paradigm of selfhood or some uniform ideal of social relations: 'such a proceeding would be as ridiculous as that of a general who would have all his soldiers dressed in a uniform of the same size.'[9]

So the anonymous republican supports sodomy, contending that a number of men and women are naturally disposed to sex with others of the same gender and that the close correspondence between the oval shape of the anus and the circumference of the penis discloses how nature made each for the other; he calls for public houses where members of each sex can gratify any desire they imagine on the grounds that lust, the expression of 'Nature's voice,' should not be 'stifled or legislated against' but should be 'satisfied in peace';[10] he opposes laws against adultery and promiscuity on the grounds that nature implanted multiple desires in each of us and that acceptance of these practices would be better than letting the state intrude so far into personal life; he opposes theft, unless it occurs in a system of inequality, but counsels the law to stay out of the matter; he endorses rape on the grounds that nature authorizes it my making rapists stronger than their victims; and he refuses to endorse laws against murder on the grounds that the risk of revenge from friends and family is a safer form of control than arming the state with too many weapons of control. This Sadeian 'republican' supports a minimal state while refusing to make optimistic assumptions either about the regulatory power of the market or harmonizing authority of community.

The Sadeian strategy is first to sever the connection between God and nature, by revealing through the endless repetition of examples how impossible it is for each to hear the same voice of God there, and then to endorse, perhaps ironically, a standard of nature devoid of God. The Enlightenment view of nature combined the idea of nature as that which enables and determines life with that which sets the end or purpose of life. But if God is subtracted from it, nature no longer has a will, intelligence or law (as command) inscribed in it; and if the designer has disappeared from nature, so has any design, purpose or end. The two elements, previously coordinated carefully under one rubric, are now separated; and nature becomes a fund of forces, materials, drives and limits which shape and condition life.

Nature now allows anything and everything. If one now wishes to ascertain whether some act is natural, one needs only to ascertain whether it can become an object of desire. And if one doubts the possibility, Sade will demonstrate how the desire can be incited in some and, often, how it has been operative in certain historical periods. Desires, even those requiring extensive social cultivation, are authorized by nature, and nothing *in nature* itself overturns any desire which becomes intense at a particular moment. By thus purporting to abide by the standard of nature Sade gradually slides desire and will themselves into the superior position, for to be desired now becomes the criterion of what is natural.

Take murder. Every creation in nature involves destruction of something because everything is created out of something else. Perhaps, though, we should let nature do the killing and refrain from it ourselves? But murderous impulses too are expressions of nature, and they flare up in many *some* of the time.

But they are Nature's impulses man follows when he indulges in homicide; it is Nature who advises him, and the man who destroys his fellow is to Nature what are the plague and famine, like them sent by her hand which employs every possible means more speedily to obtain destruction of this primary matter . . . Let us deign for a moment to illumine our spirit by philosophy's sacred flame: what other than Nature's voice suggests to us personal hatreds, revenges, wars, in a word, all those causes of perpetual murder? Now, if she incites us to murderous acts, she has need of them; that once grasped, how may we suppose ourselves guilty in her regard when we do nothing more than obey her intentions?[11]

'Let us deign for a moment to illumine our spirit by philosophy's sacred flame . . ' Sade's narcissistic individualism taunts and ridicules the transcendental narcissism governing the thought of Hobbes and Rousseau. If they can indulge the extravagant demand that nature glow with God's love or law for humanity, he will indulge the imperious wish that it authorize the link between pleasures of the self and cruelty to others. The Sadeian storm of passion and cruelty, raging within four walls of an imaginary bedroom, underlines the cosmic proportions of his opponents' narcissistic delusions: they demand that God inscribe guidelines and protections for the human comedy in the text of nature; they insist that the design of nature itself revolve around the fate of humanity! The reference to 'philosophy's sacred flame' can be read as either an ironic repudiation of nature as a guide to morality or an ironic endorsement of it because it authorizes those actions its own moralists tried to condemn.

Either way, after Sade nature no longer glows with a sacred flame capable of illuminating the life of an entire people. Each future attempt to reincarnate God or reason in nature is stymied by oppositional tactics similar to those adopted by Sade, even though the later battles never become as heated as this original conflagration. Sade remains as an exemplar of the attractions, dangers and ironies of trangression: by exploring forbidden territory transgression opens up new possibilities of action and new domains of knowledge about the human condition; by breaking down established limits it unleashes energies of violence and destruction; by calling the status of established dualities into question it brings the power that maintains them down upon itself. Certainly, after Sade's exposure of the relation between cruelty and desire, the deceits inside virtue, and the drives nature inscribes upon the body, any political theory of the self must now establish space for unconscious drives and self-conscious clarification, and any psychological theory of the stratified subject renders itself susceptible to a political reading.

But Sade himself, once the flame has been extinguished from nature, disappears as the agent of darkness. The attack on the rhetoric of nature – on nature as the medium of reason, or holy law, or divine love or a social contract – is misdirected once those who would ground a theory of modern politics have migrated to other fields.

The politics of pornography

If the Sadeian demolition of the standard of nature loses historical pertinence after political theory retreats from the myth of nature and contracts, Sade lives on as the paradigmatic pornographer, as the one who draws philosophy, desire, violence and degradation together into a persistent alliance of perversity. The word pornography, crafted from Greek words for harlot and writing, did not achieve currency in English until the middle of the nineteenth century. But by 1893, according to the *Oxford English Dictionary*, Sade had come to represent the prototype pornographer.

Given a dictionary definition of pornography as obscene writing, there is indeed pornography on every page of *Philosophy in the Bedroom*. But the pornographic dimension, in a more fundamental sense, advances as the text proceeds through the induction of Eugenie into the connections between pleasure and cruelty to the closing scene in which Eugenie takes revenge against her mother for being her mother. Desire is now assimilated with revenge in a mixture which becomes, I shall argue, definitive of the pornographic.

Eugénie has particular motives for seeking revenge against her mother; Dolmance and Madame de Saint-Ange have generic reasons.

The mother, representing nurturance, moral restraint and the acceptance of authority, is a bearer of arbitrary power concealed under the cloak of objective virtue; she thus provides a generic object of visceral revenge. Her punishment is necessary to the elusive freedom the libertines pursue.

Subjecting Madame de Mistival, the now trapped mother and wife, to a series of insults under the banner of the virtues she embodies (honesty, politeness, chastity, obedience), Madame de Saint-Ange defines her to be a whore, a woman who sells sex to her husband in exchange for security, status and support. Indeed, a whole series of redefinitions, tyrannically reversing in one room a set of categories which tyrannize libertinage outside this sanctuary, determines the course of revenge the trio plots. The victim is finally set straight:

Listen to me whore! I am going to explain everything to you! . . . You are a victim sent us by your own husband; you have got to submit to your fate; nothing can save you from it . . . what will it be? I've no idea; perhaps you'll be hanged, wheeled, quartered, racked, burned alive; the choice of the torture depends upon your daughter . . . As for your cries I warn you they will be to no purpose . . .[12]

The symbol of moral righteousness and obedience is now the object of immoral power; the previous objects of power are now completely in charge; the forces normally brought to bear against them are now either neutralized or accentuated and deployed upon the mother. 'Nothing can save you' here; 'your cries . . . will be to no purpose': neither your husband nor the state nor conventional morality nor God can intervene in this place. They are as powerless here to protect you against us as they are unwilling in the larger order to protect us against the tyranny of your morality. That seems to be the message in which the libertines take delight. This reversal of control without appeal is impressed upon her body as the trio enacts its revenge against this carrier of virtue and order. For it is the body which the order represses in exercising its control over the libertine.

The mother is thus sodomized and injected with syphilis. Finally, her lower bodily orifices – the body's openings to pleasure, reproduction, intimacy and elimination of wastes – are sewn together by her daughter. The one who restricts sex to marriage and reproduction, who idealizes obedience to the husband and the order, who regulates her daughter's conduct by a puritan economy of desire and restraint, whose very self-definition requires the moral castigation and repression of libertinage, provides the consummate object of Sadeian revenge. The ambiguous opening through which the daughter was brought into being and the mother established her claim to virtue and chastity is sealed shut by a daughter who now opens herself only to the pleasures of desire and power. The hypocrite who symbolizes a sanitized ideal of purity and virtue, who claims to contain bodily impulses within a spiritual ideal, becomes the victim of revenge inscribed with uncanny precision upon the body.

As this closing scene suggests, neither the pornographer nor his most adamant opponents can tolerate the play of ambiguity. The first concentrates its attack upon the element of hypocrisy in virtue, while the second refuses to engage the ambiguity of desire itself. In a connected way, neither Rousseau nor Sade ever speaks affirmatively of things the other idealizes, leading one to suspect that together they create a series of gaps between virtue and pornography which neither is able to fill with a discourse of words.

In this Sadeian text multiple acts of revenge are portrayed in perfectly protected and enclosed spaces: the text sets the acts in a room where control is complete and sound is contained; it sets the room in an order where control aspires to a totality in which sounds of dissidence and resistance can be muffled; it sets itself between the covers of a book where the fantasy of power and revenge is unbounded and where sounds of protest and pain are silenced. Each of these spaces engenders its complements. And in the contrived order of this text, itself portraying an indefinite series of contrived orders, nature is reinvoked as the author of reactive impulses to torture, mutilation, degradation and revenge. Human nature becomes a contrivance of desire.

Is the wilful authority of husbands and the arbitrary power of the social order to produce and punish otherness assaulted through this closing fantasy of reversal? If so, that irony is itself muffled beneath the repugnance of the acts portrayed and the inability of the text to fill the space between virtue and pornography. Philosophical pornography (perhaps the only kind there is) wreaks revenge against the new order by imagining an infinite regress of counter-violences, silences, fabrications and containments. Its agents represent themselves to be persecuted by official agents who regulate and suppress pleasures of the body, and they respond to their persecutors by fashioning a counter-economy of desire and cruelty: they take revenge upon the bodies of those who would organize their souls. Perhaps these imaginary acts reveal something about the mind/body/order problem in early-modern life. And perhaps Nietzsche will later enable us to peer more deeply into the pool from which this pail of revenge is drawn and replenished.

What can we learn through this classic text about a phenomenon which extends beyond the age in which it is located? Is understanding of pornography advanced if we think about Hobbes, Rousseau and Sade in relation to each other?

In a contemporary discourse, either the agents of pornography are treated as independent sources of an evil to be eliminated or the act of regulation is treated as an evil worse than the phenomenon itself. The questions are familiar. Does pornography cause violence or does it open a safety-valve of fantasy for those who would otherwise be violent? Does its regulation protect women from victimization by men or does that regulation foster a police state that victimizes men and women together? Should it be tolerated in the name of freedom of expression or eliminated in the name of a basic human right to dignity? Each of these questions is correct enough, and none should be erased from the field of debate.

But the questions themselves are incomplete, failing to pursue relentlessly how the phenomenon around which the debate rages is constituted as an object. Arguments about the definition, causes, significance and effects of pornography abound, but they are not often enough connected to reflection into the network of institutionally constituted identities and differences which render its definition possible, incite its occurrences, predetermine the acceptable range of responses to it, and excite a new set of resistances to these responses. Pornography is said variously to be rooted in the nature of men or the structure of capitalism or the breakdown of natural law or the effects of modern anomie and alienation. Any or all of these theories may harbor truth. But each of these analyses takes some particular network of identity and difference to be natural or unalienating or self-evident, and this background of naturalized arrangements limits the ability of the analyst to reach more deeply into the historically constructed character of the complex in which the phenomenon occurs.

A reading of Hobbes, Rousseau and Sade in relation to each other might make it possible to think about the constitution of the phenomenon itself – the social creation of its definitional space – in the context of the social construction of an entire field of personal identities, public moralities and instrumentalities of order. For, as we have seen, both Hobbes and Rousseau are alert to the created character of the identities they affirm and the differences they oppose; and both develop strategies to eliminate or reform modes of difference which threaten these identities. And, as we have also seen, Sade's assault on the standards of nature and God functions to call into question the grounding Hobbes and Rousseau would give to the constructs and exclusions they endorse. Reading Hobbes, Rousseau and Sade together in this way we can look with a new eye at the forms of otherness required to maintain the identities the first two idealize. Pornography is one of them.

If the field on which it moves constitutes the phenomenon, pornography still retains its reality and still generates real effects upon that field. But any effort to reconstitute pornography (rather than simply to take revenge against it) must now be linked to a reconstitution of other elements on the same terrain. Such an analysis would not simplify the task at hand: it would rather complicate and problematize it, while indicating how simpler strategies help to determine the phenomenon they oppose.

If, through a critical reading of texts by Hobbes and Rousseau, we can comprehend the modern stratified subject of reason, self-interest, virtue and desire to be a complex artifice which maintains itself through the redefinition and strategic containment of that which differs from it, then we can also glimpse how historically specifice dualities of mind/body, rational/irrational, virtue/vice, responsible/irresponsible, natural/unnatural, health/sickness provide the field upon which new forms of otherness are engendered and regulated. The way in which these dualities are filled in and out, emphasized and de-emphasized, graded and hierarchalized, creates the space in which that which was coarse, debauched and libertine eventually becomes recrafted into pornography. If the libertine was one who affirmed sins of the flesh over the call of spirituality, the pornographer invokes reason and power to degrade women who accept their terms of existence as social bearers of virtue and responsibility. The tightening and intensification of the affirmative standards of reason, order, virtue and responsibility creates a subordinate space within which pornography attacks this entire network of ordering concepts.

Pornography is the perverse revenge bodies take against the modern terms of their spiritual organization.

While pornography can be read as a sign of destructiveness built into established definitions of selfhood and otherness, its perversity resides in its radical intensification of destruction and its selection of the female body as the special object of its wrath. Perhaps this particularity of the pornographic object is set up by the singular status of the female as an essential participant in early-modern life (she is neither mad nor vicious by definition) who nonetheless fails to measure up to paradigmatic standards of freedom, reason, citizenship and knowledge. Does this structurally imposed ambiguity set women up to be privileged objects of pornographic assault?

Sade becomes the first pornographer – or at least the congealed symbol of a pornography forming itself upon a modern field of discourse – when sins of the flesh become defined as a 'special kind of madness' functioning in opposition to affirmative standards of reason, nature and virtue. And this process tracks a series of other shifts in the regulation of sex, such as the conversion of onanism as a sin against God into masturbation as an activity which courts madness by pumping too much blood too rapidly into the brain. Pornography comes into its own when this new regime of bodily regulation is challenged by textual acts of revenge against these standards of reason, virtue, interests and health.

There is perhaps a two-tiered process involved in the formation of pornography. The first tier involves a series of official redefinitions: sin into perversity; perversity into madness; madness into sickness; with pornography finally emerging as a specific mode of perverse desire filled with mental disturbance and social danger.

The second tier involves a reactive strategy of textual revenge enacted by the targets of these definitions; it is aimed at agents who authorize them and applied to subordinates who passively accept them. Pornography emerges as pleasurable acts of degradation and cruelty perpetrated upon those who willingly or innocently embody standards which degrade themselves. They 'get what was coming to them'.

Sadeian pornography seeks conceptual clarification through confrontation of identities with the differences they engender and subjugate. It is analytic philosophy applied to a socially established organization of bodies, desires and restraints. But in striving to expose and incite bodily resistance to a system of identities it pursues a simple strategy of reversal, attributing to the adversary all the evils officially attributed to it and projecting on to those who consent to subordination in the existing order its own grossly exaggerated versions of the penalties already imposed upon them. The typical effect of this strategy is to press most constitutencies to endorse publicly (often to keep authorities off the track of its secret powers of attraction) the very definitions pornography seeks to oppose. The pornographic strategy of revenge thus sets up its own agents to become the objects of new cycles of official vengeance. The two parties maintain each other through their complementary strategies of opposition.

Pornography is therefore simultaneously a joint production, an assault on established identities and a source of renewal for the system of identities it mirrors; it maintains difference as otherness and folds resistances back into the system of identities which engendered them. Understood in isolation from its conditions of existence, it is a sickness which jeopardizes natural standards of dignity, rights, reason and normality. Interpreted as an effect of the system in which it participates it shoots tremors of doubt and uncertainty into the complex itself. For pornography installs itself as these standards become perfected. As a joint production its most extreme opponents now become its most perverse allies: they oppose the phenomenon while obstinately refusing to rethink the complex spiral of enactments and re-enactments through which it is isolated as otherness to be subjugated; they mark the phenomenon they oppose to give definition to the identities they endorse. (This structural alliance is not dependent upon the familiar and plausible charge that adamant opponents of pornography are drawn psychologically to the texts they condemn.)

To dismantle pornography, on this reading, is to install a series of modifications on the field upon which it is defined, elicited, attacked and consolidated; it is to rethink the relations among pleasure and desire, desire and personal identity, personal identity and bodily disciplines, virtue and order, masculine and feminine, reason and unreason, collective identity and the claims of difference. Anything less participates in the cycle of vengeance and revenge. For if pornography is a perverse strategy of revenge against official definitions, many of the weapons through which it is combated move too close for comfort to those of the adversary.

Because Hobbes, Rousseau and Sade together illuminate the constructed character of complex systems of identity and difference, they together provide a textual background for rethinking this particular network of identitites and differences. Such a reconsideration can be launched by recalling that Sade was a voracious reader of Rousseau as the prototype theorist of the standards he most despised, and that Hobbes and Rousseau both concerned themselves overtly with restraints, disciplines, penalties and exclusions essential to the standards each affirmed. Such a rethinking of pornography and its conditions of existence can be launched through reading each of these three thinkers with and against the others; but it cannot be completed in this way. For the operative standards of subjectivity, normality, order and pornography have evolved over the last 200 years.

Once this limitation is acknowledged it is perhaps even more pertinent to pose a couple of questions to these three thinkers that might identify a persistent line of continuity connecting them to each other and to contemporaries standing on both sides of this issue. If revenge is inscribed in Sade's portrayals of women, reason, nature, faith, virtue and civil order, is it also imprinted in the definitions of madness, passion, drunkenness, atheism, unnaturality, unreason, civil-resistance, vice, unfreedom and women constructed by Hobbes and Rousseau respectively? And if a spirit of revenge does infiltrate into definitions advanced by these latter two idealists of order, what are its sources and who or what are its most fundamental targets?

4

Hegel: The Politics of Inclusivity

Madness and knowledge

Hegel does not endorse philosophizing 'by the light of nature.'[1] For if I look into nature through my heart or my intuition and find ultimate truths there which you do not discern, there is no higher standard we hold in common to which the issue can be referred. If he sees light and she is blind to it, there is nothing more to be said except that neither can be assured that either perceives the light of nature. The consequences of such a doctrine are abysmal.

In other words, he tramples underfoot the roots of humanity. For it is the nature of humanity to press onward to agreement with others; human nature only really exists in an achieved community of minds. The anti-human, the merely animal, consists in staying within the sphere of feeling, and being able to communicate only at that level.[2]

Hegel endorses a politics of inclusivity, a politics rooted in an ontology that identifies Being with a God realizing its essence gradually through the historical process. God is incomplete until divine principles are realized in the world, and this process of worldly completion can only be carried by a humanity which expresses these principles more completely as it perfects its own self-consciousness. God requires humanity to perfect itself and humanity cannot recognize its essence without expressing God's will in its own subjectivity and community. 'It is the nature of humanity to press onward to agreement' means that instilled within us is a purpose to pursue each historical moment of concord until the contradictions within it become visible and compelling and then to forge new and higher forms of concord which express more fully both the essence of Being and the essence of humanity. Each agreement captures some new moment of that essence, and the moments together enable the highest and most inclusive form of human community to emerge, a community housing diversity in a complex, harmonious and self-subsistent totality. It is part of the essence of humanity to seek truth by pressing onward to agreement, and the highest form of politics, to be realized finally in the modern period, is one where the sphere of fundamental agreement is all-inclusive, virtue is highly developed, rationality flourishes and freedom reigns. Put another way, the implicit purpose of human history is to eliminate otherness – all that escapes knowledge, reason and normality – by pressing onward to agreements which assimilate it to higher forms of knowledge, reason and normality. The politics of inclusivity engenders the assimilation of otherness.

The politics of inclusivity requires a world which is knowable in its essence: nothing fundamental can remain finally outside the sphere of absolute knowledge. But for the world to be knowable in this comprehensive way Being must in its essence be Spirit; it must contain within it purpose and intelligibility susceptible to knowledge. And Spirit, in its ultimate determination, is God. Hegel thus seeks to redeem politics by saving God. To do so he must rescue God from the uncertainty and doubt into which he has been sunk by modern faith. Faith must be converted into knowledge if God is to be lifted from the darkness into which Hobbes and Rousseau, along with other figures of the Enlightenment and Reformation, have plunged him. This fundamental task must be accomplished if reason, truth, freedom and political legitimacy are to be realized. The politics of inclusivity and the ontology of comprehensive intelligibility are bound together. For the ontology of comprehensive intelligiblity postulates a time when the world as a totality is available to knowledge and where the highest purpose of humanity is incorporated into its frame; and the revelation of this totality to reason can occur only during a time in which the state is capable of encompassing all of the worldly elements of this totality within its orbit. Such a totality can be projected abstractly; but it can be known only through its concrete realization. Hegelian politics thus depends upon the view that the Christian God, understood properly and philosophically, is the subject whose truth is revealed both to itself and the world in history.

God is dead in the modern age unless he can be brought to life in history through the medium of human self-consciousness. And politics is reduced to power and strife unless God can be revived as a living force in the public life. The two sink or swim together in the Hegelian system. And Hegel is a swimmer. 'The Christian religion is the religion of *reconciliation* of the world with God.'[3] To save God Hegel must reinstate his presence more firmly on earth; and to reinstate God on earth humanity must be elevated, through the historical dialectic of self-consciousness, to a level at which it can discern God's essence. This philosophy of reconciliation, in which each moves closer to the other it needs to realize itself, leads some to accuse Hegel of atheism and others to accuse him of pantheism. But it must succeed if the dialectic of inclusivity is not to turn into a politics of realization through repression.

We shall consider further the imperatives which impel Hegel to construct an ontology of spirit realizing itself progressively through time. But first it will be helpful to exemplify what the politics of inclusivity means. Madness is a paradigmatic form of otherness. As such it can and has been construed in a variety of ways, depending upon the assumptions and aspirations of the theory through which it is encountered. Madness might, as we have seen, be treated as a sign from God. Because it at once stands outside divinely sanctioned standards of life and inside the community of God's creations, it reveals darkly truths which transcend the human capacity for understanding. The knowledge it bears is too much for any human to take. When madness is construed this way, it may be excluded or it may be tolerated until it interferes too much with life. There is no call, though, to try to reform it so that it can be drawn fully into the life of the community.

Madness can also be viewed as the price of extreme sinfulness, as the consequence of excessive pride, or resentment or desire. Hobbes tended to construe it in this way. He was not interested in curing it, therefore, so much as explaining it, controlling it and warning subjects against falling prey to it. Though the mad may be enemies of the state, they are not signs of its failure or of its need to develop better cures.

Madness, to demarcate a third position, could also be defined merely as unreason. From whatever cause, perhaps unknown causes, it lowers its victims below the level of reason. We can learn nothing from it, and it contains no value for us. It must simply be confined, or excluded or eliminated.

Madness might also be constituted from a Nietzschean point of view. Its cause is neither simply in the self who bears it nor simply in the world which recognizes it to be at odds with its standards of normality. It stands at an intersection between the human imperative to complete itself within a particular form of life and the fact that the human animal was not designed to fit neatly into any way of life. Each form of life drives some people crazy and some people are so constituted that they will mesh poorly with any way of life. This perspective is compatible with a variety of responses. Some will draw from it an ethic of letting be, an ethic which tries to increase the social space in which difference can be without subjecting so much of it to treatment, drugs, therapy, control, correction or punishment. An alternative response, reflecting additional elements folded into the theory, might treat the mad as enemies to be defeated or conquered. This ontology of madness creates its own room for ethical debate, then, but since it does not define madness as a fault residing simply within its bearer, the space it establishes for ethical debate does not revolve simply around alternative strategies for controlling or curing the mad.

Hegel thinks that madness, with the exception of a residual category which is not really madness, is rationality gone awry. And this interpretation is an artifact of his presumption of the ultimate, comprehensive intelligibility of the world, or, as more briefly characterized, his ontology of Spirit. Insanity is a falling away from rationality. 'In considering insanity we must, as in other cases, anticipate the full-grown and intelligent conscious subject, which is at the same time the *natural self* or *self-feeling*.'[4] If rationality, as it develops historically, is an achievement through which the self comes closer to truth and spirit, insanity is 'a disease of mind and body alike' which disturbs the unity of the normal subject who 'subsumes each special content of sensation, idea, desire, inclination etc., as it arises, so as to insert them into their proper place.'[5] The insane retain a semblance of reason, but they lack 'the dominant genius' in the self which organizes the multitude of ideas and feelings and experiences coherently. The insane lack the unity which a well-formed subject develops:

When the influence of self-possession and of general principles, moral and theoretical, is relaxed, and ceases to keep the natural temper under lock and key, the earthly elements are set free – that evil which is always latent in the heart . . . It is the evil genius of man which gains the upper hand in insanity, but in distinction from . . . the better and more intelligent part which is there also.[6]

The passions of vanity and pride are chief sources of this inability of the self to keep its evil genius under lock and key. The normal self in modern life encounters the world through work and reason. When reality contradicts its feelings of vanity or pride it learns to adjust these reactions through the experience of family and work, as well as other social transactions; and when the 'dominant genius' in the self is challenged from within, experience in conversation and debate helps it to discern the internal contradictions which beset the challenging elements. These influences help it to acquire and retain 'self-possession.' Hegel, then, proposes a curative treatment made up of work and critical conversation strategically aimed at pointing out the contradictions in the delusions of the insane. These strategies, fitting beautifully into Hegel's philosophy of historical progress and individual development, draw deranged individuals back into the fold of normality. The strategem of refutation through conversation is the one Hegel emphasizes the most, citing several examples of successful treatment. In one case a 'lunatic' thought he was dead, refusing to eat because nourishment was incompatible with death:

The lunatic was put in a coffin and laid in a vault in which was another coffin occupied by a man who at first pretended to be dead but who, soon after he was left alone with the lunatic, sat up, told the latter how pleased he was to have company in death, and finally got up, ate the food that was by him and told the astonished lunatic that he had already been dead a long time and therefore knew how the dead go about things. The lunatic was pacified by the assurance, likewise ate and drank and was cured.[7]

The lunatic is cured by a strategic therapy aimed at creating the appearance of an internal contradiction in his system of beliefs. He has retained the commitment to internal coherence but has lost contact with the larger world in which it is set. Once he has been brought back to life through trying to live death as the dead appear to live it, the *telos* of life itself could begin to take over. Because Hegel identifies the intersubjective background in which modern madness occurs as the highest achievement of Spirit in history to date, because he thinks that Spirit's progress through the medium of humanity is established painfully by the formation of progressively more inclusive systems of intersubjectivity, and because he insists that otherness is always a sign either that the system of intersubjectivity must be broadened further or that those who have fallen out of it must be drawn back into its fold, he defines modern madness as a defect in its bearers susceptible to treatment through a therapeutic version of dialectical reason. The dialectical theory of reason and Spirit is defeated unless each form of otherness constitutes a defect of reason, to be remedied through the vale of tears which governs history or through education and therapy which bring modern individuals into touch with the highest level Spirit has achieved. The ontology of Spirit demands a politics of inclusivity, and the politics of inclusive community cannot be at peace with itself unless it can sustain an ontology of Spirit.

If Hegel cannot sustain the ontology, many of the strategems he endorses to 'keep the natural temper under lock and key' will appear as a set of subtle tyrannies applied by the world to the individual and by the individual to itself. But how can he defend this ontology of Spirit? Hegel does so, first, by showing how the epistemological strategies governing theories during the Enlightenment are doomed to fall apart and, second, by introducing a phenomenological strategy which promises to redeem itself not at the beginning of inquiry but at the end of Spirit's tortuous journey through history.

The problem with the modern orientation to knowledge is that it either gives primacy to epistemology or insists that knowing can be achieved through ineffable intuition. It is the first fault to which we now attend. To give primacy to epistemology is to claim that knowing cannot proceed until a secure foundation for knowledge has been established: we must first learn how to know and then we can begin the process of acquiring actual knowledge. But every theory which gives primacy to epistemology eventually falls victim to the dilemma of epistemology. The epistemologist treats the knowing faculty either as an instrument by means of which knowledge is acquired or as a medium through which knowledge is received. For example, the mind might be construed as an instrument of knowledge and perception might be understood as a medium through which knowledge is received. But then there is no guarantee that the 'light of truth' will shine undistorted by the medium or the instrument. It 'is obvious that the use of an instrument on a thing does not let it be what it is for itself, but rather sets out to reshape and alter it.'[8] And a medium also affects whatever is passing through it. A passive medium does 'not receive the truth as it is in itself, but only as it exists in and through the medium.'[9]

To establish a medium or instrument by which to attain knowledge and then to use it to know is to guarantee that the initial optimism in which modern epistemology begins will issue in a dismal skepticism. The Enlightenment slides from Descartes to Hume. For each attempt to test the instrument or the medium for accuracy ends up either by introducing another one itself in need of redemption or reiterating the one which needed to be checked. It thus falls either into an infinite regress or a vicious circle. Theorists who invoke different criteria of knowledge have no final court of appeal in common. Even if they do concur upon a final court of appeal *for us* as humans they can never know whether the knowledge concurred upon reaches beyond the world as it appears to us into the world as it is in itself. The latter limitation is as fundamental to Hegel as the former: unless we can participate in absolute knowledge, Spirit and humanity can never achieve reconciliation; and unless such a reconciliation can be achieved, there might always be otherness around capable of disrupting life from the inside or defeating it by surprises from the outside. Established knowledge would not be merely fallible and correctible: it would also contain the possibility of radical disruption and reconstitution within itself; and this very possibility would haunt the actual legitimacy of established conceptions of self, ethical practice and political responsibilities, especially with respect to those who are treated as insane, unethical, perverse, rebellious or irresponsible by those standards. Reconciliation requires absolute knowledge.

The epistemologist tries to begin inquiry without presuppositions of any sort, but the insistence that the faculty of knowledge is an instrument or a medium is filled with them. 'To be specific, it takes for granted certain ideas about cognition as an *instrument* and as a *medium,* and assumes that there is a *difference between ourselves and this cognition.* Above all, it presupposes that the Absolute stands on one side and cognition on the other.'[10] Hegel thinks it is this presupposition which eventuates in skepticism. He replaces it, not exactly with another presupposition, but with a promise to be redeemed at the end of inquiry rather than its inception. He will bring us phenomenologically not to a place where 'the refraction of the ray' reaches us, but where 'the ray itself' arrives. The initial case for phenomenology, then, is supported by the case against the primacy of epistemology.

Phenomenology is not a direct examination of things; it is an examination of modes of consciousness which contain within them both standards of knowledge and elements of knowledge. By examining modes of consciousness as they have evolved historically we can avoid importing any external and unredeemable standards into inquiry. And as we detect how each mode falls apart as, for instance, it discovers contradictions between specific knowledge it has acquired and the standard of knowledge it has endorsed, we will observe the internal advance of consciousness through history. We will not adopt the simple tactic of 'understanding' – a mode of consciousness which falls below dialectical thought because it thinks in fixed, dichotomous categories – and reject everything in the history of consciousness beset by internal contradictions. Rather we will record and carry forward the advances it has achieved while remembering how each mode of consciousness fell into its particular set of contradictions. Phenomenology, as Hegel practices it, remembers the internal life of the past and records the tortuous course by which it has advanced to the present.

But when a mode of consciousness breaks down, how do we know which of its elements constitute an advance to be carried forward and which constitute a mistake to be transcended? How can we transcend those modes of consciousness which fall apart into states resembling collective madness, where 'thought can find no peace,' where it 'troubles its thoughtlessness, and its own unrest disturbs its inertia?'[11] This is the anxiety which plagues Hegel and which energizes his thought. He stills the anxiety with a promise. By pursing the historical course of consciousness phenomenologically we will reach 'the point where knowledge no longer needs to go beyond itself, where knowledge finds itself.'[12] At that point we will not simply have a system of coherent elements into which all otherness has been folded, but a system which expresses Spirit as it has perfected itself through history. This is Hegel's promise.

In pressing forward to its true existence, consciousness will arrive at a point at which it gets rid of its semblance of being burdened with something alien, with what is only for it, and some sort of 'other', at a point where appearance becomes identical with essence, so that its exposition will coincide at just that point with the authentic Science of Spirit. And finally, when consciousness itself grasps this its own essence, it will signify the nature of absolute knowledge itself.[13]

Hegel replaces faith in God as the guarantor of reason with faith in reason as the vehicle of God's manifestation on earth through the progressive realization of Spirit. He is driven to this new attempt to save reason by the defeats recorded in the thought of his recent predecessors, including Hobbes, Rousseau and Kant. He will redeem what they lost. The timing and location of redemption have been changed but its spirit continues to pervade this text as it did the texts of his predecessors.

Community and subjectivity

'The history of the world is none other than the progress of the consciousness of Freedom; a progress whose development, according to the necessity of its nature, it is our business to investigate,' writes Hegel.[14] Freedom, self-consciousness and the inclusivity of the state progress together in history. This progress is the aim to which 'the enormous sacrifices' recorded in each historical epoch 'have been offered.'[15] Hegel thinks the individual may suffer in vain, even entire peoples may be sacrificed to a future which leaves them behind, but humanity does not suffer in vain. That is at once the faith of the Hegelian system and its justification for past calamities.

In its earlier stages western history does not have a conscious aim. It aims only vaguely or abstractly at the realization of Spirit. It knows not what it does. Its people lack self-consciousness. That is, they are conscious of the standards they follow and committed to them, but they neither understand the role they have had in creating those standards nor do they differentiate the individual sharply as an independent center of judgment, conscience, reason and purpose. The early (pre-Platonic) Greeks were sunk in objectivity. They did not define the self as an independent subject and they experienced the common ethic as 'a necessary of life.' They were conscious members, but lacked self-consciousness. 'Of the Greeks in the first and genuine form of their Freedom, we may assert, they had no conscience; the habit of living for their country without further reflection, was the principle dominant among them.'[16]

History takes a step forward through introduction of the principle of subjective freedom and self-consciousness, but this progress destroys the beautiful unity of Greek life. 'That very subjective freedom which constitutes the principle . . . of Freedom in *our* world – which forms the absolute basis of our political and religious life, could not manifest itself in Greece otherwise than as a *destructive* element.'[17]

Hegel's account of the origin and effect of self-consciousness proceeds along two tracks. The first track, located under the headings 'Self-Consciousness' and 'Reason' in *Phenomenology of Spirit*, abstracts its development from the broader historical setting in which it is placed and focuses attention on the logic governing the experience of those implicated in it. The second track begins with the section entitled 'Spirit'; it focuses attention on the formation, dislocation and reformation of the cultural context in which self-consciousness emerges and advances itself.

It is in the formation and consolidation of the relationship of lordship and bondage that the seeds of self-consciousness are sown. Hegel begins the elucidation of this moment with a summary statement: 'Self-consciousness exists in and for itself when, and by the fact that, it so exists for another; that is, it exists only in being acknowledged.'[18] I can know myself fully only if others recognize me to be a center of reason, freedom and conscience, and I, by reacting to that judgment, internalize it as my own. But the participants in this early dialectic could not know this yet. Each feels a lack in himself, and each senses only that the other might be used somehow to still this restless emptiness. Perhaps the early combatants in the struggle for supremacy which results are Greek warriors, each acknowledged to be noble in his own clan, and each seeking to wrest the recognition he needs from another noble being. But in leaving the dialectic unspecified Hegel reminds us that its echoes continue to reverberate within cultures which have transcended the objectivity of early Greek life.

The implicit mutual desire for recognition takes the form of a struggle. The willingness to risk one's life for recognition is part of the claim to deserve it. If the battle ends in a draw or if one kills the other, it carries no implications for the advance of self-consciousness. But if the victor forces the vanquished to serve him, and if the vanquished one, to retain his life, agrees to recognize the conquerer as his Lord, then the fateful dialectic of self-consciousness has been set into motion. The victor is now recognized by one who was noble, and he can now recognize himself to be a superior being. The vanquished, through working for the Lord, confirms the superiority of his Lordship, recognizing himself to be enslaved and the other, by contrast, to be free. Each knows that one of them supersedes the other.

But mastery is a dead-end for self-consciousness. One being is recognized by an-other who *only* recognizes, by one who is no longer his equal, by one whose 'essential nature is simply to live or to be for another.'[19] The Lord is recognized by a bondsman. His victory has not stilled the yearning that drove him to this 'trial by death.'

But for recognition proper the moment is lacking: that what the lord does to the other he also does to himself, and what the bondsman does to himself he should also do to the other. The outcome is a recognition that is one-sided and unequal.[20]

The experience of servitude, however, drives the servile one to examine his own life: 'as a consciousness forced back into itself it will withdraw into itself and be transformed into a truly independent consciousness.'[21] The servile one, because he has been forced into servility, lives in circumstances propitious to the seed of self-consciousness. First of all, he is in a perfect position to examine his life in the face of death. His life had recently been in the hands of another who could have chosen to take it, and he still runs the risk that his life might be snuffed out by the other at any time. He lives in dread that reaches to the very core of his being. 'For this consciousness has been fearful, not of this or that particular thing or just at odd moments, but its whole being has been seized with dread . . , and everything solid and stable has been shaken to its foundations.'[22]

The prospect of death leads one to concentrate the mind, to plumb the priorities of one's life and the depth of one's commitment to life. By examining these priorities in explicit knowledge of the contingency and finitude of one's own life one begins to give shape to one's self, forsaking those goals because they are unimportant or not expressive of one's best potentialities, accentuating these because they are fundamental to one's highest purpose. One begins to form oneself more definitively as a subject. Moreover the one whose life is in jeopardy begins to wonder about a world that requires servile people like himself and seems to subject the most important issues to fate. Wonder spurs thought and thought spurs wonder. The bondsman begins to become conscious of the circumstances through which his service self is formed, and he begins to desire to be what he is not: a free agent whose life is whole, as the Lord's life appears to be.

But the bondsman is also forced to work for another. He labors and the other enjoys the fruits. By struggling with the world, by making nature conform to his purposes, he experiences himself to be an active, competent being who can make a difference in the world. He makes things accord with his thoughts and designs. Through service to another the servile one establishes a sense of self. He begins to win through work what he sought through struggle; and he wrests from the world a semblance of that which was lost in defeat. For work not only shapes the thing, it requires the self to organize itself so that it can shape the thing: it is 'desire held in check, fleetingness staved off.'[23] The bondsman becomes more than a bearer of fear and desire. He becomes a self who establishes priority among its desires, and he thereby makes the self more than a 'fleeting' or ephemeral thing. 'Through this rediscovery of himself by himself, the bondsman realizes that it is precisely in his work wherein he seemed to have only alienated existence that he acquires a mind of his own.'[24]

The bondsman is still enmeshed in servitude. But through absolute fear and enforced work he has begun to acquire a more coherent self and an enhanced consciousness of it. He can think now about what freedom means for the individual and what kind of world will enable that freedom to be, though his capacity for action will be outstripped by his thoughts and his thoughts, at this stage in the history of freedom, will fall short of the mark at which they aim.

This dialectic of Lordship and Bondage exemplifies beautifully the character of dialectical reason. It illustrates the ironic victories, apparent defeats, abrupt reversals which mark dialectical advances; it points out the ugly and unpromising beginnings from which great advances are formed; it thematizes the agonies and sacrifices that make the progress of history a 'vale of tears' for its bearers; and it brings out secret attractions in a mode of thought that openly repudiates the utopian promise to erase suffering from the face of the earth while promising that ultimately such suffering will not be in vain. Hegel's dialectic provides a refuge for the politics of redemption.

The dialectic of self-consciousness continues. The moments of stoicism and skepticism represent attempts by those who remain enslaved to the world to wrest freedom out of unfavorable circumstances. Each moment is defeated by internal contradictions which eventually become visible, but together they point out, first, to what extremes of thought seekers of freedom will go to secure the appearance of freedom in conditions of enslavement and, second, how the internal life of the self is fundamental to the real experience of freedom. These modes of self-consciousness finally issue in the longer moment of the unhappy-consciousness, a priestly being who internalizes the relationship of Lordship and Bondage within itself, granting the powers of agency, goodness and intelligence to a mysterious, external God and leaving itself with the impossible task of moving closer to the spirit of God from a lowly position of sinfulness and powerlessness. But we will leave the history of self-consciousness to this split-consciousness for now, turning to the level of Spirit to get another angle on the moment when an entire culture must be furrowed under to enable the seed of self-consciousness to take root.

'It is the concrete Spirit of a people which we have distinctly to recognize, and since it is Spirit it can only be comprehended spiritually, that is, by thought.'[25] That which governs a way of life is its spirit, and Spirit at the most general level is the fundamental substance which realizes itself through the medium of dialectical history. Because it is Spirit, it can be comprehended by thought. That is the crucial demand of the Hegelian system, and that is why Hegel equates substance, that which is in itself complete and independent, with Spirit. If Spirit is thought, it is in principle intelligible to thinking beings. If human thinkers bear the advance of Spirit in their consciousness, they might eventually hope to incorporate the advance of Spirit into their explicit thought.

'Spirit is thus self-supporting, absolute, real being. All previous shapes of consciousness are abstract forms of it.'[26] When we examined the dialectic of Lordship and Bondage, we were examining an abstract form of Greek Spirit, an early form of life which, like the relationship it contained, could not sustain itself. The Spirit of Greek life is the most fundamental set of self-understandings and aspirations inscribed in its common life. In the case of Greek culture those customs were the immemorial principles of the community 'given' to the members as absolute injunctions. The Greeks attained the beautiful unity of a community in which each was defined by his or her connection to the common life, but Greek culture lacked the ability to subject conflicts between absolute injunctions to a critical analysis which could resolve them into a higher unity. The Greeks were members, not individuals.

Greek culture lacked the critical distance and self-consciousness operative in a way of life which mediates between the independent individual and the standards of the common life, and which can hope to resolve through reflective discourse among independent individuals conflicts sewn into the fabric of the common life. Lacking the principle of subjectivity, it treated fundamental conflicts which beset it as manifestations of fate, as expressions of a higher force in which it was entangled but over which it had no real control. As Hegel says, referring to pre-Platonic Greece, 'it was the Sophists who first introduced subjective reflection and the new doctrine that each man should act according to his own conviction.'[27] But this introduction destroyed the communal Spirit which had enabled Greece to be. It thereby destroyed the culture itself.

We turn here to the spiritual mirror of the dialectic of Lordship and Bondage, to that moment when the beautiful unity of the implicit Greek community was broken and the principle of subjectivity was unleashed upon a world that could not assimilate it. We turn to Hegel's reading of Antigone.

Antigone brings out the tragic flaw in Greek unity. The culture was one in which all of the elements fit together implicitly into a communal way of life. Man and woman were given specific duties; divine and human laws governed each sphere of life; and the family followed its dictates within a larger community oriented to the highest ends of the people. Each of these elements coordinated implicitly with the others, and the life of the whole presupposed unconscious harmony among them.

In Sophocles' play, Polynices, the brother of Antigone and Ismene, has borne arms against his native city, and Creon the ruler and bearer of the 'human law,' has decreed that Polynices must be left on the edge of the city unburied after his defeat and death. Ismene, Antigone's sister, follows the law which subordinates women to men. 'Remember,' she says, 'we are women; we're not born to contend with men.'[28]

But Antigone is pulled by the divine law which dictates that a member of the family must be buried, that its spirit will know no rest unless it is. Antigone and Ismene each obeys one law and disobeys another. As Antigone says to her sister, 'your wisdom appealed to one world – mine another.'[29]

Creon's ruling made sense on its own terms, particularly to a theorist such as Hegel, who, as we shall see, gives so much priority to the interests of state. 'Our country,' says Creon, is our safety. Only while she voyages true on course, can we establish friendships, truer than blood itself.'[30] Moreover, the ruler must never allow a woman to disobey his edicts, for that is a double transgression fraught with fateful consequences, going against the law of the ruler and the law which subordinates women to men. But the divine law, carrying its own absolute authority, insists that Polynices be buried and that a member of the family assume special responsibility for this task. Antigone does not represent herself as an independent agent deciding to do one thing rather than another. She is rather the bearer of a divine injunction which is absolute. She says to Creon,

that you, a mere mortal could override the gods,
the great unwritten, unshakeable traditions.
They are alive, not just today or yesterday.
They live forever, from time immemorial,
and no one knows when they first saw the light.[31]

Antigone expresses two dimensions of Greek spirit. One is the demand to follow the laws of the community as absolute injunctions and to treat their very immemorial status as the ground of their truth. The other is to obey the law to bury her brother, acknowledging the sacred character of the familial bond. Creon shares the first dimension with her, but he is equally bound, as male and ruler, to obey the principle that the enemy of the state must not receive the honor of a burial and to punish a woman who disobeys his edict. The community, bound by its own injunction of absolute obedience, lacks the ability to resolve this internal conflict. Fate takes over, 'a dark terrible wonder – neither wealth nor armies, towered walls nor ships . . . can save us from that force.'[32] And fate drives the community to anarchy, the condition all parties wish to avoid above all because it rips up families and destroys cities. Hegel concludes that in this setting each party must interpret the other as a perpetrator of outrage against the common life.

Since it sees right only on one side and wrong on the other, that consciousness which belongs to the divine law sees in the other side only the violence of human caprice, while that which holds to human law sees in the other only the self-will and disobedience of the individual who insists on being his own authority. For the commands of government have a universal, public meaning open to the light of day; the will of the other law, however, is looked upon in the darkness of the nether regions, and in its outer existence manifests as the will of an isolated individual which, as contradicting the first, is a wanton outrage.[33]

More fundamentally, Hegel concludes that in this culture each of the parties must be guilty. For while each did what the law required of it, each also broke an inviolable law of the community. Guilt in Greek life does not reside so much in the evil intention of the agent, for agency is, by later standards, undeveloped or at least underdeveloped. It resides in those whose actions assault the law of the land even if they did not intend this result and could not have acted differently. Antigone and Creon are *bearers* of guilt, for each disobeyed one law in obeying another; they are *necessary* bearers of guilt, for neither could avoid disobeying one law or the other.

The tragedy which results brings out the inner contradiction in the life of community unmediated by subjectivity. For the law requires that it always be obeyed, but it generates circumstances where obedience also requires disobedience. Its inner contradictions introduce the spirit of subjectivity, but the spirit of subjectivity in this setting can only display the endless array of actual and potential conflicts in the traditions of the land, revealing the utter lack of unity in a world which demanded that unity exist. Antigone displayed the contradiction in Greek Spirit, and the Sophists, on Hegel's reading, revealed both its need for the principle of subjectivity and its inability to assimilate it. Greek life is forced to go under.

Hegel tries to show, first at the level of self-consciousness and then at the level of Spirit, that early Greek life could not sustain itself with subjectivity and could not sustain itself without it. Once the principle of subjectivity has been unleashed, Spirit will not realize its essence until a way of life emerges which can accommodate the principle of the self as a free, independent subject within a way of life which sets just limits to subjectivity and harmonizes it within a larger, institutionalized ethical life. This is the demand of Hegelian theory and a perpetual worry for Hegel. It may well be that he himself feared that the world requires subjectivity but that no way of life could domesticate it effectively. His official position, though, is that the modern state, with its complex layering of the independent agent, the family, the mechanisms of market society, the universal orientation of the civil service, the will of the monarch and the unifying power of rational identification with this totality, is capable of housing each of these elements in a common life which harmonizes them together. Modernity will transcend the tragic character of Greek life.

Faith and Enlightenment

Antigone, as the woman who challenges the law of the state in the name of divine law, embodies in a dark form the spirit of individuality; in the world in which it manifested itself it had to be subdued. 'The community . . , by dissolving self-consciousness into the universal . . , creates for itself in what it suppresses and what is at the same time essential to it an internal enemy – womankind in general.'[34] Individuality cannot be acknowledged without destroying the Greek world. The stage we now turn to reverses this imbalance. It expresses vociferously the principle of individuality: it insists that individual reason, or individual conscience or individual feeling must be given priority both in the life of the self and in the life of the whole. In its purest manifestation it seeks to universalize individual reason, making it available to every individual and founding a common ethic upon the principles each finds when consulting reason properly. Because it treats as complete a form of Spirit which is incomplete, it meets an adversary which is the mirror image of the one created by Greek community. Its adversary is Faith, a form of consciousness that acknowledges God to stand above the principle of individual reason. The Enlightenment is marshalled into being as a battle between Insight (reason in its pre-Hegelian form) and Faith (religion in its pre-Hegelian form). Each defines itself through reference to its opposition to the other. Hegel separates the parties to this debate, but our insight into the thought of Hobbes and Rousseau will be greater if we think of each as embodying some version of the conflict between Faith and Enlightenment within the frame of a single theory. We turn first to two manifestations of insistent individuality operating at the level of self-consciousness.

Hedonism grows up in a world where people are alienated from the larger life. It is a philosophy of life which tries to snatch victory out of the jaws of defeat. If meaning has been drained from the larger life, perhaps it can be secured from that which is most subject to the control of the individual. My body is mine, and it can serve as a medium of my pleasure. Hedonism universalizes this desire into an ethic: each individual should pursue his own pleasure, and no other understandings or principles such as love, science, law, custom or the good of the community must be allowed to inhibit the pursuit of pleasure. 'It plunges therefore into life and indulges to the full the pure individuality in which it appears . . . The shadowy existence of science, laws and principles, which alone stand between it and its own reality, vanishes like a lifeless mist which cannot compare with the certainty of its own reality.'[35]

But the law of pleasure soon confronts the necessity of life. For if pleasure is everything, and there is no higher meaning, then death is the end of everything. Those committed to a common way of life, to the future of their children and their children's children, can identify with activities now which will benefit others later; they can even hope to be remembered after death by some of those who profit from the legacy they leave. But death for the hedonist is simply the end. It is a pointless necessity, ending the individual's life and serving no higher purpose. Some hedonists may react to this realization by living for the moment, but they die off soon. Others, to extrapolate a little, may react by living in dread of that which takes meaning away. They become cautious, wary, worried and suspicious. For if another hedonist wants pleasure with me, he or she will not be moved to reduce it by warning me of the dangers and risks involved for me. Such a warning would give priority to obligation or concern over pleasure. Perhaps the other has AIDS. Suspicion devolves into paranoia in a universe of hedonists.

The pleasure now goes out of hedonism. It is 'smashed to pieces' through experience of a necessity which transcends the intentionality of hedonism. For even individuality can realize itself only in a community in which its life is linked to others and its death is marked by a contribution to the life it leaves behind. Individuality must be mediated at least by the sense of respect each bestows upon the others.

The defeat of hedonism fosters a reversal which moves on the same plane. If I cannot secure meaning through the law of individual pleasure, I will follow the law of my heart. I will cultivate the pure heart, concerned only about the good of others. You can recognize me in the sweetness of my voice and the softness of my demeanor. I am concerned to help you. And if everyone would follow the law of the heart, the world itself would be a beautiful and peaceful place. 'What the world needs now is love, sweet love . . .'

The law of the heart knows 'it has the universal of law *immediately* within itself.'[36] To be a principle of individuality it must find the law immediately within itself, unmediated by customs, traditions, rules of reasoning or a recorded history of experience which transcends the immediacy of the individual heart. Indeed for the law of the heart to find pure expression these intersubjective experiences, law and customs must be interpreted as external impediments. They violate and obstruct its law. They stand in the way of a universe of loving individuals, and they must be removed.

When these violent impositions are removed, he can express his own law, a law which has 'the value of a universal ordinance'. But the translation of his heart into a universal meets with unexpected resistance, for others are now expressing the laws of their hearts, and these laws too are to have universal validity. He intended to oppose the rigid, reified laws of the world, but now he finds himself opposed to heartfelt laws of others with whom he would be aligned. For to let my hearth throb is to still yours – unless the two just happen to coincide. But since the law of the heart opposes mediating arrangements as defilements of its purity, it opposes exactly those kinds of arrangements which might draw people together under the umbrella of shared principles. Only bare coincidence could produce unity between two unmediated hearts, and even this precarious pair would be forced to constitute itself as one faction amidst a million others.

'The heart-throb for the welfare of humanity therefore passes into the ravings of an insane self-conceit, into the fury of consciousness to preserve itself from destruction.'[37] To preserve the law of its own heart it is forced to condemn the law of other hearts. It ends, then, by opposing the individuality it had celebrated at its inception. It ends, destructively and violently, in a 'frenzy of self-conceit.'

Hedonism and the law of the heart stand in opposition to each other. The first celebrates its own pleasure and the second pursues the good of others. Indeed, the first called the second into being as a response. In showing that these opponents also share affinities, in showing, further, that each defines itself through its opposition to the other, Hegel teaches us how to deepen political thought. Each believed that it could reach the universal through the resources of the individual; each opposes tradition and mediating institutions as impediments to pure individuality; each seeks an immediate universal rather than a mediated one; each defeats itself by coming to terms with the way in which the implication of its program flows from its insistence on contrasting itself primarily with that opponent which opposes it on one plane, but shares with it fundamental assumptions and aspirations thematized clearly by neither. My earlier effort to identify affinities between the opponents Hobbes and Rousseau was informed by this general teaching of Hegel's. When opponents love to oppose each other, they are likely to share some fundamental premises and demands neither is ready to thematize. The very sharpness of the debate expresses and obscures the fundamental character of that which remains unthought within it. Perhaps we will be in a position later to apply this lesson to the thought of Hegel.

These moments of individuality occur within a larger movement of culture, the Enlightenment. They prepare us for its more complex dynamic, for while they operated at the level of individual reason, it operates more explicitly at the level of Spirit. The Enlightenment is the time when the spirit of subjectivity tries to install itself against the power of tradition and religion. It is thematized by Hegel as the unequal contest between Insight and Faith.

Faith is a mode of religious consciousness which has been weakened by unconsciously assimilating the air in which Enlightenment breathes. Hobbes, for instance, as a precursor of the Enlightenment, embodies a version of Faith with resemblances to the position Hegel has in mind. Hobbes linked God to reason through nature, letting faith ground the linkage. Faith also sees God as the essential, unknowable and external ground of being who must be worshipped; and it drops nature as an element of mediation between humanity and God. It is also more suspicious of the reason it nonetheless must call upon in its daily life. Faith has become 'essentially merely a belief.'[38] It lacks the ability to defend itself against attack by any means other than reiteration of its belief.

Insight defines itself above all as the worldly adversary of Faith. It treats the essence of life as absolute self, as the pure self of reason which resides in every human being. 'It therefore seeks to abolish every kind of independence other than that of self-consciousness, whether it be the independence of what is actual, or of what possesses intrinsic being.'[39] It seeks, therefore, to judge everything by the court of autonomous reason, which it knows itself to be; and it strives, by removing the fog of superstition, myth, tradition and unreflective belief, to 'make pure insight universal.'[40]

From Hegel's point of view – 'our' point of view as he calls it – Insight and Faith flow from a common substance, which has become divided and emptied; and each embodies the error it can discern only in the other. Each, in its purity, locates truth in an empty vessel: the empty space of a pure self unmediated by identification with a larger world developed through the historical advance of Spirit or the empty point of an external God abstracted from the concrete world in which Spirit develops itself historically. Neither can fulfill itself positively until the two are reconciled, until the self expresses its self-identification with the concrete rationality of a larger world, and the deity manifests itself in the realization of a rational community through history. But at this point both are blind to their common error, and Insight, capable of doing negative work, is poised to empty Faith of the content which has guided its religious experience.

Insight wants every consciousness to become what it is implicitly: 'Be for yourselves what you all are in yourselves – reasonable,'[41] It realizes reason by attacking superstitions that cannot meet the test of its reason. 'Just as it sees faith in general to be a tissue of superstitions, prejudices and errors, so it further sees the consciousness of this content organized into a realm of error, in which false insight, common to the mass of people, is immediate, naive and unreflective.'[42] It attacks the truth of the Bible by questioning the authenticity of its human recorders, the correctness of their interpretations, the reliability of those who carried this record forward; and it attacks particular rules and rituals enjoined by church authorities on the ground that they could not be received by finite beings from an infinite God who is known only by Faith. Priests are treated as manipulators who insist on exercising religious authority over the masses for their own power and advantage. The priesthood conspires with despotic rulers to dupe the people, taking their own reason away from them.

The effectiveness of Enlightenment is determined partly by the ineffectiveness of Faith. Already breathing the atmosphere of Enlightenment reason and evidence, it feels compelled to answer each challenge with a review of the historical record on its behalf:

If faith wants to appeal to historical evidences in order to get that kind of foundation, or at least confirmation, of its content that Enlightenment talks about . . . then it has already let itself be corrupted by the Enlightenment; and its efforts to establish and consolidate itself in such a way are merely evidence it gives of its corruption by the Enlightenment'[43]

The problem for Faith is that it naively accepts Enlightenment dichotomies while still believing in the holy status of its own material symbols of divinity. They are treated by it both as manifesting pure essence and as simple things of sensory experience.

The believing consciousness weighs and measures by a twofold standard: it has two sorts of eyes, speaks with two voices, has duplicated all ideas without comparing the twofold meanings. In other words, faith lives in two sorts of non-notional perceptions, the one the perceptions of the *slumbering* consciousness . . . the other those of the *waking* consciousness which lives solely in the world of sense; and in each of them it has its own separate housekeeping.[44]

The naive consciousness of Faith makes critique easy for Insight. It wants to touch an infinite consciousness through the things of the world, but is unable to defend itself against the finite categories which govern Enlightenment thought. Is this a thing or a spirit? Is that mind or body? Is this a fact of nature or a category of thought? Is God known through reason or felt through feeling? Is God unlimited, but then how could limited beings understand him? Is he limited, then why should we worship him? Enlightenment thinkers tend to be theists with a minimal conception of God, deists who think of God as simply the first cause of the world, or atheists who deny the existence of God. And the categories through which they think make it impossible to give a rational account of a more robust Being. Enlightenment merely separates into distinct categories unities which Faith had accepted naively in its slumbering life of belief while living its waking life through the same categories. So Faith is purged of specific texts, rituals and symbols which connected finite life to infinite being. It becomes a 'sheer yearning' for that which has become a mere abstraction. Faith becomes 'unsatisfied Enlightenment' because it is now governed by categories which leave it with a sense of restlessness about the larger meaning and inherent purpose of the world. Insight becomes 'satisfied Enlightenment' to the extent it has purged the earth of the content which Faith had imposed upon it.

But Enlightenment, now that it has cleared the field for its positive action, will come to realize that its essence is identical to the position it has defeated. As it finds Faith guilty of unthinking belief and self-deceit, it unwittingly convicts itself of the same faults. For it has trust in the ability of a mode of reason constituted purely by the self to comprehend the world and to found a universal ethic. And trust, as Hegel says, is faith. The Enlightenment has faith in reason, but it will find out that *its* reason is unable to sustain itself once Faith has been defeated. It cannot, as we have already seen, resolve the dilemma of epistemology which Hegel has identified – and which is one of the issues he himself promises to resolve.

To see the world as objects known through their use-value is to drain any intrinsic significance or Spirit from the world; but it is also the most promising route to enable Enlightenment to take charge of the world. For now nothing intrinsic in nature inhibits consciousness from using it or bending it so that it becomes more useful. Enlightenment tries to construe everything from the vantage point of utility, including human beings, who by pursuing self-interest in market transactions inadvertently (by an invisible hand) serve the material and political interests of the collectivity, and including religion, which turns out for some figures to be a valuable set of beliefs because it stabilizes the life of society.

It would appear that the self and the world are now bound together into a coherent unity, a unity in which the self gains knowledge and freedom by constituting things as useful. But there is a hidden ambiguity which, at least on the reading I can make here, eventually undoes this unity. For what is useful is useful only because it 'has enduring being in itself.'[46] What acts as a means can only do so because it has the appropriate enduring properties. A mountain of rock is not readily convertible into soil for cultivation, but a flat prairie land is. So being in itself is not eliminated by Enlightenment. Utility must still confront it. What if the thing is resistant to the uses to which reason seeks to harness it? This resistance might be reduced or overcome by *making* the thing over into the useful object. And here we discern connections among a world constituted according to utility, an ethic which gives the highest status to the increase of use-value for human benefit, and an economy built around production of use-objects out of raw materials. It is very understandable, as the relationship of Lordship and Bondage has already intimated, how the Hegelian quest for deep reconciliation inspires the reply of radical reconstitution through a revolutionary remaking of the world.

The guiding aspiration of Enlightenment is to remove impediments in the world to human freedom. But now that it has emptied the world and the self of intrinsic content (except in its vacuous category of reason) moral impediments to making the self an object of use or disposal have also been removed. Without a theory of intrinsic significance in the world, the embodied-self, which can be seen to be both a subject in itself and an object susceptible to use, loses the ability do demarcate its own intrinsic significance with authority. It can now be made more useful by reshaping it to fit the needs of production or civic docility. Better stated, the categories now available to Enlightenment begin to contradict its aspiration to realize and protect the free and knowing self. The category of the useful is now free to infiltrate into everything . That, at any rate, is how I read Hegel's warning about how the 'antitheses' of self and world are about to collide:

Since the useful still has the form of an object for pure insight, it does have a *world*, one which, it is true, is no longer in and for itself, but yet a world which it distinguishes from itself. Only, since the antitheses have emerged at the summit of the Notion, the next stage will see them come into collision, and the Enlightenment will taste the fruits of its deeds.[47]

The Enlightenment, of course, is divided into camps. Some parties give primacy to rights and others to utility; some think they can support a correspondence theory of truth and others adopt a more pragmatic theory; some think there is no God and others think that a God with a limited earthly presence is necessary to the integrity of reason, morality and politics; some incline toward the market and others toward the state; some favor democracy and others a bureaucratic politics; some celebrate individual freedom and others believe that freedom can exist only in community. The very diversity of its determinations is a sign, from the Hegelian perspective, that each maintains itself by detecting defects in the opposition while it thwarts its own quest for primacy by its inability to resolve internal defects apparent to its opponents. Hegel's account of the logic of Enlightenment is also an account of how and why certain of its particular expressions glow brilliantly at one moment while others pale by comparison. We have now reached the moment when the communal side of Enlightenment achieves hegemony over the individualist side.

Enlightenment must now achieve what it found Faith to obstruct – a harmonious way of life which earns the allegiance of its members because they are certain it manifests the highest freedom available to humanity. It must realize freedom by removing every impediment to it, and the freedom to be realized involves more than unconscious identification with traditional customs or the creation of a little clearing in which the individual can do what he wants while obeying more generally the dictates of the state and the market. Freedom involves self-conscious willing of the standards and ends governing all. Once the world is defined as utility, the will can act untrammeled if it is not met by other wills which oppose and obstruct it. Indvidual wills, then, must be gathered together into a common will in which each, in giving itself to the will of the community, exercises its own will in obeying the will of all. This is the moment of absolute freedom: the 'moment when heaven is transplanted to earth below.'[48]

The pursuit of absolute freedom sounds at first like the instantiation of Rousseauian theory. While this is true in one respect, it is false in others. Rousseau never defined the object as mere utility; he insisted that a set of established traditions must be left untouched by the general will; he set severe limits to the size of the polity; and he established several additional restraints around the exercise of the general will. Hegel, though, is concerned not with Rousseau's theory in its purity, but with the way its core idea of pure freedom through the communal will enters into the more complex mode of consciousness actually manifested in the French Revolution. And that movement drew from Rousseau even in trying to realize what Rousseau would resist: absolute freedom within a large state in which the will of God has been drained from the human experience of nature. Rousseau's importance in crystallizing one of the elements entering into absolute freedom reaches beyond the scope of his actual intentions because the 'cunning of history' is more devious and profound than the theory any single thinker could articulate before absolute knowledge has consolidated itself.

It comes into existence in such a way that each individual consciousness raises itself out of its allotted sphere, but grasps itself as the *notion* of will, grasps all spheres as the essence of this will, and therefore can only realize itself in a work which is work of the whole. In this absolute freedom, therefore, all social groups or classes which are spiritual spheres into which the whole is articulated are abolished; the individual consciousness that belonged to any such sphere . . . has put aside its limitation; its purposes is the general purpose; its language universal law; its work the universal work.[49]

To gain absolute freedom, where each wills everything and everyone wills all, all particularities must be abolished. Equality is necessary, and no estate or group should represent others or execute policies by itself or initiate action independently or specialize itself in any way. All 'difference' is to be eliminated in the name of a general and unified will. Each public act 'is a work of the whole'; each individual consciousness is absorbed into 'the universal work.' This general will which demands immediate expression – rather than mediation through a variety of specialized groups and functions such as farmers who cultivate the soil, women who assume primacy in the family, representatives who crystallize the will of constituencies, an executive which enforces the laws, a monarch who symbolizes them, etc. – seeks to guarantee its purity through purging its participants of all particular perspectives, interest and priorities. Only in this way can the general will ensure that nothing breaks loose to become an impediment to its will; only by this route can every will be a general and free will.

But the general will so constituted is incapable of any positive action. It can only act as an agent of surveillance, identifying and punishing those whose particular will seems to stop the general will from finding its pure expression. Absolute freedom fosters absolute terror.

This 'fury of destruction' bursts onto the scene as the members find that, though their will is good, the unity they demand is lacking. The cause must be, given the assumptions of the pursuit, in the inner will of particular individuals. For that is the only source of resistance identifiable within this mode of consciousness. Thus after the overt opponents to the regime have been removed, the universal will must look more deeply into particular selves to locate the obstacles which frustrate it. It turns to any particular mode of agency which has tried to take positive action on behalf of the state. Since no positive accomplishment is possible without embodiment in particular individuals and institutions, every positive attempt contradicts the standard of purity governing the movement. Each government must be defined as a faction and its members killed. 'When the universal will maintains that that what the government has actually done is a crime . . . the government, for its part, has nothing specific and outwardly apparent by which the guilt . . . could be demonstrated.'[50] But it must be guilty. For the general will has not been realized, and the active agents of change have assumed the visible form of a particular will.

Later, when no agency of action can come into being out of fear of being defined as a faction, the universal will must look more deeply into the soul of suspects, detecting guilt now in a secret unwillingness to give the self completely to the cause. Hence, '*being suspected*, therefore, takes the place, or has the significance and effect, of being guilty.'[51] Those whose inner will is found to be guilty are killed as enemies of the state. The executions bring out both the purely negative power of the unmediated general will and the emptiness of the inner being of those reduced to being nothing but bearers of a universal will without content. The highest determination of absolute freedom is a self emptied of any specific character, drained of everything particular; its highest power is the ability to kill those who fail to conform to an imaginary point called the universal will.

The sole work and deed of universal freedom is therefore *death*, a death too which has no inner significance or filling, for what is negated is the empty point of the absolutely free self. It is thus the coldest and meanest of deaths, with no more significance than cutting off a head of cabbage or swallowing a mouthful of water.[52]

The Enlightenment comes to its end in this fury of destruction. It has, unknowingly and dialectically, carried consciousness close to the point where it can transcend the defects of Enlightenment and Greek ethical life together. And the determinate negation of Enlightenment, understood in the context of the history of consciousness which led up to it, makes it possible now to glimpse the outlines of a mode of being in which the dualities of the Enlightenment are resolved into a complex, higher unity: particularity and universality; finitude and infinity; the right of the individual and the will of the community; the diversity of different estates and functions and the unity of a common ethic; the way of the world and the claims of Spirit; the claims of knowledge and the demands of passion – are all to be brought together into an expressive harmony where each infiltrates into the inner being of the others and each sets limits to the excesses to which the others are prone on their own.

The Enlightenment, in purging Faith of its 'picture thoughts,' has purified it and brought its successors to the point where it comprehends the need and possibility of comprehending the Spirit of God through concepts. Pure Insight, on the other hand, can now discern its own limitations. It cannot generate an ethic, or realize freedom or establish knowledge out of itself alone. In defeating Faith, it lost what Faith had known darkly and defended weakly: without a world invested with intrinsic significance which transcends the resources of the pure self alone, the ethic, freedom and knowledge it seeks cannot be created; pure insight on its own is only capable of destruction.

Faith and Insight can be elevated to a higher unity which contains several essential characteristics. First, both recognize in the common ethic which has been evolving through the history of consciousness a set of standards and limits which enable and delimit the individual subject. Second, both recognize substance to be essentially Spirit, realizing that Spirit as it unfolds through history becomes lodged in the inner *telos* of the self and the common ethic of the society. Third, both realize that because substance is Spirit and Spirit is essentially thought, Spirit can and will realize itself through the advance of human consciousness in history. When these three elements are instantiated in the life of the society, Faith and Insight become absorbed into one another: the first acknowledges the internal connection between reason and recognition of intrinsic significance in the world and the second recognizes the internal connection between intrinsic significance and the commitment to reason. Neither can be without the elevation of both. And when this elevation occurs, the otherness each had confronted becomes internalized into the complex diversity of a harmonious whole. The circle of consciousness 'that returns into itself' becomes complete in 'the circle that presupposes its beginning and reaches it only at its end.'[53] The riddle of epistemology dissolves into the inclusive circle of absolute knowledge.

The perfection of Enlightenment

Hegel seeks to realize the Enlightenment quest for knowledge that is certain of itself, fearing that the failure to fulfill this project will result in nihilism. The two opposing parties in the dialectic of Enlightenment concurred with each other in this quest: the first locating absolute knowledge in a God who could be experienced but not known by humanity and the second grounding certainty in the human self when it is rational. To achieve the result at which they aim each would have to accept some elements from the opponent, and both would have to fold these elements into the understanding that substance is Spirit and Spirit, because of its essential character, is susceptible to being known. But while Hegel could make a good case that the ontology of Spirit was essential to absolute knowledge and that absolute knowledge was necessary to fulfillment of the aim implicitly governing the Enlightenment, those first two arguments do not show that the aspiration to absolute knowledge itself can be realized.

In place of a simple proof of absolute knowledge, Hegel offers a layered interpretation, drawing the inner certitude of Faith into the compass of a comprehensive theory of contemporary experience inspired by Insight's confidence in reason, and filling the comprehensive theory with the inward experience of realization or fulfillment which inspired Faith. So absolute knowledge is both comprehensive and certain of itself because it covers all experience and because it expresses the inner and inter-subjective essence realized in the modern experience. It unites revelation and knowledge by giving the former the shape of conceptual understanding and the latter the inner experience of fulfillment. Each layer folds into the other, but the comprehensive theory of contemporary experience is more fully developed in *Philosophy of Right* and the concentration on the inner experience of subjective and intersubjective fulfillment is more fully expressed in *Phenomenology of Spirit*. Departing somewhat from Hegel's own insistence that each of these layers establishes its certainty only in conjunction with the other, we will concentrate most of our attention on the expressive dimension here, paying more attention to the systematic dimension in the second interlude.

The expressive dimension brings out the deepest aspirations which govern members, corporate entities and the transcendent state which draws these elements together into a diverse unity. This dimension, that is, folds comprehension of the modern world into the purpose which resides within it and is brought to its essential realization in this world. When this realization is attained, it enters into the lives of members, corporate entities and the state. Though only the philosophical consciousness will recognize it adequately, others, playing particular roles in the family, civil society and the state, will become more responsive to interpretations and institutions that remind them of the common purposes they help to realize.

Hegel's account of the experience itself carries a religious resonance, a resonance which recalls the historical vicissitudes of a Christian faith which has advanced now to the level of knowledge. Knowledge and inner purpose become united. 'For this reason it must be said that nothing is *known* that is not in *experience*, or, as it is also expressed, that is not *felt to be true*, not given as *inwardly revealed* eternal verity, as something sacred that is *believed*, or whatever other expressions have been used.'[54] The recognition of absolute knowledge flows in part from the alleviation of restlessness in thought and alienation in life which had troubled consciousness up to this point.

If Hegel's theory of modern life contains such a teleological component, how could one subject it to critical scrutiny? In *The Will to Power* Nietzsche says: 'If the world had a goal, it must have been reached. If there were for it some unintended final state, this also must have been reached.'[55] Nietzsche is wrong in saying that a final end could not be posited for the world unless it has been reached by now, but right in calling attention to the fact that any theory of an immanent purpose which is held to be both installed in the world and knowable to human consciousness must also claim to discern the configurations of the final result in the outlines of the present. Otherwise Hegel's promised culmination of history, 'which happens to be known to me because I have traversed the entire field,' would stand as an article of faith, contradicting its own promise of certitude. Hegel's theory would be seen to contain the sort of debilitating uncertainty and contestability he exposed in other theories. So Hegel has to discern the outlines of the end in the shape of the present, and he has to claim that lived-experience in this foreseeable future will be filled with the inward feeling of an essence realized, a purpose fulfilled, a restlessnes stilled. Of course, none of these results will be complete or unqualified, for particularities are both essential to realization of the universal and restricted in their ability to embody it. Modernity cannot dissolve the problem of evil or the enigma of human guilt altogether. But the inner history of the realized future must nonetheless transcend that of the alienated past.

This expectation sets up a test of sorts of the Hegelian ontology of Spirit in the lived-experience of modern life. And that experience belies the Hegelian expectation of fulfillment at several crucial points: the untamed forms of subjectivity which Hegel identified have been maintained and extended rather than drawn into the orbit of a larger life; religious faith has not found itself lifted into the sphere of knowledge but if anything it has become more sectarian, divided, grounded in faith, and insistent in its assertions of faith; secular consciousness on the other hand, has not become infused with the life of Spirit, but has drawn itself further away from modes of consciousness which locate a purpose or design in the world itself; many people in modern life do not experience the common norms and understandings which govern them as media of fulfillment but as external impositions of alienating requirements; identification with the state as an internal medium of justice and freedom is volatile and uncertain, while immediate identification with it as an agent of power in the international arena also fits poorly into the Hegelian expectation; and the future is not viewed benignly in the present, but dismal possibilities such as ecological catastrophe, a degeneration of state relations into recurrent cycles of state and non-state terrorism, and the extinction of humanity through nuclear war compel the present to face the future unfolding before it with anxiety and uncertainty.

To the extent these actualities and projected possibilities infect the inner experience of modern life they expose an element of insistence inside the philosophy of Spirit pedaled by Hegel; they drain confidence and certitude from the comprehensive theory he advances. Realized Spirit does not find expression in the inward life of modernity; a spirit of restlessness, resentment and anxiety infiltrates into a world in which the order of things seems fragile, laced with power and coercion, and susceptible to catastrophe.

Hegel's expectation of the realized state reveals itself retrospectively to be a chain of faith which bound his theory together, enabling him to interpret the past and the present from the vantage point of a fictional future for which he yearned. One can continue to have faith in this vision, of course, but because that faith is thoroughly contestable it loses the authoritative status required for it in Hegelian theory.

Hegel reveals how previous modes of consciousness rested upon a faith which defeats their claim to universal acceptance once it is discovered. A faith which is indefinitely revisable, questionable and contestable 'tramples underfoot the roots of humanity' by defeating the human quest, as Hegel defines it, 'to press onward to agreement with others . . . in an achieved community of minds.' But Hegel's own theory stands among those he has so identified; its sustaining ontology of Spirit, too, loses its credibility once the ground of absolute knowledge slips away beneath it.

The ontology of Spirit must be known to be believed, but the claim that it is knowable always collapses into an act of faith. If certainty is stripped from this ontology then the determinacy and directionality which discipline the Hegelian dialectic are also peeled away. For the theory was to be established not by assumptions it proves at the beginning but by the authoritative result it achieves at the end. Absent the promise of the end, it is contestable which direction must be taken whenever a particular mode of consciousness is negated. Does the relation of Lordship and Bondage advance the future of freedom when it introduces subjectivity into a world which cannot house it? Or does it expose permanent and unresolvable conflict between the claims of individuality and the demands of order? Or does it manifest resentment against the finitude of the self and the lack of transcendent purpose in the world which themselves must be overcome before freedom can be advanced? Or does it reveal a tragedy lodged in the human condition to which we must somehow become reconciled? The Hegelian reading at the close of that dialectic anticipates a result to be established at the end of the journey of consciousness through history; and the necessity of his own reading is no greater than the certainty of the result it anticipates.

The result at the end was supposed to draw otherness into the frame of knowledge and a common ethic. But when the standard of absolute knowledge is called into question, the project of assimilating otherness into a diverse and inclusive unity is too. Perhaps otherness, in the spheres of ethical life, normal individuality and knowledge, should be treated as a sign of human finitude and the absence of Spirit in the world, and perhaps the quest to assimilate otherness into higher forms of community should be understood as the demand to imprison difference within the frame of a unity shaken by any sign of its own limit and uncertainty. Similarly, if the known is surrounded perpetually by a fringe of the unknown, it is constantly possible that disruptive effects from the fringe will undermine radically a whole system of previous beliefs. And if what counts as knowledge shifts radically in any direction, the interpretation of those modes of consciousness which led up to the established synthesis will shift globally too.

The incredibility of the Hegelian ontology, then, unravels the determinacy and the directionality of the negations through which its dialectic of consciousness advances. It opens space for alternative readings of the same phenomena. And it calls into question the Hegelian project of folding otherness into an expanding sphere of knowledge, ethical life and normality. The normal, modern self which 'keeps the natural temper under lock and key' assumes a different appearence when the Hegelian model of selfhood is no longer circled by a halo of certainty.

Nonetheless, even these findings reveal how much is gained from exploring the Hegelian dialectic. For the Hegelian theory reveals to what extremes thought must go if it aspires to lift itself to absolute knowledge, and it also suggests that theories of knowledge and freedom which require a robust theory of truth to sustain themselves will face debilitating difficulties as they pursue the implications of their quest. Hegel stands at the end of such quests, waiting to show more modest thinkers how their own projects presuppose a philosophy of Spirit they refuse to endorse. Hegel teaches questions to ask and criticisms to pose to theories which try to return to any of the moments he has investigated. If the Hegelian ontology has lost its power to persuade, Hegel's critical examination of alternative philosophies still retains a measure of power and significance. And the defeat of his own project opens thought to possibilities previously thought to be closed.

It is through engagement and re-engagement with Hegel that one might judge whether contemporary thought can still pursue the stable consensus sought by Mill, Marx, Dewey, Habermas and Rawls, or must step onto the more slippery terrain charted by Nietzsche, James, Heidegger, Freud and Foucault. The theorists of the first set, disagreeing significantly amongst themselves on epistemological, moral and political issues, nonetheless construe the phenomenon of otherness to be a tractable issue facing a theory of rationality, knowledge, individuality, alienation, community or justice. The latter thinkers, also disagreeing amongst themselves, are touched both by Hegel's critique of previous modes of consciousness and his failed attempt to transcend them. They interrogate any attempt to reinstate the problematic of the Enlightenment or to dissolve its dilemmas into a pragmatic conception of community. They treat otherness as a mysterious or intractable feature of existence, reacting back upon forms of knowledge, individuality, community and freedom which compete for hegemony in modern life. Whichever way one turns, reading and rereading Hegel's *Phenomenology of Spirit* provides a superb way to clarify the multiple issues involved.

Second Interlude:
Hegel, Marx and the State

The unity of the state

Hegel's theory of the modern state is designed to show how freedom comes to fruition in modernity. The modern state is the one entity capable of encompassing the principles of subjectivity and expressive unity in one diverse and harmonious whole; and freedom cannot be lifted to its highest level until these two media of realization are drawn together in the same life. The essence of the state is implicitly on the verge of realization in modern life, according to Hegel, but one more ingredient is required to bring it to its fulfillment: 'It requires to be grasped in thought as well; the content which is already rational in principle must win the *form* of rationality and so appear well-founded to untrammeled thinking.'[1]

When the implicit rationality of the state is rendered explicit, not only will its appearance change but its real structure will shift too. For now the members will recognize more fully the freedom which is theirs, the limitations they must accept to protect this freedom, and the ethical life they must endorse to enable the state to achieve its highest level of existence. And this recognition will infuse the life of the individual, the family, corporate associations, the market, the civil service and the relations all these entities bear to the state.

The structure of *Philosophy of Right* differs, then, from that followed in *Phenomenology of Spirit*. Both texts are dialectical. But while the first dialectic is historical, embodying moments which advance consciousness until it becomes inclusive, the second is structural, beginning with the simplest and most abstract self-understandings of modern life and advancing through more complex self-interpretations to the achievement of full self-consciousness. The first level lives modern life through the categories of abstract right; the second through the understandings of interests and moral principle available to civil society; and the highest level lifts the first two to a common ethical life inscribed in the predispositions of members and institutions and brought to a pinnacle of self-consciousness through the state. We progress, then, from Hobbes, Locke and Kant through Adam Smith and Montesquieu, ultimately reaching Hegel himself; and that progression is already available to some degree in the implicit experience of modern life.

Each of the simple levels of consciousness is brought through awareness of its internal insufficiency to a higher and more encompassing level of understanding. Thus, at the first level, Locke is right and so is the simple consciousness he represents: property is an essential right of human beings. But this formulation also misleads. It is not merely good to a personality which is already formed and demanding it; it is not merely the right of a natural person. The institutionalization of property helps to form the self as a person or agent.

The key distinction here is between a mere possession and property. Property is the social recognition that something belongs to me. For that recognition to be realized a whole system of laws, rules of contract and exchange, standards of responsibility, understandings of freedom, definitions of crime and punishment have to come into being. These norms, given institutional form by civil society, constitute the self as a person with rights; they introduce first personhood and then subjectivity into the self. (Note: Hegel distinguishes person from subject; the first is a bearer of rights and the second advances freedom into the entire realm of morality. We cannot explore those distinctions here.)

Thus 'contract presupposes that the parties entering into it recognize each other as persons and property owners.'[2] A similar relation is implied with respect to crime. For there is no institution of property and contract unless it is a crime to break a contract or steal another's property. In a hunting and gathering society, for instance, the self is not recognized as a bearer of rights, the contractual form does not define much of the common life, and responsibility is likely to be diffused among individuals, groups and the gods. So, through the institutional recognition of property, contract and exchange, I am seen and see myself to be an agent, capable of owning, acting according to private will, entering into contract, establishing my own career, accountable legally and morally for stealing from others, and worthy of being held responsible individually for the successes and failures in my life.

The institution of property, embodied in a reciprocal web of recognition, endows the self with the sort of recognition the two parties sought implicitly in the relationship of Lordship and Bondage. They could not achieve it because its institutional preconditions were lacking.

'The self-consciousness of heroes (like that of Oedipus and others in Greek tragedy) had not advanced out of its primitive simplicity either to reflection on the distinction between act and action [or] between the external event and knowledge of the circumstances. On the contrary they accepted responsibility for the whole compass of the deed.'[3] Socrates and Christ, later, could project the idea of subjectivity, but it could not become installed fully and securely in a way of life until property and civil society unfolded together.

But this means that the moment of individuality – of self as an independent agent of rights, interests, conscience and knowledge – is enabled and delimited by the institutional setting which makes it possible. It means that the self as a person and the idea of property are actually constituted by the institutional setting in which they reside. There is, then, no absolute right to property nor an untrammeled right to follow the conscience of the individual. Both must be limited to the extent needed to maintain their institutional conditions of being, and both must be brought to a higher level of self-consciousness by attending to the arrangements and understandings which make them possible.

We are thus lifted by these (and other) considerations to a higher level of self-understanding. We begin to discern how the institutions of civil society constitute the forms through which we achieve identity and how reconciliation to the imperatives of this institutional matrix is essential to maintaining and perfecting that identity. Civil society consists roughly of the individual, the executive and enforcement branches of government, the family, the corporation and the market. It is these entities in their institutional interactions and modes of consciousness. It is the state experienced as an external entity, understood to act upon the self, but not yet understood to enter internally into the very constitution of the self and the ethical life which hold the totality together.

Hegel is very impressed with civil society, calling it 'the achievement of the modern world.'[4] For the market, in conjunction with the other institutions, provides both room within which the principle of modern individuality can flourish and the combination by means of which it can be kept under lock and key. When each pursues private ends as an entrepreneur, banker, worker or farmer, he experiences himself to be an agent with rights, interests, conscience, responsibility and freedom. The activities tend to concentrate each participant on its particular interest or concern, drawing attention away from the whole which enables these interests to be pursued together. But civil society, through its principle of coordination through organized competition, implicates the individual unwittingly in the life of the whole. In it my interests can only be attained through exchange with others, and so out of self-interest I produce or trade with others, and they do so as well: 'The particular person is essentially so related to other particular persons that each establishes himself and finds satisfaction by means of the others.'[5] Civil society, with the entrepreneur and the market as its core, introduces subjectivity into the world and harnesses it for the common good.

But civil society, by itself, is constantly on the verge of going too far, of destroying itself in the clash among particular interests, desires and principles. It does contain two mediating institutions which help to instill the principles of ethical life into its members and into institutional relations. The family, whose interior form finds its rational basis in the different 'physical characteristics of the two sexes,'[6] educates its members into ethical life. The wife is determined naturally to concentrate on the internal quality of family life, while the husband represents the family in public life. The recognition of each of the unity they establish out of difference, and the importance that child-rearing carries for the future of the order, constitute the micro-experience out of which implication in the larger ethical life can develop. Because of the substantial interest the whole has in the health of the family as an institution, divorce must not be based on the whim or desire of the parties alone; it must be determined by a representative of the state whether the marriage can be restored or not. The corporation similarly mediates between the particularities of civil society and the ethical life.

But even with the family and the corporation, civil society is not self-subsistent. Two of its limitations are particularly important, for they strike at the heart of subjectivity and universality as Hegel understands them. The first flows from the tendency of entrepreneurs, in the competitive pursuit of profit, to squeeze as much out of the workforce as possible. The increase in wealth which results benefits the entire order. But that is only 'one side of the picture':

The other side is the subdivision and restriction of particular jobs. This results in the dependence and distress of the class tied to work of that sort, and these again entail inability to feel and enjoy the broader freedoms and especially the intellectual benefits of civil society.[7]

If work, as Hegel argued in *Phenomenology*, is fundamental to the achievement of agency and self-consciousness, then this tendency of civil society is self-destructive. It 'alienates' an entire portion of the populace from the common life, pushing it outside the reach of ethical life and making it susceptible to coordination only through force and coercion.

The second self-destructive tendency of civil society, again flowing from the very competitive system which enables subjectivity to be and regulates it excesses, is to drive the income of those at the lowest level below subsistence – below the level needed for one to function effectively as a 'member of the society.' This class of paupers becomes a 'rabble,' unjustly treated in itself, resentful of the ethical life it is called upon to follow, and destructive of the larger life through its resistance and the orientation toward it instilled in the public. This tendency must be reversed, but the state confronts a dilemma when it tries to do so. It might adopt welfare programs to lift paupers to a subsistence level; it might call upon private charity to maintain them; or it might give them public employment. But the first two responses violate 'the principle of civil society and the feeling of individual independence and self-respect in its individual members,' and the third exacerbates the evil which produced unemployment: 'an excess of production and . . . the lack of a proportionate number of consumers who are themselves also pro-ducers.'[8]

On the issues of alienated work and pauperism, then, Hegel anticipates Marx, but his response is un-Marxian. These effects of civil society reveal it to be incomplete on its own, but it still remains necessary to enable the modern principle of subjectivity to be. These dislocations, along with others to which civil society is susceptible, require that it be drawn into the orbit of a comprehensive state, a state which preserves the moment of individuality fostered by civil society by filling it with an inward ethic and surrounding it with more objective institutional form.

In contrast with spheres of private rights and private welfare (the family and civil society), the state is, from one point of view, an external necessity and their higher authority; its nature is such that their laws are subordinate to it and dependent upon it. On the other hand, however, it is the end immanent within them, and its strength lies in the unity of its own universal end and aim with the particular interest of individuals.[9]

The state is the only self-subsistent entity. It draws the other essential elements into an inclusive totality which can sustain itself; and it enables each of the elements to maintain its difference from others while harmonizing with them in a self-subsistent whole. The primary institutions of the state are its constitutional law, an executive branch, a legislative branch, a monarch who is the sovereign power, and a class of civil servants who have their eye on the universal interest or the interests of the state as such.

We cannot explore its institutional structure in detail. But the essence of the state is that through its public and written laws, its sovereign power to resolve the most fundamental conflicts, and its personification of sovereignty in the hereditary monarch, it transcends the sphere of unconscious regulation. It articulates or brings to self-consciousness principles and understandings which govern the land; it is the sphere of self-conscious action in support of the common good; and it nurtures and protects the customary ethic which infuses the inward life of the well-ordered subject, family, church, corporation and civil society. The state is the locus of Spirit, and Spirit comes to its highest and most differentiated *political* expression in the state.

The . . . substantiality of the state consists in the fact that its end is the universal interest as such and the conservation therein of particular interests since the universal interest is the substance of these . . . But this very substantiality of the state is Spirit knowing and willing itself . . . The state, therefore, knows what it wills and knows it in its universality . . . Hence it works and acts by reference to consciously adopted ends, known principles and laws which are not merely implicit but are actually present to consciousness; and further it acts with precise knowledge of existing conditions and circumstances.[10]

The state without Spirit

What would the Hegelian state look like if Spirit were drained from it? I do not mean, How would it look if every expression of loyalty, identification, patriotism, and principle were subtracted from the common life? But, How would it appear if the ontology of Spirit, which Hegel thinks finds its highest political expression in the institutional life of the modern state, were subtracted from it? There is no way to answer such a question with precision or assurance. For maybe some of the identifications Hegel perceives to be manifestations of Spirit would remain as the more mundane respect of citizens for principles and structures which nourish the life they prize. Nevertheless, it may be fruitful to pretend we could remove Spirit surgically from the state while retaining room for modes of identification which might emerge in a world without Spirit. The pretense enables us to think critically about Hegel's theory of the state, even if it does not allow us to prove or refute the theory he has offered.

While Hegel allows room for contingency in the modern state, its most fundamental institutions are held to embody rational necessity: each plays an essential role in maintaining the integrity of the state. This conviction, expressive of the view that Spirit installs itself more fully in actuality as history progresses, compels Hegel to endow actuality with rationality wherever it is indispensable to the state. Hegel's philosophy of

Spirit thus renders him, with respect to modernity, a philosopher of empiricist-essentialism. There are, though, at least four areas where Hegel's explicit treatment of an actuality as expressive of an emergent rationality might be called into question: the division of responsibility between men and women, the role of war in the internal life of the state, the issue of work, and the issue of pauperism. We will consider the first and the second now, and then discuss briefly Marx's alternative reading of the sources, effects and remedies for pauperism within the frame of civil society.

Hegel invests marriage and family with a heavy load of *telos*. Rejecting the mind/body dualism of many Enlightenment theories – which brings with it an insoluble set of problems – he defines the self as essentially embodied, with embodiment entering into the thoughts, judgments, purposes of the self. Definite and uniform bodily difference signifies, then, a difference of immanent purpose. It is not only that 'our objectively appointed end and so our ethical duty is to enter the married state,'[11] making those who remain single incomplete beings. But bodily differences between male and female signify objective differences in the mental and intellectual capacities of men and women, and these together reveal the different purposes each is to serve. It is this essential difference which makes each incomplete without the other, which invests the union between the sexes with spiritual significance, and which prepares them to appreciate the more comprehensive union realized through the state. The key is in the rational difference between masculinity and femininity flowing from the 'physical differences between the two sexes.'

Women are capable of education, but they are not *made for* activities which demand a universal faculty such as the more advanced sciences, philosophy, and certain forms of artistic production. Women may have happy ideas, taste and elegance, but *they cannot attain* to the ideal. The difference between men and women is that between animals and plants. Men correspond to animals, while women correspond to plants because their development is more placid and the *principle that underlies it* is the rather vague feeling of unity.[12]

This account of gender difference, which completes itself by reserving the home to women and civil society to men, is not an incidental feature of Hegel's ontology of Spirit. It is fundamentally expressive of it. For Spirit must invest itself in actuality, and actualities which persist for centuries and are drawn into the frame of modernity are thus fraught with spiritual signification. Thus bodily difference between the sexes is said to have a 'rational basis' and to be invested with difference in intrinsic purpose; each bearer of difference is incomplete until completed through union with the other in a family; and the family helps to lift its members to participation in the higher unity of the state. As long as the ontology of Spirit infuses the account, gender role differentiation cannot be defined as subordination; bodily differences which cut across and through gender lines are not given ontological weight; and the claim of the state upon the life of the family is not treated as intrusive.

To criticize Hegel's theory of gender difference is to call into question the ontology of Spirit with which it is infused. Hegel, as we saw in the *Phenomenology*, recognized a self-destructive dialectic lodged in the early Greek world. The unity it achieved established different roles for men and women, but it lacked a principle of subjectivity capable of mediating between them when fundamental conflicts arose between role imperatives. Greek life 'creates for itself in what it suppresses and what is at the same time essential to it an internal enemy – womankind in general.' This finding of Hegel's about Greek life could only be articulated after the modern world had clarified the principle of subjectivity and the role it can play in ethical life. Similarly, the modern world of nineteenth-century Europe and America, viewed now from a perspective accepting Hegel's systematic account minus its ontology of Spirit, inverts and exacerbates that classical contradiction. It introduces the principle of subjectivity into ethical life, civil society, politics, and intellectual life, and then informs women that they "cannot attain to the ideal." It creates its own internal enemy, giving it the principle of subjectivity as its goal and weapon in the battle.

The profundity of Hegel still glows amidst this defeat. For on Hegel's theory of complex interdependencies among the elements of the modern state, the full extension of the right of individuality to women would introduce powerful pressures for change in several sectors of life. We have seen some of these changes occur, in the increased intrusions of the state into the life of the family (which accompanies the demise of a single authority to resolve internal conflicts), in patterns of child-rearing, in the incidence of divorce and the nature of its settlements, in the occupational system, in cultural norms and educational expectations, perhaps in a dialectical expansion of the principle of subjectivity into new areas of life as it is extended across gender lines.

But such a massive contradiction was not supposed to occur in the realized state of modernity. Its actual occurrence presses against the ontology of Spirit. The occurrence does not prove the ontology to be dispensable to achievement in modernity of inward identification and institutional unity amidst diversity. It rather suggests that this ontology was invented to fill a need rather than discovered as the principle of its fulfillment. To encounter Hegel in this way is to come to appreciate at once the need which occasioned the ontology of Spirit, the forms of subordination buried within its rhetoricity, and the issues facing late-modern theory and practice in a world without its presence.

Hegel's account of the *telos*, of war in the modern state contains the same lessons. For while Hegel treats the state as a self-subsistent whole, its self-subsistence does not consist simply in its internal composition and the inward identifications of its members. The centrifugal forces of civil society are too powerful for that. The internal dynamic of civil society presses each individual and corporate interest to concentrate exclusively on itself and to forget its dependence upon the whole. But the threat of external enemies does for the state as a whole what the risk of death did for the self in the relationship of Lordship and Bondage. It draws particular interests together in awareness of their membership in the state, and it teaches each that sacrifice for the whole is a condition of both membership and individuality. War is not, then, a contingent feature of the modern state, nor is it an evil always to be avoided. It is a necessity expressing a higher purpose.

Here as elsewhere, the point of view from which things seem pure accidents vanishes if we look at them in the light of the concept and philosophy . . . War is the state of affairs which deals in earnest with the vanity of temporal goods and concerns . . . War has the higher significance that by its agency, as I have remarked elsewhere, 'the ethical health of peoples is preserved in their indifference to the stabilization of finite institutions; just as the blowing of the winds preserves the sea from the foulness which would be the result of a prolonged calm, so also corruption in nations would be the product of prolonged, let alone perpetual peace.'[13]

Here, Hegel invests a necessity of the modern state system with spiritual significance. Because war inevitably emerges between sovereign states without a common authority, it reveals Spirit at work fulfilling an inner need. Without periodic war the modern state cannot keep the principle of subjectivity in rein: it must either lose its capacity to maintain the health of the whole in which subjectivity is set or it must maintain its internal structure in a coercive way. Either response corrupts the life of the state, so war must arise periodically to crystallize the minds and identifications of its members. War disciplines subjectivity while allowing the principle itself to remain intact in civil society.

But the late-modern possibility of nuclear holocaust throws this entire identity between system necessity and its fulfillment into disarray. Today war means the risk of extinction, either of civilization or humanity. If it is a need, it is one that must not be fulfilled. Perhaps the late-modern state needs war to maintain itself internally but must resist it to defer the risk of total destruction. That contradiction places the internal structure of the state and the Hegelian ontology of Spirit under the same critical lens. It does not give much comfort, either, to those theories of the modern state which have not peered so deeply as Hegel has into the internal dynamic of subjectivity, civil society and commonality in modernity. For these criticisms cast doubt upon the spiritual unity of the system of interdependencies Hegel examined; they do not show that the system can avoid internal contradictions without Spirit.

Pauperism and politics

Marx, in his early writings, sought to reveal contradictions in the Hegelian model of the state, to replace it with a more equal and less mediated idea of community, and to sustain the idea of community without drawing upon the 'idealist' philosophy of Spirit in which Hegel situated the state. It is as though in a world without Spirit the perfection of human collectivity constitutes the only hope Marx can imagine to bring the excesses of modern subjectivity under control.

In an early essay on pauperism in Germany and England Marx outlines an anti-Hegelian reading of the state in civil society. Hegel had construed pauperism to be an effect of civil society which the state must eliminate if its inward unity was not to be destroyed through disaffection, conflict and the extension of coercive measures. But while exposing contradictions in policies devised at the level of civil society, Hegel failed to delineate a viable response available to the realized state. Marx picks 'a Prussian' – who in the wake of a local uprising of workers had called for a political response to pauperism – to be the immediate target of his critique. But Hegel hovers in the background both as a source of key concepts deployed and the spiritual object of Marx's wrath.

The 'Prussian' explained German misrepresentation of the sources of pauperism by the fact that Germany was undeveloped politically. Marx disputes this explanation and the remedy it implies. If it is admitted that England is the most political country in Europe, with organized interests, contested elections, and competing parties, it 'will also be granted that England is the country of pauperism, for even the word itself is of English origin . . . In England the misery of labor is not partial but universal; not confined to the factory districts but extends to the rural districts.'[14] And movements against pauperism have a longer history in England than in Germany.

In England, each of the contending parties has a solution to pauperism, and each blames the other for not resolving the problem.

Insofar as the English bourgeoisie grants politics any responsibility for pauperism, the Whig regards the Tory, and the Tory regards the Whig as the cause of pauperism . . . Neither party finds the cause in politics in general, but rather in the politics of its opponent; neither party lets itself dream of reforming society.[15]

Each party selects as cause something that the other could remedy if only it had the will to act. In this way both parties converge in defining the problem of pauperism to reflect a failure of will. One party blames the problem on 'defects in the administration' of the poor laws, laws designed to provide charity for the poor. But the perfection of these instruments seems merely to expand the number of poor coming for aid. The other party blames 'the evil disposition of the poor,' endorsing the Malthusian view that 'charity is folly' and that the state must 'leave the poor to their fate.'[16] So the first calls for reform of the laws and the second calls upon the state to control the poor through punitive measures. Each call for action refers to policies available to the state, and each party is therefore able to blame pauperism on the failure of will of the other: 'Where there are political parties, each finds the cause of every evil in the fact that its opponent instead of itself is at the helm of the state.'[17]

Both parties together seek the source in areas of action that are legitimately available to the state now: 'Every state seeks the cause of its ills in accidental or intentional defects of administration and therefore seeks the remedy in reprimand of the administration . . . Why? Precisely because administration is the organizing activity of the state.'[18]

The state cannot detect the source of the problem in the basic organization of the civil society over which it presides. For it represents civil society; all of the pressures applied to it flow from civil society; and its ability to act is confined by the necessity to protect the operation of civil society.

If the modern state would want to transcend the impotence of its administration it would have to transcend the present mode of private life. If it wanted to transcend private life it would have to transcend itself . . . No living being, however, believes that the defect of his specific existence is rooted in the principle or essence of his life.[19]

Hegel could not devise a remedy for pauperism nor, by extension, for alienation in work, because the state he celebrates expresses the contradictions in civil society that would have to be resolved. Hegel, like the Prussian, has too much faith in the independent power of politics to resolve fundamental issues. He has unfounded faith in the healing and unifying drive of Spirit as it expresses itself within the politics he celebrates. But the issues are so fundamental that they can be resolved only by more revolutionary action designed to replace civil society itself by a higher form. When civil society is fraught with contradictions, politics becomes one of the modes by which they are concealed from participants.

The principle of politics is will. The more one-sided, and the more perfected political thought is, the more it believes in the omnipotence of will, the blinder it is to the natural and spiritual restrictions of the will, and the more incapable it is of discovering the source of social ills.[20]

Hegel could not resolve pauperism because every political answer he imagined defeated itself without the support of a fictive Spirit. In the absence of Spirit, civil society spawns competing and inadequate responses to pauperism. Some responses make the state too punitive; others separate recipients of charity from the principles of self-reliance and self-respect central to civil society; others draw the poor into forms of organization and control which contradict the same principle of civil society from another direction. The issue is left hanging, because only a revolution which transforms the structure of civil society could solve it. And Hegel insisted that the French Revolution was the last revolution modernity needed or could take.

Marx, in his early writings, seeks a form of community which transcends civil society and the 'abstract' state which accompanies it. The community envisaged will resolve pauperism, but it echoes the ideal which Rousseau had already explored and Hegel had already criticized:

Human emancipation will only be complete when the real individual has absorbed into himself the abstract citizen; when . . . in his everyday life, in his work, and his relationships he has become a species being, and when he has recognized his own powers, so that he no longer separates his social abilities from himself.[21]

In criticizing the structure and effects of modern civil society, Marx first denies the ontology of Spirit which gives Hegel faith in the curative and unifying power of the state and then tries to discern another way to regulate (or coordinate or harmonize) the principle of subjectivity which flourishes in civil society. His answer is to elminate civil society itself and to fold individuality into communal life. This idealism becomes more attenuated and cautious as Marx matures, but the initial impulse never changes its direction. In *Kapital,* for instance, Marx reiterates a version of it:

The religious reflex of the real world can, in any case, only vanish when the practical relations of everyday life offer to man none but perfectly intelligible relations with his fellows and to nature. The life process of society does strip off its mystical veil until it is treated as production for freely associated men, and is consciously regulated by them in accordance with a settled plan.[22]

It appears that the debate between Hegel and Marx moves within the same sort of circle Marx discerned in the debate between Whigs and Tories. Each party, in opposing its adversary, first blames observed difficulties on practices or principles celebrated by the adversary and then responds by inflating a principle deflated by the opponent. Hegel celebrates bourgeois life, but contains it in Spirit; Marx denies Spirit but insists all the more that bourgeois individuality must be contained within communalism. One gives room to civil society; the other thinks it must be eliminated if modernity is to realize itself. One incorporates otherness within a complex totality which emphasizes differentiation and inequality; the other dissolves alienation in a social form which supports more equality and commonality. One thinks nature itself will become intelligble as Spirit is realized within it; the other thinks that nature becomes intelligible through human mastery of it. One believes that reconciliation to a particular role in a complex whole is the key to freedom; the other thinks revolutionary achievement of a communal whole unlocks freedom. One thinks foreknowledge of death is essential to the historical dialectic of self-consciousness; the other ignores the relation of life to death while extending the possibility of self-consciousness to all members of the realized community. There are certainly broad and fundamental differences between these two thinkers. What encloses each in the same circle with the other?

The state of modernity

Both Hegel and Marx reject early-modern theories of a self which is transparent to itself. This theory of the foundational individual tended to emphasize the role of introspection in self-knowledge, and it treated the individual as the best judge of his or her own desires, interests and conscience. Individualism found its most confident justification in the simple theory of the foundational self. But Hegel and Marx together pull this foundation away.

For both Hegel and Marx transparency is a *goal* of the self, to be realized only after a review of the history of consciousness and through understanding of the intimate links between the structure of the social whole and the internal composition of the self residing within it; it is thus attainable in a full sense only in modernity when the realized society becomes transparent to itself. Freedom presupposes self-consciousness and self-consciousness presupposes the achievement of a transparent society whose fundamental principles of operation are visible and whose visible principles are also known to be true and legitimate. The self-conscious self will thus include in its self-consciousness a deep understanding of the link between its identity and the identity of the whole, its interests and the interests of the whole, its freedom and the freedom of the whole. Hegel invests this capacity for self-conscious harmonization politically in the state and intellectually in the sphere of philosophy, indicating that all other segments of the diverse whole participate in this knowledge variably and imperfectly. Marx invests it in the community as a universal entity. But despite this difference, Marx shares in the Hegelian aspiration to self-consciousness and the transparency of the social whole. He anticipates a world in which 'the practical relations of everyday life offer to man none but perfectly intelligible relations with his fellows and to nature.'

But if knowledge of the whole in which the self is implicated reveals the structure of the whole to be the basis of self-realization and the vehicle of collective realization, if it supports individual and collective freedom and binds them together in a transparent totality, then politics must play a modest role in the Hegelian and Marxian ideals of social life. These are depoliticized ideals of modern life.

Of course each ideal contains a political dimension. Hegel's order consists of a diverse populace, each segment tending to be blind to some truths which are apparent to others. There is a politics through which each tends to press its particular perspective too far, and each is brought closer to an understanding of the common good through involvement in mediating institutions. The Hegelian order depends upon civil servants, the monarch and philosophers to enlighten those sunk deeply in the particularities of civil society about the commonalities which unify them objectively. The first constituencies, then, are brought to a deeper *recognition* of what the common good requires by agents who are themselves above politics. And the Marxian community, less differentiated and more democratic in form, also recognizes a politics through which the common will is crystallized. But both theories enclose politics within an ethic of objective realization; politics becomes a means by which the common good is known and brought into being, by which the dictates of the good life become transparent to members.

These are depoliticized visions of life from the vantage point of a perspective which insists, first, that common understandings form the background for collective action in modern society; second, that decisions binding upon all members must be made in a complex society; third, that the resources of social knowledge are perpetually insufficient to select a single decision with confidence from the array of possibilities; fourth, that a case typically can be made for some of the choices ignored or foreclosed by any decision actually taken; and, fifth, that political conflict, disruption, disturbance is one crucial way to educate members about the uncertain and contestable elements in common understandings and to alert them to the ineliminable element of arbitrariness in the very necessity of common action amidst conditions of persistent indeterminancy in knowledge.

From this latter perspective, then, Hegel and Marx both depreciate the importance of politics in the realized society because each has too much faith in the possibility of transparency and harmony in the realized state. Each tends to absorb politics into the medium of administration, one by glorifying the relation of civil servants to the universal and the other by espousing the collectivization of administration. Seen from the vantage point of a perspective which finds these ideals of self-consciousness, transparency and collective realization to be mad dreams, each theory becomes a vehicle through which politics is contained, disruptive and contestable elements in the common life are suppressed, and the bureaucratization of the common life is legitimized. Because each theory denies that otherness will persist once the state or the community is actualized, because each seeks to draw all otherness into the sphere of a realized state or community where it can fulfill its essence, each theory is unintentionally repressive in its implications. What, though, are the presumptions in each theory which make it appear repressive from a perspective denying them?

It is not simply that each gives too much to commonality (and thus could resolve the imbalance simply by giving more to individuality), but each invests too much ontological significance in the artifices through which common purposes are defined and the common standards by which conduct is governed. By demanding that commonalities, necessary to life, also be seen as products of knowledge and realization, Hegel and Marx put politics on ice: the importance of its disruptive dimension is subtracted from the value of its unifying dimension, squeezing creativity, contestability and tragedy out of the sphere of politics and converting it into professional or collective administration. This tendency is masked by the critiques each gives of actuality and the robust role each gives to politics in unrealized states; it becomes pronounced in the projections each gives of the world to be actualized.

Marx explicitly repudiates the ontology of Spirit which permeates Hegel's theory of the modern state. Such a theory, according to the Marxian critique, divests agency from human beings and invests it in a fictitious power. This mystification of agency issues in a mystified theory of the state, pulling the will of the state too far from the actual will of the people and harnessing the state too closely to the particular will of capital in civil society. But Marx then fills the vacancy left by the departure of Spirit. If nature does not become filled progressively with Spirit as history advances, it does, through the historical course of the dialectic, progressively become more susceptible to human mastery. Nature becomes the object of a settled plan; it becomes transformed from a world of alien things standing over and against humanity into a deposit of resources harnessed for human ends and purposes. For the 'settled plan' through which the community regulates its internal relations is also the productive plan by means of which it transforms its relations to nature. The operationalization of the plan transforms nature until 'everyday life offers none but perfectly intelligible relations with his fellows and to nature.'

The explicit ontology of Spirit is displaced by an implicit ontology of plasticity in nature. If the world, including external nature and the embodied self, is not filled with an inner *telos* which becomes reealized through history, it is transformable through human science and activity into forms available to the civilization of productivity and abundance. For the Marxian ideal presupposes the universalization of abundance, and the universalization of abundance presupposes the convertibility of nature into resources for human use. The embodied self can be designed to fit into the realized community and the realized community can reshape the things of nature to conform to its needs. We have here a theory of freedom as the assimilation of otherness and a corollary understanding of otherness as malleable material susceptible to mastery. The Marxian theory, then, does not merely require a theory of the unalienated self; its theory of the unalienated self requires an ontology of nature as the locus of pliable material susceptible to human mastery.

Amidst their opposition Hegel and Marx share a fundamental pattern of insistence. Both, through their theories of freedom and transparency, insist that the world must be *for us* in its most fundamental structure. It must either express a Spirit through which we finally achieve realization or it must be susceptible in its inner structure to our most ambitious dreams of mastery. In giving up the demand that the world be formed for us Marx insists all the more fervently that it be susceptible to formation by us. This is Hegelianism by other means. It is the conversion of Hegelianism into a set of presumptions more credible and amenable to modern sensibilities.

Suppose human bodies (the organic material from which the modern self is formed) and external nature (the world of earth and things, gravity and atoms) contain elements stubbornly opaque to human knowledge, resistant to incorporation into human projects, recalcitrant to assimilation into the modern model of selfhood. Under these conditions, each worthy design we enact will subjugate some characteristics while releasing others, create new resistances while dissolving previous ones, and engender new contingencies while taming old ones. From the vantagepoint of this set of presumptions neither Hegel nor Marx evinces enough appreciation of that in the world and the self resistant to human designs and opaque to human knowledge. Each insists upon an ontology in which otherness can be dissolved into higher unities; neither affirms one in which every project and achievement engenders otherness as it realizes itself.

The ontology each accepts is a precondition to the credibility of its theory of freedom and realization. But, again appraised from a perspective which rejects the assumption of Spirit or Plasticity, each advances a theory of freedom which supports suppression and subjugation in the name of realization for the self and the community. Because each ideal projects the possibility of drawing all otherness into the whole it endorses, any otherness which persists will be interpreted as irrationality, irresponsibility, incapacity or perversity. It can never be acknowledged as that which is produced by the order it unsettles. Both of these parties place too much in the self and the community under lock and key. This trait is signified in Hegel's reading of madness and Marx's confidence in the inclusivity of his settled plan. Each is doomed to see vice, irrationality, incapacity, perversity or madness where otherness resides, and each constructs an ideal of order which produces the forms of otherness it is supposed to transcend.

These affinities with respect to the transparent society, politics, freedom and ontology create a further and common blindness in the thought of Hegel and Marx. While they debate what form modernity should take, both support a model of modern development which cannot sustain itself unless it can be generalized eventually to the entire world. For late-modern states interact closely and necessarily with second and third world countries, inspiring in the latter the desire to become what the modern world appears to be and to resist impositions it imposes upon them. Modernity must either be generalizable to the rest of the world or engender conflicts with other states and non-states which jeopardize its own integrity. If it is not a universalizable form, if the continuation of established modern states requires the subordination of others, a new and more global master–slave dialectic is set into motion.

But modernity does not appear, in either its capitalist or its socialist forms, to be a universalizable form of life. These civilizations of productivity depend upon the continued existence of areas with 'undeveloped' economies and ecologies; and self-destructive ecological ramifications would be set into motion if every area in the world were to replicate the life found in America, Japan, Europe and the Soviet Union. When one thinks late-modern states in terms of their place in the world system, the repetition on a global scale of Hegel's judgment of the Greek world appears: it 'creates for itself in what it suppresses and which is at the same time essential to it, an internal enemy' – a third world.

A further reflection may be pertinent here. Late-modernity has become a systemic condition without a corollary center of political action. It is a time but not a place. The internationalization of capital and ecological damage in a world of nation-states can serve as a symbol of this development, and acid rain, illegal aliens, drug traffic, non-state terrorism, corporate flight, resource shortages, disinvestment controversies, the accelerated pace of disease transmission across state lines and the nuclear capacity for global destruction can serve as some its signs. These developments magnify a feature endemic to modernity all along. First, the very systematicity of the late-modern world – the worldwide web of interdependencies and conflicts which constitute it as a condition – enables critical thought to pose the question of the legitimacy of late-modernity itself. Is it self-sustaining? Can it realize the standards of justice it celebrates in the world drawn into and around its orbit? Are received categories of political thought appropriate to this new condition? Does the system embody a world destructive trajectory built into its defining projects? But, second, late-modernity also lacks a political entity (a state, a coordinating center of action) large and efficacious enough to respond to those issues posed about it as such. Political thought thus loses its potential efficacy when it reaches its appropriate level of reflection. Late-modernity is a general condition without an inclusive state.

This fundamental asymmetry between the appropriate level of reflection and the actual capacity for collective action cannot be eliminated by any discernible means. It is a defining element of the late-modern condition. And this truth, I think, renders both the ideal of the Hegelian state and the aspiration to Marxian community anachronistic. The two consummate theorists of the nineteenth century do not provide a frame within which thought about the late-modern condition can advance because neither discerns how this development calls consuming projects of the modern age into question. The task today is to rethink the projects of attunement through the realized state or mastery through a civilization of productivity and abundance. No state can be inclusive enough to realize itself in the way required because every state is contained within a complex web of global interdependencies which determines some of its projects and nullifies others. No project of mastery can establish a settled plan of the scope and scale needed to attain the freedom and control it seeks.

This gap between the level of state efficacy and the level of world systematicity helps to explain the extension of internal discipline in late-modern states. The late-modern state has become a medium through which world systemic pressures are transmitted to its most vulnerable domestic constituencies as imperatives of discipline. These imperatives are legitimized as 'necessities' or 'requirements of progress' through state institutions and rhetoric which reify the modern projects of growth, productivity and abundance that called them into being. But the very ambivalent location of the late-modern state calls the viability of these ideals and projects into question.[23] The attempt to realize nineteenth-century ideals in the circumstances of the late-twentieth century now ushers in a visible future which promises to defeat them.

Neither Hegel nor Marx reflected deeply into this predicament or its implications for his theory. The inapplicability of the Hegelian ideal of the realized state to the dependent position of the contemporary state and the insufficiency of the Marxian theory of imperialism to the new world condition provide indexes of this fact. The absence of reflection on the right scale is due partly, of course, to differences between the circumstances operative in the middle of the nineteenth century and those prominent in the later decades of the twentieth century. But it cuts deeper than that. It is also inscribed in the ontological assumptions governing each theory. Nietzsche is a pertinent counterpoint to both of these theories today because he counters relentlessly Hegel's ontology of Spirit and Marx's vision of the potential transparency of social relations within a world susceptible to human mastery. The counter-ontology of resistances within human constructions which Nietzsche pursues exposes the presence of these ontologies inside the major conceptions of each theory. It also exposes and contests subdued versions of these assumptions in a whole range of contemporary theories which pretend to dispense with them. The Nietzschean counter-ontology becomes, in effect, a series of thought experiments through which one can detect and reconsider such implicit assumptions in one's own thinking.

There is no neutral place from which to assess the theories of Hegel and Marx. One can accept a perspective derived from one or both of them; or, alternatively, one might try to expose and reassess patterns of insistence operating in these theories by 'adopting' a perspective which challenges assumptions each relies upon the most. The affinities and deficiencies I have discerned in these two theories are identified from a place closer to Nietzsche's assault on teleological theories than it is to either Marx or Hegel. To locate this space in a preliminary way, it might help to review a charge Nietzsche aimed at Hegel and thinkers like him. 'German philosophy as a whole – Leibniz, Kant, Hegel, Schopenhauer, to name the greatest – is the most fundamental form of romanticism and homesickness there ever has been . . . One is no longer at home anywhere: at last one longs back for that place in which alone one can be at home: the *Greek* world.'[24]

In the realm of theory, homesickness is the demand, the insistence, that one realize within theory what one yearns for most in life. It becomes translated into presuppositions and assumptions one treats as the unquestionable standard by which all other elements in the theory are to be judged. Hegel insisted that the unity which had been destroyed in Greek life must achieve realization at a higher level in modernity. To sustain this demand Hegel postulated the presence of Spirit realizing itself gradually but insistently in the world. His homesickness found its resolution in the ontology of Spirit. Marx, who could have been added to Nietzsche's list homesick German philosophers, rejected Spirit, insisting nonetheless that modernity provide the time and place for consummate realization. He resolved his homesickness in the insistence that the design of humanity enables it to master the world and that the design of the world renders it susceptible to mastery. Since neither Hegel nor Marx could resolve the dilemma of epistemology Hegel had delineated so dramatically in the *Phenomenology,* neither succeeded in endowing the most fundamental elements of insistence in his theory with the status of knowledge. These elements emerge, then, as articles of faith which hold each theory together rather than as findings established by the truth of the theory in which it is housed.

Facsimiles and remnants of these articles of faith are silently insinuated into a wide range of contemporary theories which celebrate some version of modernity as the realized state for the individual or the collectivity or which yearn to return to a world we have lost. The individual, the community, the light of reason, the medium of language, the original contract, the Constitution all provide hiding places where faith can do its work for a while free from the glare of critical thought. But Hegel and Marx, if they were unable to ground their own ideals in certainty, nonetheless taught us how to peer more deeply and skeptically into the foundations of alternative theories. They released the critical element of Enlightenment while inadvertantly putting its quest for certainty on ice. These lessons, once released into the air, cannot be filtered out, however toxic they may seem. The attempt to purge them from the atmosphere of contemporary thought would require a systematic assault upon subjectivity; it would involve a thorough-going repression of thought comparable to the most serious assaults which have preceded it in modern life. Perhaps, then, it is better to follow the trail further.

If a task of contemporary thought is to give faith no place to hide, to draw it into the open so that it can be acknowledged and assessed, then Nietzsche is the modern thinker most acutely in need of attention. If thought which veils its faith is dangerous while thought which strives to lift the veil is too, then Nietzsche insists upon thinking dangerously during a time of danger. Questioning discloses danger and possibility.

What political theory today does not lean upon fragile and unstable suppositions bound together by insistence? What pattern of insistence today can sustain itself after it recognizes the element of insistence within it? Is it possible to locate every point at which insistence operates in contemporary theories? Is it possible to reconstitute the relation between insistence and existence so that the balance inclines more toward the latter?

5

Nietzsche: Politics and Homesickness

Truth and homesickness

Modern thinkers, as we have seen, demand a solution to homesickness. Homesickness has always been with us, but the death of God makes it all the more apparent. We killed, we moderns, the God who could ground an entire way of life in common injunctions and assurances. When previous understandings of God's hand in the world wilted, early modern thinkers tried to enliven them by transplanting God into reason, or nature, or Spirit or the subject. But each of these responses encounters its own internal problems as it strives to perfect itself. Hobbes demands faith in reason and its God, but he cannot instill a common faith. Rousseau idealizes nature and nature's God, but he cannot recapture its purity at a more complex level in a will which is both general and singular. Hegel rationalizes faith, but his Spirit must be known to be believed by moderns, and there is no way to demonstrate its truth.

From Nietzsche's 'perspective' – a term of art in Nietzschean discourse – each of these thinkers embodies the spirit of nihilism. Each demands a definitive standard which he cannot sustain; each idealizes nothing and yearns to give it a content; each insists that life cannot go on unless the standard for which he yearns can be realized. Each expresses and fosters an empty longing: 'God is dead; but given the way of men, there may still be caves for thousands of years in which his shadow will be shown.'[1]

These thinkers are not to be spurned or ridiculed. They manifest an urge built into the human condition. The 'caves' Nietzsche refers to reside within us, and these thinkers allow us to illuminate such dark places. They bring out the compelling character of the urge to find a home in the world and explore alternative routes to its realization. They teach through the brilliance of their defeats and the power of the insights they uncover along the way. Their mistake is not in expressing the desire to find a home in the world; it resides in the demand that there be a way of life or afterlife which synchronizes with this urge.

The drive to establish commonalities and to seal them in truth is well grounded in the human condition as Nietzsche defines it. It is gounded, first, in the essential incompleteness of the human before it is given social form; second, in the practical requirements of coordination among beings whose activities would not mesh without social rules enforced by moral and civil sanctions; third, in the restrictive provision of socially established identities in any structured way of life; fourth, in the character of beings who must reduce much of the common life to implicit rules, routines, habits, traditions and recipes to avoid overloading their limited capacities of conscious reflection with too many explicit rules and conventions; fifth, in the dense medium of language through which a common world of standards and judgments is crystallized; sixth, in the psychic disturbance which wells up when the conventional character of socially established identities, implicit standards and explicit norms is exposed.

These requirements and demands demarcate the human as the 'herd animal.' They join with one additional feature to fix it as the 'sick animal.' For if the human is the animal which requires social formation and coordination to fix itself and its conduct, it also encounters elements of resistance in itself to any specific form imposed upon it. It thus becomes the animal which requires reasons to live this way rather than that and then demands that these reasons too have their reasons. Its sickness resides in its quest to reach the end of a trail which has no such terminus.

Nietzsche is misunderstood by those who think his philosophy makes it impossible to affirm anything. His philosophy asserts that we are filled with beliefs, habits, principles, pragmatic rules before we have begun to reflect into them and that we are invaded as well by secondary habits, anxieties and reflexive dispositions which tend to protect these identities from dissipation once they have become fixed. Nihilism is more likely to result from the disharmony between one set of contingent dispositions in self and competing sets of similar strength or, just as likely, from the inability to accept the contingent character of the principles which govern the life of an indivdual or a people. Nihilism haunts modern life because one set of understandings lodged in its culture about the conventional basis of commonalities collides with another set of demands lodged in the character of herd animals to ground conventions in truth. The theories of nature, contract, general will and spirit we have encountered were designed to resolve this discrepancy. Nietzsche's philosophy, then, spawns an encounter with nihilistic tendencies in modernity while others strive to resolve them before they get out of hand. From his point of view their resolutions contribute to the phenomenon.

Nietzsche would not liquidate all fixity and normality in human life. Rather, so much about the human condition conduces toward the establishment of common settlements and their condensation into truth that the need is to bring out the temporal, contingent and discordant elements inside these settlements. The cumulative power of the first set of compulsions constantly works to suppress the value of the second. But freedom is located in that space of tension between these two drives; and in most settings most of the time the powers that be – inside and outside the self and in and out of the academy – press in favor of the idealization of established conventions and the condensation of settled practices into truth.

It is not that if Nietzsche's view of the self, language, truth and morality is adopted then 'anything goes'; it is that to accept it is to agree that any particular settlement is potentially susceptible to disturbance. 'Given the way of men,' we must live in herds to be, but it is nonetheless dangerous to suppress the ambiguous character of herd existence. Indeed, some must insistently affirm its ambiguity, forcefully calling attention to the underside of particular settlements, if there is to be space for freedom within the commonalities of life. Maybe life is this struggle between commonality and resistance to its dictates, and perhaps the attempt to stifle the struggle manifests a will to lifelessness, to death.

Human life is paradoxical at its core, while modern reason, penetrating into new corners of life, strives to eliminate every paradox it encounters. This is a dangerous combination, with repressive potentialities. It is dangerous to deny the paradox, either by ignoring the urge to unity or by pretending that it can be realized in life. The denial, often expressed in liberal theories of the 'open society,' overlooks ways in which the urge finds expression in the life of the present, and the pretense, expressed in communitarian protests against the anomie of liberal life, hides the political character of actual or ideal settlements behind a smokescreen of transcendental imperatives. Both responses go well with a sublimated politics of inclusivity, a politics in which the world is treated as a place susceptible to human mastery or communal realization and everyone is organized to fit into these complementary projects; a politics in which that which does not fit into the organizational scheme is defined as objective incapacity, or irrationality, or sickness, or perversity, or irresponsibility or enemy; a politics in which some of those defined as other become subversive, others become perverse, others yet become sick, and still others become terrorists; a politics in which everything always remains to be done because each new triumph breeds a new set of enemies to be conquered.

Does Nietzsche say this? Well, this message is contained in what he says. He defines ineliminable sources of the urge to find a home, but sometimes he also seems to look to a world where the urge itself disappears; he attends to the struggle within the self to overcome belief that the world is designed to become a home, and sometimes he acts as though those who do not or cannot conquer it should be subordinated to those who do; he exposes what happens when moderns try to master the world, but many of his formulations then seem to call upon a 'overman' to master it more completely.

Nietzsche's affirmative politics is open to alternative readings. Instead of exploring each of those readings here I will concentrate on that element in his thought which calls all attempts to find a home in the world into question and which reveals how a shadow of longing trails modes of thought which purport to have left homesickness behind. I will then mine the Nietzschean problematic to see if an alternative to the ethics of mastery is discernible within it, not worrying too much whether that alternative itself is the only one which Nietzsche himself pursued. Perhaps thinking is advanced further today by reversing the normal patterns of charity and suspicion: give more charity to Nietzschean theory and less to those theories grounded in transcendental conceptions of the subject, or the embodied self, or nature, or knowledge or language. Perhaps it is more conducive to thought about the late-modern condition to treat the Nietzschean philosophy as a problematic which excludes transcendental and teleological theories but contains a diverse set of ethical and political possibilities within itself. Such a strategy might help theorists, for instance, who think they have left Hegel behind to problematize the residue of Hegelian teleology clinging to their own theories. It might open alternative lines of thinking by scrambling the network through which thought has been organized.

A problematic sets a frame within which questions are posed and a range of possible responses are opened to reflection and debate. The objective here is to uncover the Nietzschean problematic and then to articulate one of the political possibilities residing within it. It is less important to me whether Nietzsche actually explored that possibility carefully or consistently, more important whether the problematic he unfolds enables one to think in these ways; less important whether the reading already has competed successfully with alternative views within this frame, more important whether it can compete with some success; less important how this position appears to those who insist upon an alternative which denies the problematic character of its own foundations, more important how it appears to those who make this crucial concession.

This approach to Nietzsche finds some support in his own texts. He did not write systematically, thinking that the 'will to system is a lack of integrity.'[2] He tried on alternative perspectives within a problematic which defined the attempt to establish one system of thought as the one and only truth as a form of intellectual deceit informed by the will to tyrannize. Each of the thinkers we have examined manifests 'the will to system,' and by focusing on the Nietzschean problematic we will be able to discern how and why he thought it to represent a 'lack of integrity.' In opposition to the will to system Nietzsche conveys another intellectual mood: 'Profound aversion to reposing once and for all in any one total point of view; refusal to be deprived of the stimulus of the enigmatic.'[3]

I will treat Nietzsche as the thinker who seeks to rethink modern versions of the wish to find a home in the world. This is my Nietzsche – the one who cracks the ice on which we stand to show how thin it has become, the one who thinks that thick ice freezes too much of life.

We who are homeless – Among Europeans today there is no lack of those who are entitled to call themselves homeless in a distinctive and honorable sense: it is to them that I especially commend my secret wisdom and gaya scienza . . . We children of the future how could we be at home in this today? We feel disfavor for all ideals that might lead one to feel at home even in this fragile, broken time of transition . . . The ice that still support people today has become very thin; the wind that brings the thaw is blowing; we ourselves who are homeless constitute a force that breaks open ice and other all too thin 'realities.'[4]

Truth is ice. And a wind gathering strength in early modernity is thawing it out In *Twilight of the Idols*, Nietzsche provides a one and a half page history of truth in the west, converting Hegel's dialectic of truth into an account of 'How the "Real World" at least Became a Myth: History of an Error.'[5] There are six stages in the unfolding of this fable of the western world. Each stage is best understood as an attempt to preserve something from the wreckage left behind by its predecessor.

1 'The real world, attainable to the wise, the pious, the virtuous man.' Plato discounts the sensuous world of change, growth, decay and finitude to attain the true world of ideas. Plato is to Nietzsche the first Christian. The sphere of ideas brings the pious and virtuous man to truth and it establishes a set of standards by which the mundane world must be

evaluated. This is the first and most confident expression of the western will to truth, of the will to interpret the world in human terms and then to pretend that the interpretation reflects the world as it is in itself. 'Oldest form of the idea, relatively sensible, simple, convincing.' Everything that follows is a devolution of this pure will to truth, a devolution forced by the self-defeat encountered by each new attempt.

2 'The real world, unattainable for the moment, but promised to the wise, the pious, the virtuous man (to the sinner who repents).' The sphere of ideas becomes more remote; it becomes God; it 'becomes more subtle, deceptive, more incomprehensible – it becomes female, it becomes *Christian*.' The shift from Platonism (Nietzsche indicates elsewhere that Plato himself may not be a 'Platonist') to Christianity puts the attainment of truth off into the future. Realization cannot succeed on earth, but it will in heaven for the sinner who repents. God is truth. It is a sin to think one has it on earth; it is also a sin to deny that it exists, that it governs this world, that it sets the standard for earthly life, that it shows the things of this world to be low and mundane. It is revealed, darkly and imperfectly now so that it can be 'promised' as a reward later.

3 'The true world; unattainable, undemonstrable, cannot be promised, but even when merely thought of a consolation, a duty, an imperative.' The true world remains an imperative of faith, but it is even more remote: 'the idea has become elusive, pale nordic, Königsbergian.' Kant, the resident of Königsberg, is the definiive figure here, but this new retreat applies in basic respects to Hobbes and Rousseau as well. Kant demonstrates the inability to know the world in itself. Human reason and knowledge only apply to the apparent world, to the world as it is constituted by the categories of reason. But Kant retains a vague, 'pale' idea of the real world, of the kingdom of God. By showing that reason cannot penetrate to this sphere he saves a place for faith. Reason is corrosive in its sphere, but faith is immune to its corrosive power. Faith needs these limits to reason to save itself. Kant then 'postulates' the existence of God, a postulate which gives reason its final and unknowable justification. Hobbes did this more bluntly when he insisted that God 'hath made men rational.' Together they set limits to knowledge and console us with faith that what reason enjoins upon us brings us closer to immortality. They provide reason with a hook to elevate itself above other faculties.

4 'The real world – unattainable? Unattained, at any rate. And if unattained also *unknown*. Consequently, also no consolaton, no redemption, no duty: how could we have a duty to something unknown?' This is

the effect Hegel sought to ward off. Hegel, says Nietzsche elsewhere, held off atheism for a couple of generations. But, understanding the vicissitudes of faith, he demanded *knowledge* of Spirit to validate the inequalities, sacrifices and losses embodied in his own idealization of the modern state. And he could not deliver on this requirement. The defeat of Hegelianism (this modern Platonism) calls positivism into being. 'The cockcrow of positivism' is the attempt to know firmly that which is knowable and to forget about the rest. Its seeks a foundation for knowledge in the mundane, sensuous world; it puts its faith in facts and data. But it also underplays how slippery facts are, how open to multiple interpretations things are when the ontological ground has shifted beneath them. And it has no response to the dilemma of epistemology delineated by Hegel.

5 'The "real world" – an idea no longer of any use, not even a duty any longer . . . an idea grown useless, superfluous, *consequently* a refuted idea: let us abolish it.' It seems to be an occasion for celebration. The world has become lighter; the weight of the ideal world has been lifted from the actual world. So 'free spirits run riot.' This, I think, is the moment of pragmatism and utilitarianism and scientism. The true is exhausted in human use and organization of the resources of nature. Organize that which is susceptible to organization and forget the rest. Look to experience itself for guidance. Simply naturalize Hegelianism (for example, Dewey, G. H. Mead, Richard Rorty). But, somehow, this apparent devaluation of the real world is too light-headed. Too much 'cheerfulness' here. It fails to discern how thoroughly its own practices and aspirations are permeated by the tradition it claims to have abolished. It fails to come to terms with *resistances* in the world and the self to those practices and aspirations. It ignores the politics of resentment. It lives in a house with rotting foundations and plants flowers in the backyard. But, still, it constitutes an indispensable step in the revaluation of truth.

6 'We have abolished the real world: what world is left? The apparent world perhaps? But no! *With the real world we have also abolished the apparent world!* (Mid-day; moment of shortest shadow; end of the longest error; zenith of mankind; *incipit Zarathustra*).' The abolition of the non-sensuous world is not enough. Its ghost still haunts life, and we must come to terms with it. What does it mean to say that the abolition of the real world is also the end of the apparent world? Is this another idealism (the world is what its most consummate constituters take it to be)? No. The world of appearance has always been defined through contrast to the real world, to the world as it is knowable in itself. If the latter disappears,

the world defined by contrast to it must too. They come and go together. If there is no Knower who can know the world in itself, then we must begin to think about the enterprise of knowledge differently. We must stop comparing belief to the pure model it seeks to copy and start appraising beliefs according to standards of the living. We might even begin to discern that knowledge – an authoritative organization of experience – is both a support and a danger to life.

We must come to terms with the relation between knowledge and power: to affirm life even when the ineliminable element of power in it is acknowledged, even when every transcendent standard is lifted from it. With the disappearance of the real world goes the last remnant of faith in the idea that the world was designed to coalesce today or tomorrow with our highest needs and that we were designed to realize a unified essence. Knowledge now becomes a mode of power for Nietzsche, a way of imposing form on the self and the world so that they can be manageable and comprehensible, so that human beings can comprehend each other and act in the world. Life is incomplete and incoherent without form, but it cannot be given form without the application of power. Form may not be the result of power alone, but it always involves an element of power.

To link knowledge to power is not to say that knowledge simply is power and power simply is domination. Power now becomes a more labile term: the will to power is the will to give form to something and to fix it in its form despite resistances it may offer. And knowledge is a particular, distinctive 'form' or 'tool' of power. A saw, a hammer, a drill, a screwdriver and a level are all tools of carpentry. Each does things the others cannot do, and if one of these tools is substituted where another is needed, the result is usually a mess.

Knowledge is a distinctive tool of power. There 'is in us a power to order, simplify, falsify, artificially distinguish.'[6] and 'knowledge works as a tool of power.'[7] Knowledge does special work, work which other forms of power are ill equipped to do. It is more akin to sandpaper than it is to a hammer or a saw; or perhaps to a sculptor's chisel. It shapes and smooths and simplifies and refines. Nor is it simply a polish on top of a world which remains as it was underneath; it actually reshapes the world and refines its contours. The will to knowledge transcends the will to *see* the world in particular ways: it emerges as the will to *organize* the world to become a certain way. It is honest with itself when it shifts from the pretense that it discovers that the world 'is thus and thus' to the admission that it wills 'that it shall become thus and thus.' The function of knowledge, the function which has emerged from the devaluation of those interpretations which made it a form of discovery is 'to humanize the world, i.e., to make ourselves more and more masters within it.'[8] The will to knowledge is the will to change the world so that it corresponds more closely to human capacities for conceptualization and organization. Knowledge does not correspond to the real world; it arranges a world for us in which our existence is made possible: it renders the world 'calculable, simplified, comprehensible, etc., for us.'[9]

Now it seems either that Nietzsche is a pragmatist or that he assumes a world in itself to which knowledge co-responds. But these two pre-packaged alternatives do not rovide room enough for Nietzsche's thought. Nietzsche, I think, denies the pragmatist assumption that the world is readily susceptible to the forms we are able to establish upon it. If the world is not the product of a transcendental design, we are likely to encounter resistance to forms we seek to impose upon it. Thus a residue of the providential view of the world clings to the categories through which the pragmatist seeks to organize it. The pragmatist *naturalizes* Hegel and forgets that a naturalized world may not be as responsive to human capacities as one filled with Spirit. The ghost of Hegel's Spirit still roams the world of pragmatism.

Wherever Hegel projects Spirit, there Nietzsche projects an element of resistance. Wherever pragmatism projects a pliable material, readily susceptible to some particular formation, Neitzsche projects an element of recalcitrance. Wherever idealism treats the world as exhausted by the categories which organize it, Nietzsche projects that which escapes, eludes, subverts, disturbs categorical organization. And wherever there is resistance, recalcitrance or subversion, power is needed to secure form.

But, then, what is this talk about the world? What is this resistance to knowing? If Nietzsche is not a pragmatist, must he not postulate a 'real world' which offers this resistance? Things get tough here. But notions of the real world, the true world, the thing in itself always invoke a thing which is known or knowable to some being: to Plato, or priests, or Hegel's philosopher, of the ideal community or God. There is no world in itself for Nietzsche because we have no ground for believing that the world corresponds to any being's capacity for cognition. The assumption that it does, when made overtly, has always fostered its own devaluation, as Hegel showed inadvertently and Nietzsche's 'history of an error' summarizes explicitly. So Nietzsche's resistance is not the resistance emanating from a world knowable in itself. It resides in gaps, disjunctures, anomalies, discordances and uncertainties which constantly plague every system of knowledge.

Why, then, bother to postulate resistance rather than, say, speaking with the pragmatist of the incompleteness and fallibility of knowledge? The Nietzschean idea that an element of resistance is encountered in every formation – in the various formations of the human through history into a coherent self, in every form of social life, in every organization or use of nature – is a coordinate of his treatment of being as will to power. If we 'need' "unities" in order to be able to reckon,' if a 'species grasps a certain amount of reality in order to . . . press it into service,' the will to establish those unities becomes the will to power only because it encounters resistance: the 'will to power can manifest itself only against resistances.'[10] The presumptions of resistance and power engender each other; neither functions until it is called into being by the other.

The question now becomes, What is the status of Neitzsche's projection of resistance? Isn't it, as Nietzsche's opponents love to insist, self-contradictory to deny that we can know the world in itself and then to claim that one knows the world itself engenders resistance to human formations? It depends on the status of this projection in Neitzsche's thought.

It has, I think, three sources. The first is in Nietzsche's effort to become more appreciative and alert to the great variety of ways in which human life has been lived and organized. If the variety is great, and if most forms seem to express somewhere in their organization a measure of estrangement from their own forms (think of the history of religious experience and the modern experiences of alienation), then perhaps each encounters resistance because no actual form of life speaks to every drive and tendency in the species. Perhaps each form of life has to suppress some appealing possibilities to enable others to be, and perhaps the religious dimension of life expresses (among other things) a yearning for that which has been sacrificed as well as a sanctification of that which has been enabled.

The second source flows from Nietzsche's review of how providential interpretations of the world and its Creator have tended to defeat themselves in western history as they tried to perfect their understandings. These defeats call the idea of a world Creator with a grand design into question. But if the self and the world are not predesigned by a master designer, then it would be surprising if any historical form of self and society cohered smoothly with everything residing in the material from which it is formed. Such a neat fit would be unexpected in a thoroughly contingent world. And it would not be unsurprising to see every transcendental theory run into internal difficulties as it tried to shore up its own foundations more securely.

The third source flows from Nietzsche's effort to expose ways in which a dense legacy from the past pervades contemporary self-interpretations even though many contemporaries overtly reject the ground upon which this legacy was built. The presumption of resistance exposes this sedimented material wherever it is hidden and compels it to defend itself explicitly – if it can. It converts presuppositions which have appeared to be necessary or natural into contestable assumptions which must defend themselves against an articulated alternative.

This third motivation may be indicated in the following aphorism:

Even the *thought of a possibility* can shake us and transform us; it is not merely sensations or particular expectations that do that! Note how effective the *possibility* of eternal damnation was![11]

The possibility of eternal damnation, never demonstrable, shook and transformed people for centuries. Every aspect of modern life has been infiltrated by the history of belief in that possibility. So Nietzsche counters that belief with the possibility of eternal recurrence, and, to extrapolate from the context of this statement, he counters holist and teleological theories with the possibility that every human formation and every thing (for a thing is a formed unity to Nietzsche) is forged and maintained against a measure of resistance. The presumption of resistance challenges the legacy of the presumption of createdness wherever it clings to life. It exposes how pervasively its competitor continues to invade modern life; it makes familiar forms and unities appear more artificial and strange as it identifies elements of power in their being; and it places that defined as other by those formations in a new light.

The Nietzschean presumption of resistance carries no more or less credibility now than the presumption of creation and eternal life did previously. It is merely a possibility. But it is a valuable presumption for thought which seeks to revise the text in which it is now inscribed; it is constructive for thought which wishes to think unthought presumptions in its previous thinking; and it is disturbing and unsettling for thought which has floated unconsciously on the surface of a world in distress. This possibility shakes and transforms us when applied relentlessly to contemporary experience. It is thus a tool in the service of thought, in the service of a *Nietzschean* quest for 'self-examination: becoming conscious of oneself, not as individuals but as mankind. Let us reflect, let us think back; let us follow the highways and byways.'[12]

A genealogy of the subject

The *Genealogy of Morals* is also a genealogy of the modern self as subject. For the bearer of modern morality is a subject, and if that morality is to be placed under scrutiny its bearer must be too. Nietzsche opens this text with an arresting assertion: 'We are unknown to ourselves, we men of knowledge – and with good reason. We have never sought ourselves – how could it happen that we should ever *find* ourselves?'[13]

Self-knowledge is a defining objective of modern life. Hobbes, Rousseau, Marx and Hegel pursued it, each in his own way. Hegel converted it from a process of introspection into a quest for self-consciousness, a self-consciousness gained through a review of the dialectic in which other selves and other times have been locked. Self-consciousness brings out into the open obscure purposes and desires; it enables one to test them against standards of consistency and ethical propriety; and that process in turn enables us to extend and perfect the standards of ethical life. It makes one more free, this thematization of the internal life in its connections to social experience. For conduct which had been the effect of cloudy motives and unclear purposes can now the be product of conscious purpose; and each purpose can be appraised to ascertain how it fits into the fold of a coherent agenda. Action now become more autonomous, more the decision of a reflective subject than the effect of unknown causes. The self itself becomes more unified and coherent in the sense that its desires, purposes and principles increasingly assume the shape of a unified whole; its actions now support and coalesce with each other rather than opposing and thwarting each other; and the principles governing its unity now become open and articulable. The self becomes a free subject, less completely for particular individuals in the Hegelian scheme and more completely in the Marxist vision.

But Nietzsche will have none of this. Why are we knowers unknown to ourselves? Because, if we were not designed, there is no assurance that the human capacities for articulation cohere smoothly with those bodily impulses, sensations, inclinations, stirrings and perturbations brought to articulation. Where is the guarantee that words can correspond to bodily stirrings? Or that there is an articulation which lifts and elevates these stirrings to the highest truth at which they implicitly aim? The demand for self-knowledge presupposes a fit between inner life and the public resources of language, between the structure of desire and the logic of articulation. But if we drop that presupposition, treating it as the remains of an old theology, we can characterize articulation as a specification which organizes and forms that which it presents. It neither represents the bodily drive as it is in itself nor realizes the essence at which the initial stirring unwittingly aims. Hence we knowers could not come to know our interior selves through introspection or self-clarification.

Nietzsche here opposes both mind/body dualism and the view of the embodied self as an integrated unity. Each contender contains the same insistence. The first organizes internal experience into two different substances and then demands that a way be found to bring each into accord with the other. The second demands that the embodied self be or become an integrated unity, in Hegel's case through the medium of Spirit which infuses both the *telos* of the body and the logic of language.

Nietzsche treats the demand for integration as a social compulsion and an internal drive which do not correspond to any possibility or essence in the world. Articulation organizes the stirrings of the body into new forms. It enables more refined emotions and desires to emerge, and it disables that which does not mesh well with the resources of articulation. Language is a social product, and the quest to articulate the inner self more perfectly emerges now as the effort to insinuate socially established injunctions and standards more firmly into the interior of the self. The 'herd' becomes interiorized as part of the self, often in the name of the truth, or independence or autonomy of the self. There is no spider who ensures that the social web of language will represent, or express or perfect the network of the body without loss or suppression.

'Self-knowledge' simultaneously lifts the self to a more complex level of social subtlety and subdues that which does not fit into the elevator: 'So we are necessarily strangers to ourselves, we do not comprehend ourselves, we *have* to misunderstand ourselves, for us the law "Each is furthest from himself" applies to all eternity – we are not "men of knowledge" with respect to ourselves.'[14]

The quest for self-knowledge presupposes the actual or potential transparency of the self to itself. It is the last, slumbering outpost of the view that the world is a design. While this quest presupposes the human animal to be a medium of self-realization, Nietzsche projects another, extreme and competing possibility onto a world without a designer: 'we are necessarily strangers to ourselves.' He counters one implicit projection with another explicit one. If the social demand for self-knowledge persists among beings necessarily strangers to themselves, and if the linguistic web into which it is drawn is a social product which reduces unique and particular experiences to a common vocabulary, then the quest does not render the self transparent to itself. It inserts the imperatives of a particular social form more deeply into the interior of the individual. That which individuates the self comes from a more creative dimension of language, one which does not find ample expression in those theories which seek to bring the inner life of the self into neat coordination with the social form of language.

The quest for self-knowledge produces (rather than discovers) the interiorized self. It thus helps to produce the modern subject – the interiorized and unified self of modernity. But the production is not simply an achievement for Nietzsche. It encounters internal resistance. Dirt and denial lurk inside its form. The more we seek to perfect ourselves as subjects, the more we construct an unconscious which challenges and subverts the pursuit. The more the self strives to bring itself to fit the dictates of this socially prescribed identity, the more it comes to loathe that in itself which resists this prescription. The pursuit of self-knowledge fosters self-loathing, and self-loathing inspires the self to try to know itself even more perfectly to rid itself of this loathing.

The will to self-knowledge presents itself as a quest for individual knowledge and freedom, but Nietzsche construes it as a way in which the modern self is tamed and domesticated by modern society. For modern society (as we saw Nietzsche argue in chapter 1) is more subtly and highly organized than previous forms and to maintain itself it must penetrate more subtly and pervasively into the self than previous forms of life. The more completely the quest for transparency governs the self – in its prayers, confessions, disciplines, therapies and self-intellectualizations – the more precisely the conscious interior of the self mirrors the norms, standards and aspirations of modern society. The drive to self-knowledge is the drive to render the self more 'predictable' and 'calculable'.

The first irony in this social dynamic of self-interiorization is that it draws the self into it as an active and eager participant. The second is that even as the self is drawn into its own entrapment there is much in the human animal which continues to resist, oppose and subvert this drive to unity, transparency and calculability. The goal of transparency is never reached. There is thus (the third irony) always more work for the self to do on its self, always more dirt in the self to be identified and cleansed.

Nietzsche thus reverses the received interpretation of self-knowledge, applying the presumption of resistance to the interiorization of the self and opening the modern ideal of interiorization to rethinking. With this initial reversal we witness the strategy of genealogy at work. We can also discern the difference between the self-examination Nietzsche endorses ('becoming conscious of oneself, not as individuals, but as mankind') and the self-examination which strives to translate the deepest purpose of the self into words. For genealogy supports the first sort of self-examination while adopting an ambiguous stance toward the second.

Genealogy is the attempt to trace the small, discrete and disconnected beginnings of formations we now take for granted, and now treat as if they were natural, or given, or established by reason or expressive of an inner *telos*. One could attempt a genealogy of the subject, of the modern moral conscience, of the idea of truth, of the notion of self-consciousness, of the notion of a thing, of the logic of a legal system, of the interpretation of madness, of the idea of nature, of the idea of eternal life; or one could pursue even more familiar and less visible constructs such as procrastination, the standard of sincerity, the norm of masculinity, the notion of punishment.

Genealogy aims at a kind of self-examination: a rethinking of how one has been formed historically which encourages one to experience the dissonance in the form one has become; a rethinking which encourages the self to endorse, modify or oppose each contingent formation after coming to terms with dirt and dissonances contained within it. It clarifies cloudy formations on familiar horizons by placing them under a different sky. It applies the presumption of resistance (the reversal of the presumption of design) to areas of life in which the idea of design still slumbers, inattentive to the difficulties it will encounter in its own world of assumptions once it is shaken from its sleep.

The 'evolution' of a thing, a custom, an organ is thus by no means its *progressus* toward a goal, even less a logical *progressus* by the shortest route and with the smallest expenditure of force – but a succession of more or less profound, more or less mutually independent processes of subduing, plus the resistances they encounter, the attempts at transformation for the purposes of defense . . . the form is fluid, but the 'meaning' is even more so.[15]

This characterization merely provides a gloss on genealogy. It ignores the rhetorical strategies by which it subverts settled assumptions, the reversals it negotiates merely to show reason to be compatible with two opposing formulations, the self-exaggerations it indulges to compel thought to come to terms with its own patterns of insistence, the nasty charges it levels against those who entertain the highest ideals and the purest sentiments, the ways in which it redefines that which is defined as otherness within established discourse. Genealogy is a dirty game which can only be experienced to be depreciated. Like its closest opponents – immanent critique and dialectical reason – it is displayed most saliently through exemplification.

So we return to a genealogy of the modern self, to the interiorized subject which pursues self-knowledge even though it is necessarily a stranger to itself. Nietzsche's reversal of the master/slave dialectic (Hegel's dialectic of Lordship and Bondage) provides a viable point of re-entry. A 'noble' ethic, historically realized by a few in pre-Platonic Greece, bestows a positive valuation on whatever requires it to struggle.

It establishes itself against resistance. Good is that to be established; bad is that which resists or obstructs it. The noble ethic is 'affirmative' because its definition of good receives priority over its definition of bad or base. But, to come to Nietzsche's point, those defined as bad or low by this ethic create an adversarial, reactive ethic. The slave ethic begins with a reactive definition of evil: the evil are those unlike us, who are other, who oppress us and, it adds creatively in paranoid style, who *intentionally* aim to oppress and exploit us.

The lowly ones introduce the standard of intentionality into ethics by attributing evil intentions to a neglectful being who simply uses them without paying much attention to them. Slave morality holds itself and others responsible not merely for the effects of action but primarily for the intentions which enter into them. This is its revolution. It thus makes it more necessary to decipher the interior intentions of the other and to bring a reactive standard to bear on the appraisal of those intentions. By inventing the category of 'evil' (rather than merely the category of bad) it foments the interiorization of the self. By acting as if its opponent is already interiorized it presses it to become so.

The slave morality grows out of resentment against its condition, its self-contempt for refusing to risk life to escape it, and its self-indulgent assumption that its oppressors are as interested intrinsically in it as it is in them. These three motives condense into a definition of the evil ones, the ones unlike us slaves.

The slave revolt in morality begins when *ressentiment* itself becomes creative and gives birth to values: the *ressentiment* of natures that are denied the true reaction, that of deeds, and compensate themselves with an imaginary revenge . . . slave morality from the outset says No to what is 'outside,' what is 'different,' what is 'not itself'; and this *no* is its creative deed.[16]

Nietzsche is not saying that slavery is good. He is saying that an ethic which grows out of slavery is negative and destructive. The slave feels resentment and is obliged to contain or suppress it. When bottled rather than poured out directly, resentment turns into poison. It creates a negative, dirty, self-deceitful ethic glossed by professions of love, purity and self-knowledge. It says no to life and resents those who say yes. It redirects its desire for revenge into the desire to justify its own reactive posture and to hold nobility to standards it is already constrained to observe.

The slave morality is an ethic of lies amidst its celebration of honesty and integrity. It lies about the source of its morality in its own resentment. The subordinate ones are compelled to work, to be honest to the master, to be humble and meek, to keep their pride under wraps. But they convert these compulsions into a set of principles commanded to them by God: they invent God to convert weakness into virtue. They pretend that God commands them to do and be what their weakness requires them to do and be. They say: 'let us be different from evil (namely good)! And he is good who does not outrage, who harms nobody, who does not attack, who does not requite, who leaves revenge to God, who keeps himself hidden as we do . . . the patient, humble and just.'[17] They whisper among themselves until they have translated weakness into merit and have displaced the human demand for revenge against the strong onto a God who loves the meek and punishes evil.

The slave morality would be unimportant historically if it did not become universalized. Christianity, however, is the universalization of slave morality. But how, on this interpretation, does Christian resentment become universalized and what are the objects of rancor once the masters too have been absorbed into slave morality?

The overt resentment against concrete masters concentrates and intensifies a more pervasive resentment against the human condition found in anyone and everyone. The presentation of the slave morality allows Nietzsche to dramatize a struggle going on in everyone. Humans are incomplete outside of social form, yet any social form requires a measure of cruelty to complete humans according to its specifications. Moreover, to live we must suffer pain, injury, insults, losses, sickness and death, so we yearn to identify some higher purpose or goal to which our suffering contributes. *Human beings resent the transiency and suffering which define the human condition.* This condition can be tolerated best if humans can find some agent who is responsible for suffering, an agent who can become the repository of resentment.

This subterranean current of resentment flows in everyone, rendering each susceptible to some degree to the assurances, promises and veiled spirit of vengefulness in Christianity. We suffer from the problem of our meaning, and we seek to give meaning to our suffering. We are thus disposed to the slave morality, once it has been founded creatively by those lowly ones facing the most intense humiliation and resentment. We make ourselves into servants of God: he will save us, if we are good, and bestow immortal life upon us. God does not eliminate suffering or finitude, but God gives meaning and purpose to these necessities.

Masters, too, are susceptible to the slave morality once it has crystallized into a creationist cosmology. The human condition renders that morality ripe for universalization. The historic profundity of the slave morality is this: out of weakness it creates a God and a morality which infiltrate even into the consciousness of the adversary who encounters its accusations and hopes.

And so Nietzsche reverses the valuation Hegel gave to the dialectic of Lordship and Bondage while continuing to treat it as the site of a significant development. Even the reversal is incomplete, however, for Nietzsche wishes to salvage somehow some dimensions of selfhood made possible by the slave morality:

it is only fair to add that it was on the soil of this *essentially dangerous* form of human existence, the priestly form, that man first became *an interesting animal*, that only here did the human soul in a higher sense acquire *depth* and become *evil* – and these are the two basic respects in which man has hitherto been superior to other beasts.[18]

Today 'there are still places where the struggle [between the two moralities] is undecided,'[19] even though the slave morality has become the official morality everywhere. The political struggle, Nietzsche seems to think, is now reduced to an interior struggle within the self. It takes a keen ear to hear it. A creative prose is needed to make it audible to those who now feel its impulse only faintly. Nietzschean rhetoric is designed to incite within the self the experience of discordance between the official morality and its internal competitor, to bring the self to a point where it might 'listen to a different claim.' Nietzschean 'eloquence' reverses the Hobbesian brand; Nietzsche is uninterested in dampening and cooling emotions already too enclosed within the interior prison of subjectivity. There is a second difference as well. Hobbes, Rousseau and Hegel deployed rhetorical strategies to intensify the power of their messages; but each situated eloquence and rhetoric inside a cognitive enterprise in which it was the subordinate partner. Nietzsche reverses this priority and insists that the reversal was already implicitly at work in the prose of his rationalist predecessors. Nietzsche does not repudiate reason, but he does deploy a rhetorical style designed to bring the self up against the limits of reason. Reason is necessary to life, but it is also insufficient to it. Those who simply label Nietzsche an 'irrationalist' ignore the ambiguity in his stance to reason.

The explicit deployment of rhetoric in genealogy is necessary to its exposé of the implicit priority of rhetoric in the texts of its rationalist opponents. To hear it at work we will concentrate on the first instance in the *Genealogy of Morals* when Nietzsche enters (as I read it) the unconscious factory inside the early subject, when he slips into the dark workshop where the self manufactures its highest ideals out of its own resentment.

We encounter a dialogue between a 'rash and curious' voice in the self which wants to hear what is going on down there and a more cautious voice whose curiosity is tempered by anxiety about what it might find. The latter is normally tempted to silence the former, but now it allows it to speak: 'Say what you see, man of the most perilous kind of inquisitiveness – now I am the one who is listening.'[20]

'I see nothing, but I hear the more. There is soft, wary, malignant muttering and whispering coming from all corners and nooks. It seems to me one is lying; a saccharine sweetness clings to every sound. Weakness is being lied into something meritorious . . . '
   'Go on!'
   'and impotence . . . into "goodness of heart"; anxious lowliness into "humility"; subjection to those one hates into "obedience" . . . (they call him God) . . . his inability for revenge is called unwillingness . . . perhaps even "forgiveness". They also speak of "loving their enemies" – and sweat as they do so . . . '
   'Go on!'
   'Now they give me to understand that they are not merely better than the mighty . . . whose spittle they they have to lick (*not* from fear, not at all from fear! but because God has commanded them to obey the authorities) – that they are not merely better . . . but will be better off someday. But enough! enough! Bad air! Bad air! This workshop where *ideals are manufactured* – it seems to me to it stinks of so many lies.'

In this cellar the desire for revenge is never mentioned, but it provides the energy for the creation of both an entire morality and the kind of self who can be its bearer. If we hear this early, interior drama with a Nietzschean ear we may reinterpret the way in which Hobbes plays upon the fear of death and damnation to install the commands of God into the 'dictates of reason.' We may rethink Rousseau's idealization of the pure will. We may reconsider Hegel's plan to cure madness by perfecting the principle of subjectivity latent within it. We will discern the subject to be a formation crafted from organic material partly resistant to it. And we may listen to conflicts raging inside the contemporary subject with a new ear. In each of these instances one's hearing must be particularly acute, for the motives and aims governing these themes become muffled and subdued once they have been institutionalized and inscribed in the very conceptions available to thought. Only attention to the crude and creative work done at the historic inception of this morality can enable one to hear the muffled groans and deceits in the modern versions.

But doesn't this interpretation of the interior dialogue restore the thesis that we can know ourselves? Or at least that Nietzsche can know us and bring this knowledge back to us? Perhaps. But I think that conclusion is unnecesasry. This is an interpretation of the internal dialogue from the vantage point of an ontology of resistance. And that ontology cannot be known. By interpreting the interior of the self within the frame of this possibility we strip more familiar readings of the air of necessity and incontestability that otherwise accompanies them. We are now in a position to decide between (at least) two readings, each with the ability to make sense of the self and each fraught with implications for ethical and political life. Nietzsche invites us to listen to an alternative interpretation; he does not claim to know that it is true. 'It seems to me one is lying.'

By proceeding in this way he problematizes both orthodox readings and his own. Interpretation becomes, so to speak, politicized, not in the sense that anyone can casually reach any conclusion but that more than one detailed reading can be given to familiar experience. Does Nietzsche's interpretation make it much more difficult to accept established readings of the self to be true and necessary? Yes.

Back to Nietzsche's reading, then. Now we can listen to modern idealizations of the subject with new refinement. Thus, the subject is the agent of freedom; but when one is reminded, 'you *chose x*' or, worse, 'you *freely chose y*,' one is being accused, reminded, held responsible for the consequences of that action. Thus, the subject seeks to become more self-conscious of its internal self, but most recommendations by another that one does so are calls to confess some dirt or deviant disposition within oneself and to correct oneself according to an established standard. Thus, the subject is free, but many authoritative assertions of its freedom are accompanied by the announcement of a verdict or a warning that it will be treated institutionally as a non-subject if its conduct gets too far out of line – treated as irrational, or perverse, or mad, or abnormal, or sick, or primitive or incapacitated. Freedom is a privilege of subjectivity which can be lost if one deviates from conditions surrounding the privilege; it is thus a set of limits branded into the self as well as a set of rights the branded self can exercise.

The subject is not simply or unambiguously the self which establishes its unity, freedom, independence and self-transparency; it is also the self required to interiorize a complex set of socially imposed standards and to regulate that in itself which deviates from those norms. The subject is ambiguously an instrumentality of modern order and a claimant of rights within it, an independent centre of knowledge and a bearer of socially established criteria of knowledge, a seeker of self-transparency and an interiorizer of social norms. This ambiguity is its essence; but its denial is crucial to its identity. Is there, then, no trace of resentment in the self which bears the impress of subjectivity? Is there no drive to revenge in the accusations, corrections, improvements, verdicts and punishments subjects mete out to each other or in the treatment they accord to those falling below the threshold of subjectivity?

The modern subject, as Nietzsche construes it, emerges when this struggle between two moralities has been shifted to the interior of the self; it becomes the dominant mode of selfhood when one side in the interior contest controls most of the resources of social power in interpreting, correcting, improving and punishing the self and in isolating or defeating those whose conduct does not measure up to its norms. To be a subject is to be the locus of an internal struggle one strives to suppress; it is to lie to oneself about the origins and bearing of the self one is. A world in which the subject prevails is a world where therapy abounds.

These characterizations are central to the Nietzschean model of subjectivity. We are not born to be subjects. Nor do we contain an inner essence which draws us toward stasis and subjectivity. Nor are we indefinitely plastic beings readily adaptable to a variety of socially formed modes of selfhood (including subjectivity) without loss, strife or resentment. Nietzsche opposes and challenges those models of selfhood which have competed within the sociological and philosophical literature of modern discourse. They all deny one element or another in the formation of the human into a self: each denial deflates the dimension of resistance, resentment and revenge in the modern subject. 'The task of breeding an animal with the right to make promises ... presupposes ... that one first *makes* men to a certain degree necessary, uniform, like among like, regular, and consequently calculable.'[21]

To be a subject is to be made into a calculable, uniform, promising being, capable of being held responsible for deviant conduct and deserving of punishment for irregular acts. This is the subject from the perspective of social discipline, the subject as the effect of external and internalized pressures to make it fit for modern society.

To be a subject is to have a unity imposed on the self which stirs up resistance and struggle within the self (the unconscious, insanity, perversity, depression, etc.) and which insulates the self from connecting these effects to its own form of being. This is the interior of the subject viewed from the perspective of an ontology of resistance, a perspective which authorizes a particular reading of the resentment, violence, depression, self-loathing paranoia, etc. which shadow modern subjectivity.

To be a subject is to be an *interesting* being, one whose quest for God fosters the possibility of godlessness, one whose commitment to truth presses it to become truthful about truth, one whose interiority fosters a genealogy of interiorization, one whose very obligation to become a more coherent and transparent self opens it to the possibility of rethinking the teleological assumptions inside these standards of inner harmony.

Each of these dimensions attaches to the modern subject, and Nietzsche seems to admire achievements it enables while exposing the sicknesses it spawns. Only an interiorized, reflective subject could, after all, receive Nietzschean genealogy.

The modern subject carries around too much rancor against that in itself which resists subjectivity and that in others which deviates from its standards. That is the prinicipal objection to it. To be a subject is to be too predisposed to punishment (of self or others) or too predisposed to help (self or others) measure up to its standard. The subject oscillates between conquest and conversion in its relations to otherness. In each case, the subject refuses to accept difference in itself and others. It converts difference into otherness, into a form of deviation which must be improved, excluded, punished or conquered.

But why? What is being protected here? Nietzsche offers an answer. 'For every sufferer instinctively seeks a cause for his suffering; more exactly an agent; still more specifically a *guilty* agent who is susceptible to suffering.'[22] The Greek gods, heroically, assumed responsbility for human suffering. They absorbed guilt into themselves, reducing the store of poison to be absorbed by humans. But the single, all-powerful God of Christianity demands that humanity assume responsibility for suffering and evil. We become storehouses of guilt and responsibility. If all sufferers instinctively seek a cause for their suffering, more exactly an agent, the subject finds that agency in itself. The subject gives meaning to suffering by holding itself responsible: it redirects resentment against the human condition into itself. That is its most creative act. 'Quite so, my sheep,' the religous and secular priests say, 'someone must be to blame for it: but you are this someone, you alone are to blame for it.'[23] The priests (including later judges, therapists, teachers, confidants, spouses) deflect resentment against suffering in life back into the self, manufacturing it into energy 'for the purpose of self-discipline, self-surveillance, and self-overcoming.'[24]

What Nietzsche seeks, though the pursuit is never delineated fully, is a form of selfhood in which self-regulation and discipline are affirmed while the tarantula of resentment and revenge is refused. He doubts very much that most humans can affirm this form of self or that any human can do so consistently. But he yearns for it, at least for some. This is the Nietzschean yearning, the voice in Nietzsche with interesting resonances to its Christian counterpart. Zarathustra, the voice closest to Nietzsche's own, says:

Behold, this is the hole of the tarantula. There it comes willingly: welcome tarantula! Your triangle and symbol sit on your back; and I also know what sits in your soul. Revenge sits in your soul: wherever you bite, black scabs grow; your poison makes the soul whirl with revenge.[25]

Later he asserts: 'Mistrust all in whom the impulse to punish is powerful . . . And when they call themselves the good and the just, do not forget that they would pharisees, if only they had – power.'[26] The impulse to revenge against the human condition must be overcome. Overcoming it involves the acceptance of contingency and the refusal to seek redemption in God, Will, Truth or Spirit. But it does not eliminate the injunction to self-discipline, nor does it eradicate the problematic relation in any society between the form of selfhood consonant with its standards of commonality and that in the self which resists those norms.

Nietzsche would deliver the self from resentment and revenge through its affirmation of contingency and the disciplines necessary to selfhood. '*For that man be delivered from revenge*, that is for me the bridge to the highest hope, and a rainbow after long storms'[27]. A form of selfhood which does not resent its own mode of organization. Now this is at once a tempting and a disturbing proposal. Tempting in its call to accept contingency and dissonance in the world and the self, disturbing in its apparent disruption of interior dispositions in the self to regulate its reactions to others according to delicately established principles of reciprocity. Is it possible to internalize modes of self-regulation consonant with reciprocity without intensifying the reactive sentiments of resentment and revenge? Is it feasible to affirm a particular form of selfhood while also acknowledging elements of artifice in its being?

Nietzsche often resolves this issue by espousing an aristocratic solution in which the few – defined not economically but by criteria of relative strength in affirming the contingency of existence – separate themselves from the herd. This solution underlines his recognition of the close relatonship between the modern subject and citizenship in a democratic state. Such a resolution is certainly susceptible to criticism from the vantage point of a democratic model of politics. The connection between subjectivity and citizenship can be converted, indeed, into an argument in favor of affirming the subject as an artifice worthy of endorsement. One could even argue, as I have elsewhere, that a democratic politics provides the best way to incorporate the experience of contingency into public life. That would still leave much to be thought about the relations between the contingent subject and the forms of otherness it engenders. But Neitzsche's aristocrtic solution is also self-defeating on its own terms. It spawns the condition Nietzsche has already diagnosed: it recreates the very resentment it seeks to redress and sets its own aristocracy up to be its target.

Perhaps the rainbow arcs over a dilemma built into the human condition. Perhaps the human animal cannot be delivered from this interior struggle between civility and resentment, self-containment and revenge, but only from those doctrines which magnify cruelty to the self, hegemony over otherness, and danger to the species by pretending to transcend the struggle.

A Nietzschean ethic

Nietzsche predicts that he will be asked, 'What are you really doing, erecting an ideal or knocking one down?'[28] Here he anticipates the most common charge made against him and his followers. 'When you have cleared the world of these false ideals, nothing will be left. You can only destroy and never affirm. You are irresponsible in a destructive way (and hence must be ignored, accused, punished for your adventurism).' Nietzsche responds with a counter-charge:

But have you ever asked yourselves sufficiently how much the erection of *every* ideal on earth has cost? How much reality has had to be misunderstood and slandered, how many lies had to be sanctified . . . ? If a temple is to be erected *a temple must be destroyed:* that is the law – let anyone who can show me a case in which it is not fulfilled![29]

I take Nietzsche to say here that every ethic is destructive in the act of being constructive and that every ethic subjugates admirable possibilities in the world and the self to maintain itself. Most ethics deny the element of destruction and subjugation within them. They shroud it in a cloud of meta-idealism: the will of God, the *telos* of history, the dictates of reason, the law of nature, the general will. Nietzsche seeks an ethic which can be adopted while affirming the necessary element of destruction and subjugation in it. He seeks a brave ethic.

Nietzsche does not propound a political theory. He does not even propound an ethic in any precise sense of that word. But he does establish a distinctive problematic within which ethical debate can occur, a new frame in which a few alternatives present themselves as viable competitors while others are rejected because they do not meet minimal standards of bravery and honesty – honesty and bravery, of course, as understood within the terms of this frame. The Nietzschean frame is essentially problematic in the sense that it is undemonstrable; but it, unlike many of its competitors, affirms itself to be so.

Two candidates are given considerable play within this frame. The first understands life to be will to power rather narrowly understood and counsels humanity to complete its project of assuming mastery over the world, accepting the implication that many human beings will have to be subjugated by a few to achieve that end. This ethic has the advantage of bringing out into the open dark implications residing within the modern quest to master the world. It exposes self-deceits involved in the modern pretense that such a project of mastery could be consummated democratically in accord with liberal standards of rights and dignity.

The second alternative counsels us to come to terms with difference and to seek ways to enable difference to be. It is an ethic of letting be. It calls into question the project of perfecting mastery of the world on the grounds that, given resistances built into the order of things, the project would reduce everything to a straitjacket while pursuing an illusory goal. The second ethic stands on the same ground as the first in its acceptance of an ontology of resistance: both affirm that human life cannot be without the creation of social form and both affirm that every social form will engender that which resists it. Each ethic is a response to this condition. And each is locked into a debate with the other in the way that, say, the theories of John Rawls and Jürgen Habermas are locked into debate within the frame of neo-Kantianism. The social ontology within which intra-Nietzschean debates occur shatters the air of sufficiency or exhaustiveness surrounding those contemporary debates which presuppose together more providential ontologies. It thus opens thought to new possibilities while it reduces confidence in the adequacy of established terms of discourse. It poses questions and objections to the theories of Hobbes, Rousseau, Hegel and Marx which bring out complementary dimensions in their competing themes of self-interest and virtue, individuality and commonality, mastery and attunement, capitalism and socialism.

Nietzsche experiments with each of these alternative ethics. Without suggesting that the ethic which seeks to locate space for difference to be is finally or truly his preferred stance, I will here try to elaborate some of its dimensions. It seems to me to be a more promising stance to explore in the closing decade of the twentieth century.

Since this ethic is never developed systematically, we will restrict ourselves to three areas in which it does find expression in Neitzsche's texts, examining ethics of the self, friendship, and war and peace.

The human being is the 'sick animal,' and this sickness cannot be cured definitively. Its instinctive equipment is insuficient to govern life, but the social forms through which it is given determinacy drive some of those instincts inward. The subject is the form of selfhood in which this inwardness is the most highly developed. It is the interiorized self; the self with a long memory; the self which plans today for its future; the self which organizes itself so that it can become an agent of self-interest, knowledge and freedom; the self which monitors its desires and impulses so that they can be redirected into purposes that cohere with each other and with the norms of the society; the self whose interiority and coherence increases its sense of guilt and renders it capable of being held responsible; the self whose inner resistance to its own form renders it particularly susceptible to mental illness, criminality, delinquency; the self whose acceptance of the standards of subjectivity exacerbates its drive to revenge.

But if the subject is a social formation facing internal conflict for which it blames itself, is there a form of selfhood which could eliminate this effect? Certainly Nietzsche does not accept a theory of alienation in which one form of selfhood within a ideal society would resolve such conflicts. And clearly he does not endorse the idea of a self which simply allows the multiplicity in itself to find its variable, contradictory expressions. That would not work: it would defeat competing drives in the self to become a unity; it is inconsistent with any complex form of social life; and even if possible the result would be very uninteresting.

Nietzsche seeks a self which adopts a form of self-discipline without raging against that in itself which must be regulated and (this amounts to the same thing) without pretending that its contingent form corresponds to an essential mode of being. He endorses a form of selfhood which could only be pursued after the emergence of the modern subject and after the flaws in its mode of insistence have been exposed. His model of selfhood is only as different from the modern ideal of the subject as the early idea of the subject was from the Greek model of self. That is, it is significantly different while embodying continuities and affinities with the form of selfhood it challenges.

Its first injunction is to overcome rage against contingency (to resist the temptation to convert some contingencies into essentialities). 'What alone can our teaching be? That no one *gives* a human being his qualities: not God, not society, not his parents, not his ancestors, not he himself . . . He is not the result of a special design, a will, a purpose.[30]

The acceptance of contingency. One happens to have these parents rather than those, to be gay rather than straight, to be persistent rather than flexible, to be chaste rather than experimental, to be sensitive rather than affable. These various contingencies enter into the self; they help to compose it. But they do not automatically fit together: they are likely to collide with each other in various ways. Nor does this constellation of contingent dispositions contain, even when examined deeply, an essence which must be realized. Some of these contingencies do become branded in the self; they acquire the character of *contingent necessities*. Others remain contingent variabilities; which are which is also a matter of contingency. When a contingency becomes an ineliminable aspect of self, one must simply make the most of it, expressing, sublimating or concealing it but not repressing, eliminating or denying it. One must not rage against that which became branded into the self even before one reached the age of self-examination. Accept fate without lapsing into passive resignation; accept fate without attributing a will or an essence to it, without accusing, without attacking oneself or others for what one has become. And then work, patiently, tactically and strategically, on those aspects of self which are liable to adjustment, further harmonization, polishing.

Yes, but how?

One thing is needful – To 'give style' to one's character – a great and rare art! It is practiced by those who survey all the strengths and weaknesses of their nature and then fit them into an artistic plan . . . Here a large mass of second nature has been added; there a piece of original nature has been removed – both times through long practice and daily work at it. Here the ugly that could not be removed is concealed; there it has been reinterpreted and made sublime . . . In the end when the work is finished, it becomes evident how the constraint of a single taste governed and formed everything large and small.[31]

The self becomes a work of craftsmanship using materials readily available. Drawing on elements in one's first and 'second nature' (that is, the contingencies which become branded into the self), one strives to craft a distinctive unity which is worthy of admiration. The result is an artifact which affirms itself to be so; it is also one that the self has a hand in crafting. This is accomplished, less by subjecting the self to self-criticism or willing changes in one's character, and more by applying detailed techniques to the self so that gradually a series of modest changes evolves. Adjustments in diet, exercise, reading habits, relationships practiced over a long duration are crucial here. 'How do men attain a great strength and a great task? All the virtues and sufficiency of the body are acquired laboriously and little by little, through much industry, self-constraint, limitation, through much obstinate, faithful repetition of the same labors, the same renunciations.'[32]

This is vague, but so is every ethic of the self. It only makes sense in a context of engagement with the ethic of self-consciousness and self-realization pursued by the modern subject. Above all, this must be heeded: 'that a human being should *attain* satisfaction with himself . . . by means of this or that poetry and art . . . Whoever is dissatisfied with himself is continually ready for revenge, and we others will be his victims.'[33]

The key here is not to insist that the contingencies which have formed one constitute a pre-design which one must realize or a pre-design which one is thwarted from realizing. For these patterns of insistence necessarily foster self-loathing, and creatures of self-loathing are continually seeking revenge against whatever and whomever can be held responsible for their suffering. They punish themselves the most. And they constantly wish to compel others to live up to the design or to punish them for not doing so – even when the refusal to 'live-up' constitutes no desperate peril to life and even when the beings to be helped would thrive if only the standard applied to them were divested of its authority.

What about one's relations with others? What, particularly, about those relations in which differences of some magnitude are encountered? Zarathustra meets a hunchback who seeks to be persuaded that Zarathustra's doctrine is good for him. First, Zarathustra counsels the hunchback, whose life is difficult, against the spirit of revenge, against that spirit which inevitably rises when one is constituted differently from the norm and placed at a disadvantage by it. But each self has its incapacities and difficulties. Some selves, for instance, lack ears with which to hear subtle sounds of discord in themselves. They are ripe candidates to become creatures of self-loathing. Zarathustra refuses to indulge the hunchback for resenting his fate. He pursues the opposite course: 'When one takes away the hump from the hunchback one takes away his spirit – thus teach the people.[34]

The hunchback has a particular perspective unavailable to others without its deformity. It carries its advantages and disadvantages. In this case – but in many others too – the disadvantages are more apparent. But there is here a particular deformity which informs about the human condition, which can teach the hunchback lessons that many are unable or unwilling to confront. The deformity is a challenge. The pretense that the hunchback is 'normal' is a form of pity. It signifies repugnance to difference and the drive to regularize everyone according to some fictive model of normality. The alternative insistence that the hunchback must be helped to reach the plateau of normality is also debilitating. The friend is a spur to a battle the hunchback must fight. A friend does not repress the battle nor fight it for the hunchback.

But this is what matters least to me: to see that this one lacks one eye and that one an ear and a third a leg . . . ; for there are human beings who lack everything; except one thing of which they have too much – human beings who are nothing but one big eye, or a big mouth or a big belly. Inverse cripples, I call them.[35]

The inverse cripple is the one whose self-contempt and desire for revenge drives him to reduce everyone to a norm and to punish those who resist too intensively. If heterosexual he is homophobic; if homosexual he is heterophobic; if bisexual he is monophobic. He is crippled by the quest for revenge against the human condition. He has a 'big eye' through which he observes everyone for signs of otherness and a 'big mouth' from which recipes for reducng difference to sameness are constantly emitted. The hunchback, confronting contingency and differences in a dramatic way, is better equipped to learn this lesson of life. He can appreciate the necessity and significance of difference in a contingent world. Without contingency, no individual could be; with it, each is at odds with the norm in some ways. Without established norms, no self could be formed; with them difference faces a struggle to create space for itself.

Hobbes has a big eye; Rousseau has a big eye and a big mouth; Hegel has a big belly into which everything is digested. The friend of a hunchback will treat him 'in a hunchbacked way,' and he will thus help him to avoid the temptation to fall into one of these philosophies in which difference is depreciated, regulated and helped in the name of a true norm. Established norms will exist, of course, but the artifice in them will be appreciated, and they will serve as a spur to the expression of difference as well as a standard through which the common life is organized. Thinkers will adopt an ironic and ambiguous orientation to the norms they endorse, even to those norms they endorse in opposition to the settlements achieved in their own society. Ethical commitment becomes more layered and subtle.

It is not that the hunchback could become anything and everything. But, then, neither could anyone else. Each is confined by a set of necessary contingencies, and there is in each the wish to pretend that only one course of action is the true course to follow. The hunchback is in a better (more transparent) position to confront the paradox of freedom. 'By doing we forgo,'[36] says Nietzsche in one of his most compelling maxims. If I pursue one course, say, preparing myself for politics, I necessarily forgo a variety of other possibilities for which I was also equipped. And if this course runs dry after two or three decades of training and pursuit, I cannot return to my alternative plans to become an analytic philosopher, a concert pianist or a nuclear physicist. By doing I forgo several possibilities, but by refusing to forgo I would sacrifice my life itself to passivity. I would renounce life out of fear of death. For the fear of committing oneself to something is really the fear of facing up to the way in which human finitude fosters the paradox of freedom. We seek transcendent theories of truth, subjectivity, Spirit and Will to pretend that we do not really forgo when we do; we deny the necessity of foreclosure by convincing ourselves that the true choice contains all the highest goods within it. But this pretense fosters the disposition of revenge against otherness. For the other must now be seen either to achieve what has been closed to oneself or to require correction for deviation from the norm. The refusal to admit that doing is forgoing encourages the conversion of difference into otherness.

The desire to evade the paradox of freedom derails the freedom available to the human animal: to make itself into something definite within the limits of contingency by forgoing alternative possibilities. Those who deviate most obviously from norms of life governing a culture are both more tempted by the quest to evade the paradox and better equipped with ears to hear the sources and implications of the evasive attempt. That combination is the advantage Nietzsche identifies in the hunchback.

These first exemplifications of a Nietzschean ethic are pitched mostly at the level of the individual, though each carries implications for the character of public life. The last example is cast at the level of the state itself. Both war and peace, for Nietzsche, are ambiguous conditions. War fosters great destruction, but it enables people to come to terms with what is important to them. It enables them to establish priorities in the public life, and it gives them something to struggle for. In a nuclear age Nietzsche would clearly be on the side of pursuing peace, accepting the ambiguity inside that pursuit.

Nietzsche thinks the claim by each state in a state system that its arms are simply 'to serve the defense' constitutes the biggest single cause of war between modern states. If 'our' arms are only for self-defense 'this implies one's own morality and the neighbor's immorality; for the neighbor must be thought of as eager to attack and conquer if our state must think of . . . self defense.'[37] To establish a stable peace a strong state must 'abjure arms for self-defense' as much as for conquest. For the former disposition requires the leaders of the state to accuse the adversary of the most vicious intentions, and the mutual recriminations between states generates a war in which each fights only to defend itself against the immorality of the other.

Only a state which is strong and self-confident can break this logic. It can relinquish its weapons out of strength.

And perhaps the day will come when a people, distinguished by wars and victories and by the highest development of a military order and intelligence, and accustomed to make the heaviest sacrifices for these things, will exclaim of its own free will, 'We break the sword,' and will smash its entire military establishment down to its lowest foundations. *Rendering oneself unarmed when one had been the best-armed.'*[38]

This fits with the other commendations we have reviewed. An individual and a state must proceed from inner strength in their relations with others. Each must overcome its own fear and loathing to enter into equitable relations with others, and only an entity which has made progress in that respect is in a position to let others be what they are or must be.

In a nuclear age, Nietzsche's strategy of disarmament becomes both more pertinent and in need of adjustment. Its pertinence resides in the fact that the world hangs in the balance when nuclear arms are at issue and that the strongest country in the world must assume the initiative if the arms race is to be curtailed. The adjustment resides in the fact that unilateral reduction becomes superior to unilateral elimination in the new setting. If the strongest state reduces its arms to a minimal threshold needed for defense, it helps to break the dialectic of mutual escalation, and it deters a surprise strike against it by maintaining a capacity to reply.

These, then, are elements in a Nietzschean ethic. They bear an intelligible relation to other dimensions of his perspective. They seek to create space where difference can be while acknowledging the need for commonalities growing out of the human condition itself. They encourage the self to quell its homesickness so that it can affirm the 'rich ambiguity of existence.' They are governed by one objective (or norm, if you will) above all: to reduce the drive for revenge against human temporality by affirming the contingencies of life. They assume less the form of argument from shared premises and more the mode of preaching to those who must listen with new ears to what resides within the premises they now presuppose and must then be converted to an alternative set of premises. Argumentation merges into conversion here. There is irony in this mode, and we may as well assume that it is not alien to Nietzschean thought to affirm it: he can imagine, at least, a world in which the modern subject has been reconstituted and in which the modern project to master the world has been called into question, but he cannot imagine one in which this conversion is achieved without recourse to the style of preaching practiced by Christianity.

Nietzsche, then, can indeed affirm an ethic. He tears down ideals to construct alternative affirmations, constantly pressing us to admit that every construction also destroys and that every affirmation spawns a series of risks and foreclosures. What ethical directives is one willing to endorse upon reception of these truths? The nihilist is the one who refuses to entertain this question, who refuses to affirm when the ambiguity of existence comes into view. He would rather endorse nothing at all than affirm the ambiguity of existence.

The fate of modernity

If Nietzsche creates a problematic in which ethical discourse can occur he does not formulate a political theory. In this he is unlike Hobbes, Rousseau, and Hegel. A political theory delineates the parameters of a way of life, defending the limits it must accept in light of the possibilities it realizes. It provides answers against which we can test ourselves while rethinking assumptions and demands which called them into being. In this respect Nietzsche is a disappointment. But perhaps this deficiency is also an advantage in some respects. For it stimulates thought about presumptions within which contemporary political discourse takes place without requiring the thinker to commit oneself in advance to a single theory of politics. By pitching itself at the right level it enables thought to engage the fate of modernity.

It is because Nietzsche examines some of the most pervasive assumptions and self-understandings of the modern era as if they were the hallucinations of an alien tribe that he provides a pad from which a critical examination of the modernist frame can be launched. His alien readings – full of caricature and exaggeration as such readings must be – loosen the hold established debates and ideals have over thought, calling established assumptions about the self, knowledge and the good life into question, and opening thought to new possibilities of reflection. If this is the level at which thought engages the fate of modernity itself, it is also the level at which argumentation and debate within a common frame merge into sermons about the patterns of insistence which hold the frame together. Sermons are necessary to thought at this level, both in the commentary they make on commonly accepted theories which pretend to dispense with them and in the self-commentary they make on the problematic status of a perspective which challenges hegemonic theories. If modernity is a time in which intellectuality lost touch with its own sermons, it is also the time when an anti-christ emerged to enable a few thinkers to regain that touch.

How is it, though, that the author of 'will to power' advances a perspective in which alternative routes to mastery of the world and the perfection of subjectivity might be re-examined in a critical light? Does this doctrine not magnify the perspectives it illuminates? Is not will to power merely a condensation of modern drives to mastery and realization? It does the former and it can be the latter. That constitutes its value for the sort of critical reflection needed today. Nietzsche fosters questioning by explicitly assuming a perspective which simultaneously reveals veiled dimensions of dominant theories and disturbs the tranquility of assumptions which support them. The dogmatic assertion of will to power carries within it the corollary assertion that there is an element of resistance and recalcitrance in every human formation. And the Nietzschean presumption of resistance exposes in other theories implicit assumptions about a world susceptible to human mastery or a world designed to respond to human yearnings for harmonious community. It calls both of these projections into question together rather than allowing thinkers to incline automatically toward the first whenever the second is doubted and then to incline toward the second whenever the first is doubted. In this way it takes thought off its automatic pilot. It enables thought to probe common impulses operative in these contending perspectives, namely the insistence that the world be treated as if it were designed *for us* at the most fundamental level – either in its susceptibility to human mastery or in its resonance to the quest for unified community. The thesis of resistance, then, extends the reach of questioning into these twin inclinations of modern thought. For the ontology of discord within concordances always provides the occasion to question anything which has become fixed.

But to stand in the mist of this *rerum concordia discors* and of this whole marvelous uncertainty and rich ambiguity of existence *without quetioning*, without trembling with the craving and rapture of such questioning, without at least hating the person who questions, perhaps even finding him faintly amusing – that is what I feel to be *contemptible*, and this is the feeling for which I first look in everybody. Some folly keeps persuading me that every human being has this feeling, simply because he is human. This is my type of injustice.[39]

This discordant tissue of concordances instills an attitude of wonder and questioning in those who will engage it. Pondering it can 'shake and transform' thought; at the very least it brings those shaken by such tremors to hate the person who continues to question. For every answer can now be heard to harbor discordance within it, and no system of knowledge can pretend, within this perspective, to conform to being itself. The authoritarianism by which a political settlement is brought back to its members as the will of God, or the light of nature, or the dictates of reason, or the expression of Spirit or the findings of adminstrative rationality always falls under suspicion within the confines of this philosophy.

We require answers – settled arrangements and standards – to maintain a common life, and many epistemic, psychological and institutional features of human life conduce in this direction. This is what I have treated as the terrain of human insistence and homesickenss whenever it defeats or silences contrary pressures within life. Such a designation is intended to call attention to the dirt residing in established achievements and to the variety of theoretical/institutional strategies by which this dirt is swept under the rug. As we saw earlier, only those who fail to come to terms with Neitzsche's account of the sources and functions of 'the herd' are likely to think that a philosophy of discordant concordances would automatically engender a world devoid of common standards. It is because the inertia of life flows in the other direction that a Nietzschean strategy of interrogation is needed.

Common standards, at their best, support and enable life, but they never are merely supports. Any set of answers is also susceptible to questioning and challenge with respect to the presuppositions it expresses and the cruelties it causes. The cruelties and injuries within a particular complex of settlements (a way of life) are not to be identified by reference to another world where all such ambiguities are eliminated but by reference to other ways of life in this world where *those injuries are rectified even while others may be produced*. Politics resides in this ambiguous space between the insistent rewards of commonality and the wonder of existence. It enables each claim to find expression without giving final or full hegemony to either. It keeps the will to question alive even when the pressures of time, statecraft, private identity, collective reassurance or economic rationality press to close it down. And any theory or practice which would dissolve politics into fixed rules of morality, bureaucratic rationality, the will of a leader or the destiny of a nation squeezes the life out of politics. The philosophy of discordant concordances opens more space to politics than the alternative positions elaborated by Hobbes, Rousseau, Hegel or Marx. For while these thinkers often play politics up in circumstances preceding the state they commend, the contain it in the commended state itself. Contemporary theories of the normal individual and the consummated community follow a similar bi-polar logic. None is sufficiently attentive to the link between a robust politics and the ambiguous character of existence.

Even the ontology of discordance within a tissue of concordances could be called into question if only it first became the operative assumption of a significant set of thinkers. But certainly those dominated by the debate between capitalism, and socialism or between the idea of the normal individual and the restrictive community have so far remained deaf to these issues. To become alert to the Nietzschean critique of rationalist and teleological theories is to see that the rebuttals these opponents typically make to him either presuppose the points he has called into question or accuse him falsely of giving no affirmative status to truth, reason, knowledge, commonality or a self-disciplined self. A post-Nietzschean perspective will thus be one which responds to Nietzschean texts not as they appear to the confirmed rationalist but as they appear after his critiques of rationalist and teleological theories have been absorbed. It will be open to the possibility that Nietzsche is elaborating paradoxes and exposing existential ambiguities at those moments the rationalist is inclined to convict him of self-contradiction or incoherence.

In the meantime those who think within a critical philosophy of discordant concordances must construct theories of self, justice, and the common good appropriate both to the ambiguous character of existence and to historically specific dangers and possibilities residing in the late-modern condition. It may be that a post-Nietzschean political theory can be compounded of a Nietzschean ontology and an independent reflection into the plight of late-modernity.

Take justice for instance. Does a Nietzschean ontology rule out the issue on the grounds that the cry for justice always expresses resentment? Thinking now within the frame of this ontology – rather than within the confines of Nietzsche's own political formulations – one can make a case for the centrality of justice today. For resentment flows from two sources: from rage against a human condition which gives no transcendental purpose to suffering or death; and from institutional arrangements which impose suffering and injury on some for the benefit of others. Late-modern resentment is thus overdetermined, and each of its components deters efforts to deal creatively with the other. Such a double load of resentment fosters the spirit of revenge, and that spirit flows today into relations within and between states.

If the load of civic resentment is destructive and dangerous, if, as could be argued, it even endangers civilization as such, then those who would reduce this danger must struggle against it on two fronts. They would campaign on one front, with Nietzsche, against ontological demands and insistences which exacerbate existential resentment. They would campaign on another front, without Nietzsche, against social practices which intensify resentment by imposing heavy burdens and risks on some for the comfort and benefit of others. Rough equality, where, say, no one has more than three or four times as much income as anyone else and everyone has a hand in defining and coping with the common fate, would not only relieve social causes of resentment; it might also enable equals to combat more overtly the fund of existential resentment which continues to fester among them. It would help to expose the reservoir of existential resentment flowing under the current of civic resentment. Civic equality concentrates reflection – when informed by the right philosophy – into the deepest well of human resentment, enabling everyone and anyone to struggle against the pretense that it flows merely from socially established injustices, enabling anyone and everyone to confront human limits to the mastery of fate.

Such a prescription follows Nietzsche in tracing the deepest well of resentment to rebellion against the ultimate 'senselessness of suffering'; it tracks him too in striving to absorb a portion of resentment into a practice of justice and law; it breaks with him in its egalitarian prescription for justice. Nietzsche's endorsement of the first two points can be heard in the following formulation:

Wherever justice is practiced and maintained one sees a stronger power seeking a means of putting an end to the senseless raging of *ressentiment* among the weaker powers that stand under it . . . partly by substituting for revenge the struggle against the enemies of peace and order, partly by devising and in some cases imposing settlements, partly by elevating certain equivalents for injury into norms to which from then on *ressentiment* is once and for all directed.[40]

But what, then, could one say (still moving broadly within Nietzschean ontology) on behalf of an egalitarian standard of justice? The case would be supported by attending to the conditions of late-modernity, where everyone is entangled intimately in the fate of everyone else; where rage among the dispossessed and rejected can terrorize anyone and everyone even if it is unable to realize positive ends by itself; where power has penetrated more and more thoroughly into life partly in response to the dialectic of revenge engendered by tangled structures of inequality, confinement and exclusion; and where the order of things becomes more fragile and susceptible to deterioration even as civil power becomes more extended. It would also appeal more overtly (than Nietzsche does) to the way in which the struggle between affirmation and resentment is a universal, opening each self potentially to bonds of identification with others who are also implicated in this interior strife.

This meta-sketch of a picture of justice does not establish the conclusion toward which it gestures. Nor could a more detailed presentation do so securely, since, as the Nietzschean critique of nihilism suggests, discursive argumentation is seldom so tight and complete that it reduces opposing perspectives to nullity. Rather it, appeals to one set of assumptions and judgments lodged in common dispositions and concepts (for example, resentment, danger, destruction) while calling into question others to which they are attached. It moves in a (hermeneutic) circle, but it accentuates a particular set of elements often devalued within current circles of thought. It thereby contributes to thinking. By developing these readings of resentment, revenge, discordance and danger, a set of distinctive considerations might be introduced into late-modern discourse, perhaps helping to shift the terms within which established debates about justice, the self, freedom, the common good, politics and the role of the state occur.

Late-modernity is the era in which it is possible to understand both that the late-modern state cannot legitimize itself to the rest of the world unless its form is universalizable, and that the very form assumed by this state today makes it unsusceptible to universalization. It is additionally the time when the late-modern state is tempted to protect itself by a variety of external and internal modes of repression, and when a variety of state and non-state entities possess the capacity to destroy the world. If these four assertions are true, and if they are joined to a philosophy of discordance within concordances, it begins to look as though the competing modern projects of world mastery and attunement to an intrinsic set of purposes in the world place the most advanced modern states today on a self-defeating trajectory. Each of these historical projects demands too much from nature, from the self, from the collectivity or from the world outside the charmed circle of highly modernized states. Certainly Hobbes, Hegel and Marx did not anticipate these points, and if Rousseau anticipated them uncannily through his critique of commercial society, he responded with a solution inapplicable to the late-modern condition.

Perhaps, as I have suggested at several points in this text, late-modernity reveals the need to *relax* the drive to master the world and, thereby, to *relieve* those manifold pressures in the self and defining institutions to domesticate discordance in pursuit of discipline, productivity and order. The twin projects of mastery and attunement look self-destructive from the vantage point of a contemporary perspective which identifies a persistent strand of recalcitrance in human beings and the world to every consummate project of mastery and realization. Each fosters self-loathing against otherness in oneself and rage against those other selves who do no measure 'up' to established standards of production, functionality, normality or self-realization; each spawns too many reactive projects of control or conquest or elimination against the otherness it creates and opposes. It is because neither human beings nor the world mesh neatly with either design that we should attenuate the designer's urge within each of these perspectives. But since the twin drives to mastery and harmonization are installed in modern institutions of production and consumption, legal standards, the relation of the state to its citizens and its economy, the terms of public discourse, the operative standards of selfhood and responsibility, this counter-project must install itself in many places if it is to make a compelling difference anywhere. It is not that points of opposition and resistance to the politics of mastery and attunement are lacking; it is rather that these resistant energies can too readily be absorbed, derailed, erased or defeated as long as they must be drawn into the discourse of normal individuality, restrictive community or state hegemony to be given legitimacy. So perhaps a good place to start is with those theories of pragmatic legitimacy, the normal self, the realized community and the voluntary contract which silently put the squeeze on difference as they loudly pursue a constellation of goods.

Perhaps a reconstituted, radicalized liberalism is needed today; one which reaches into the subject itself rather than taking it as the starting point for reflection; one which challenges the hegemony of economic expansion rather than making it a precondition of liberty; one which treats nature as a locus of difference and resistances essential to life as well as a shelter and set of resources for human use; one which copes politically with the tension between the human need for a common life and the inevitable points of subjugation in any set of common norms; one which relaxes the hegemony of normalization to enable some things to be which its predecessors found to be irrational or perverse or sick; one which restrains the drive to comprehend and cure various forms of otherness by confronting first the way its own contestable standards of normality and realization help to constitute these phenomena; one which measures the legitimacy of its state's foreign policies by the degree to which they foster its ability to co-exist peacefully with the rest of the world; one which idealizes politics over administration, economic rationality or welfare dependency.

This would be a radicalized liberalism, but not in the direction of revolutionary overthrow, socialist abundance or the universalization of the late-modern state. It would be a radical liberalism in its comprehension of the depth and scope of the issues facing life today and in its readiness to dissent militantly from the settled frame in which contemporary issues are debated. It would be a liberal radicalism in its appreciation of the critical temper and its sensiti ˙   to the rights of difference against the weight of mastery and normality. It would be critical in its insistence upon opening issues currently insulated from interrogation. And it would be problematic, not only in its ability to establish itself in the current setting of political debate, but in its initial ability to specify closely its implications for particular practices of law, therapy, gender, race, the ethics of responsibility and relations with other peoples. The case for pursuing this direction thus resides less in its proven ability to inform political conduct and more in the visible ways in which established political alternatives foster a politics of discipline and destructiveness.

Such a perspective would stand to Nietzsche as Marx stood to Hegel: in a relation of antagonistic indebtedness. It would appreciate the reach of Nietzschean thought as well as its sensitivity to the complex relations between resentment and the production of otherness, but it would turn the genealogist of resentment on his head by exploring democratic politics as a medium through which to expose resentment and to encourage the struggle against it. And it would turn periodically to thinkers such as Hobbes, Rousseau, Hegel and Marx to probe more deeply what they reveal and conceal abut the dynamic of the late-modern condition; to locate the myriad ways and means by which the twin drives to mastery and realization have lodged themselves inside modern formations; and to listen to subdued sounds of strife and resistance emanating from these integrated systems of modern thought.

Notes

Chapter 1   The Order of Modernity

1 Friedrich Nietzsche, *The Gay Science,* trans. by Walter Kaufmann (New York: Vintage Books, 1974), n. 125, p. 181.
2 Ibid., n. 125, p. 181.
3 Jolandi Jacobi (ed.), *Paracelsus: Selected Writings,* trans. by Norbert Guterman (New York: Pantheon Books, 1951), p. 21.
4 Emile Male, *Religious Art in France: The Twelfth Century,* trans. by Marthiel Mathews (Princeton: Princeton University Press, 1978), p. 318.
5 Nietzsche, *The Gay Science,* n. 152, p. 196.
6 Ibid., n. 125, p. 182.
7 Friedrich Nietzsche, *The Will to Power,* trans. by Walter Kaufmann and R. J. Hollingdale (New York: Vintage Books, 1968), n. 2, p. 3.
8 Ibid., n. 866, p. 463.
9 Ibid., n. 36, p. 23.
10 Ibid., n. 12, p. 12.

Chapter 2   Hobbes: The Politics of Divine Containment

1 Thomas Hobbes, *Man and Citizen: De Homine and De Cive* (subsequent references to *The Citizen* or *On Man* as appropriate), edited by Bernard Gert (Garden City: Doubleday and Co., 1972), Preface to *The Citizen*, p. 104.
2 Quoted in David Knowles, *The Evolution of Medieval Thought* (New York: Vintage Books, 1962), p. 342.
3 Hobbes, *The Citizen,* ch. 28, p. 374.
4 Ibid., ch. 24, p. 299.
5 Hobbes, *On Man,* ch. 24, p. 73.
6 Hobbes, *The Citizen,* ch. 14, p. 275.
7 Ibid., ch. 12, p. 249.
8 Ibid., ch. 27, p. 368.

9   Ibid., ch. 28, p. 375.
10 Ibid., ch. 4, p. 154.
11 Ibid., ch. 15, p. 293.
12 Ibid., ch. 15, p. 293.
13 Ibid., ch. 15, p. 293.
14 Ibid., ch. 1, p, 110.
15 Ibid., ch. 1, p. 110.
16 Thomas Hobbes, *Leviathan*, edited by Michael Oakeshott (New York: Macmillan, 1962), ch. 8, p. 60.
17 Ibid., ch. 8, p. 61.
18 Ibid., ch. 8, p. 64.
19 Ibid., ch. 14, p. 103.
20 Ibid., ch. 13, p. 100.
21 Hobbes, *The Citizen*, ch. 10, p. 231.
22 Hobbes, *Leviathan*, Review and Conclusion, p. 504.
23 Ibid., ch. 14, p. 104.
24 Ibid., ch. 14, p. 104.
25 Ibid., ch. 15, pp. 118–19.
26 Hobbes, *The Citizen*, ch. 10, p. 231.
27 Ibid., ch. 3, pp. 137–8.
28 Ibid., ch. 13, p. 268.
29 Ibid., ch. 8, p. 199.
30 Hobbes, *Leviathan*, ch. 32, p. 271.
31 David Hume, *Dialogues Concerning Natural Religion*, edited by Henry D. Aiken (New York: Hafner Publishing, 1957), Part I, p. 6. The statement is by Philo.

Chapter 3   Rousseau: Docility Through Citizenship

1   Jean-Jacques Rousseau, *Emile*, trans. by Allan Bloom (New York: Basic Books, 1979), Book 4, p. 321.
2   Ibid., Book 4, p. 323.
3   Ibid., Book 4, p. 332.
4   Jean-Jacques Rousseau, *On the Social Contract: with Geneva Manuscript and Political Economy*, edited by Roger Masters and trans. by Judith Masters (New York: St Martin's Press, 1978), Book 1, p. 46 (subsequently each of the texts in this volume will be cited separately as *The Social Contract, The Geneva Manuscript* and *Political Economy*).
5   Jean-Jacques Rousseau, *Letter to M. d'Alembert on the Theatre*, trans. by Allan Bloom (Ithaca: Cornell University Press, 1960), pp. 12–13.
6   Rousseau, *Emile*, Book 4, p. 285.
7   Ibid., Book 4, p. 291.
8   Ibid., Book 4, p. 295.
9   Ibid., Book 4, p. 290.
10 Ibid., Book 4, p. 300.

11 Ibid., Book 4, pp. 311–12.
12 Rousseau, *Letter to d'Alembert*, p. 11.
13 Rousseau, *Emile*, Book 1, p. 37.
14 Jean-Jacques Rousseau, *The First and Second Discourses: Discourse on the Sciences and Arts and Discourse on the Origin and Foundations of Inequality*, edited by Roger Masters and trans. by Judith Masters (New York: St Martin's Press, 1964), p. 103.
15 Rousseau, *Second Discourse*, p. 102.
16 Ibid., p. 105.
17 Ibid., p. 114.
18 Ibid., p. 116.
19 Ibid., p. 149.
20 Ibid., p. 134.
21 Ibid., p. 135.
22 Ibid., pp. 148–9.
23 Ibid., p. 173.
24 Ibid., p. 159.
25 Ibid., p. 159.
26 Ibid., p. 159.
27 Ibid., p. 173.
28 Rousseau, *Geneva Manuscript*, p. 160.
29 Rousseau, *Essay on Political Economy*, p. 227.
30 Ibid., *Essay on Political Economy*, p. 221.
31 Rousseau, *Geneva Manuscript*, p. 158.
32 Rousseau, *Social Contract*, Book 2, p. 69.
33 Ibid., Book 1, p. 56.
34 Ibid., Book 1, p. 53.
35 Ibid., Book 4, p. 127.
36 Ibid., Book 4, p. 131.
37 Ibid., Book 4, p. 109.

First Interlude: Hobbes, Rousseau and the Marquis de Sade

1 Marquis de Sade, *Philosophy in the Bedroom*, in Richard Seaver and Austryn Wainhouse (trans.), *The Marquis de Sade* (New York: Grove Press, 1965), p. 203.
2 Ibid., pp. 342–3.
3 Ibid., pp. 208–9.
4 Quoted in 'Chronology of Sade' by Paul Dinnage in Simone de Beauvoir, *Must We Burn Sade?* (New York: Peter Nevill Publishing, 1953).
5 Sade, *Philosophy in the Bedroom*, p. 313.
6 Ibid., p. 308.
7 Ibid., p. 304.
8 Ibid., p. 304.
9 Ibid., p. 310.

10   Ibid., p. 316.
11   Ibid., p. 332.
12   Ibid., p. 357.

Chapter 4   Hegel: The Politics of Inclusivity

1   G. W. F. Hegel, *Phenomenology of Spirit*, trans. by A. V. Miller (Oxford: Clarendon Press, 1977), para. 69, p. 42.
2   Ibid., para. 69, p. 43.
3   G. W. F. Hegel, *Lectures on the Philosophy of Religion: Vol. III, The Consummate Religion*, edited by Peter C. Hodgson and trans. by R. F. Brown, P. C. Hodgson and J. M. Stewart (Berkeley: University of California Press, 1985), p. 65.
4   G. W. F. Hegel, *Encyclopedia of the Philosophical Sciences: Part III*, trans. by William Wallace, with *Zusätze*, trans. by A. V. Miller (Oxford: Clarendon Press, 1971), para. 408, p. 123.
5   Ibid., para. 408, p. 123.
6   Ibid., para. 408, p. 124.
7   Ibid., para. 408, p. 139.
8   Hegel, *Phenomenology*, para. 73, p. 46.
9   Ibid., para. 73, p. 46.
10   Ibid., para. 74, p. 47.
11   Ibid., para. 80, p. 51.
12   Ibid., para. 80, p. 51.
13   Ibid., para. 89, pp. 56–7.
14   G. W. F. Hegel, *Reason in History*, trans. by Robert S. Hartman (New York: Liberal Arts Press, 1953), p. 19.
15   Ibid., p. 21.
16   G. W. F. Hegel, *The Philosophy of History*, trans. by J. Sibree (New York: Dover Publications, 1956), p. 253.
17   Ibid., p. 252.
18   Hegel, *Phenomenology*, para. 178, p. 111.
19   Ibid., para. 188, p. 115.
20   Ibid., para. 191, p. 116.
21   Ibid., para. 192, p. 193.
22   Ibid., para. 194, p. 117.
23   Ibid., para. 195. p. 118.
24   Ibid., para. 196, pp. 118–19.
25   Hegel, *Reason in History*, p. 71.
26   Hegel, *Phenomenology*, para. 440, p. 264.
27   Hegel, *Philosophy of History*, p. 253.
28   Sophocles, *Antigone*, in *The Three Theban Plays*, trans. by Robert Eagles (New York: Penguin Books, 1984), p. 62.
29   Ibid., p. 88.
30   Ibid., p. 68.

31 Ibid., p. 82.
32 Ibid., p. 108.
33 Hegel, *Phenomenology*, para. 466, p. 280.
34 Ibid., para. 475, p. 288.
35 Ibid., para. 361, p. 218.
36 Ibid., para. 367, p. 221.
37 Ibid., para. 377, p. 226.
38 Ibid., para. 528, p. 322.
39 Ibid., para. 536, p. 326.
40 Ibid., para. 537, p. 327.
41 Ibid., para. 537, p. 327.
42 Ibid., para. 542, p. 330.
43 Ibid., para. 554, p. 338.
44 Ibid., para. 572, p. 348.
45 Ibid., para. 580, p. 353.
46 Ibid., para. 580, p. 354.
47 Ibid., para. 580, p. 354.
48 Ibid., para. 581, p. 355.
49 Ibid., para. 585. p. 357.
50 Ibid., para. 591, p. 360.
51 Ibid., para. 591, p. 360.
52 Ibid., para. 591, p. 360.
53 Ibid., para. 802, p. 488.
54 Ibid., para. 802, p. 488.
55 Friedrich Nietzsche, *The Will to Power*, trans. by Walter Kaufmann and R. J. Hollingdale (New York: Vintage Books, 1968), n. 1062, p. 546.

Second Interlude: Hegel, Marx and the State

 1 G. W. F. Hegel, *Philosophy of Right*, trans. by T. M. Knox (Oxford: Oxford University Press, 1967), Preface, p. 3.
 2 Ibid., para 71, p. 57.
 3 Ibid., para. 118, p. 81.
 4 Ibid., Addition, para. 116, p. 266.
 5 Ibid., para. 182, pp. 122–3.
 6 Ibid., para 165, p. 114.
 7 Ibid., para, 243, pp. 149–50.
 8 Ibid., para. 244, p. 150.
 9 Ibid., para. 261, p. 161.
10 Ibid., para. 270, p. 165. Translation adjusted slightly.
11 Ibid., para. 162, p. 111.
12 Ibid., Addition, para. 166, p. 263. Italics added.
13 Ibid., para. 325, p. 210.
14 Karl Marx, 'Critical Notes on the "King of Prussia and Social Reform" ' in Loyd East and Kurt Guddat (eds), *Writings of the Young Marx* (New York: Anchor Books, 1967), p. 342.

15 Ibid., p. 342.
16 Ibid., p. 347.
17 Ibid., p. 348.
18 Ibid., p. 348.
19 Ibid., p. 349.
20 Ibid., p. 350.
21 Karl Marx, 'On the Jewish Question' in Robert Tucker (ed.), *The Marx-Engels Reader* (New York: W. W. Norton, 1972), p. 41.
22 Karl Marx, *Das Kapital, Vol I* (New York: International Publishers, 1961), pp. 78–9.
23 In *Politics and Ambiguity* (Madison: University of Wisconsin Press, 1987) I explore, first, how disciplines are extended into new corners of life and, second, how contemporary individualist and communitarian theories tend to obscure together the extent and intensity of this development.
24 Friedrich Nietzsche, *The Will to Power*, trans. by Walter Kaufmann and R. J. Hollingdale (New York: Vintage Books, 1968), n. 419, p. 225.

Chapter 5 Nietzsche: Politics and Homesickness

1 Friedrich Nietzsche, *The Gay Science*, trans. by Walter Kaufmann (New York: Vintage Books, 1974), n. 108, p. 167.
2 Friedrich Nietzsche, *Twilight of the Idols*, trans. by R. J. Hollingdale (New York: Penguin Books, 1968), p. 25.
3 Friedrich Nietzsche, *The Will to Power*, trans. by Walter Kaufmann and R. J. Hollingdale (New York: Vintage Books, 1968), n. 470, p. 262.
4 Nietzsche, *The Gay Science*, n. 377, p. 338.
5 Nietzsche, *Twilight of the Idols*, 40–1. The quotations on the next couple of pages all come from this one-and-a-half-page 'History of an Error.'
6 Nietzsche, *Will to Power*, n. 517, p. 280.
7 Ibid., n. 480, p. 266.
8 Ibid., n. 614, p. 329.
9 Ibid., n. 521, p. 282.
10 Ibid., n. 635, p. 338; n. 480, p. 267; n. 656, p. 346.
11 Quoted in Martin Heidegger, *Nietzsche: Vol II, Eternal Recurrence of the Same*, trans. by David Farrell Krell (San Francisco: Harper and Row, 1984), p. 129.
12 Nietzsche, *Will to Power*, n. 585, p. 317.
13 Friedrich Nietzsche, On the Genealogy of Morals, trans. by Walter Kaufmann and R. J. Hollingdale (New York: Random House, 1969), section 1, p. 15.
14 Nietzsche, *Genealogy of Morals*, section 1, p. 15.
15 Ibid., Second Essay, section 12, p. 76.
16 Ibid., First Essay, section 10, p. 36.
17 Ibid., First Essay, section 13, p. 46.
18 Ibid., First Essay, section 6, p. 33.

19 Ibid., First Essay, section 16, p. 52.
20 Ibid., First Essay, section 14, p. 46. The quotations which follow immediately are from section 14.
21 Ibid., Second Essay, section 2, p. 59.
22 Ibid., Third Essay, section 15, p. 127.
23 Ibid., Third Essay, section 15, p. 128.
24 Ibid., Third Essay, section 16, p. 128.
25 Nietzsche, *Thus Spoke Zarathustra*, trans. by Walter Kaufmann (New York: Penguin Books, 1966), Part II, 'On the Tarantulas,' p. 99.
26 Ibid., p. 100.
27 Ibid., p. 99.
28 Nietzsche, *Genealogy of Morals*, Second Essay, Section 24, p. 95.
29 Ibid., Second Essay, section 24, p. 95.
30 Nietzsche, *Twilight of the Idols*, p. 54.
31 Nietzsche, *The Gay Science*, n. 290, p. 233.
32 Nietzsche, *Will to Power*, n. 995, p. 518.
33 Nietzsche, *The Gay Science*, n. 290, p. 233.
34 Nietzsche, *Thus Spoke Zarathustra*, 'On Redemption,' p. 137.
35 Ibid., pp. 137–8.
36 Nietzsche, *The Gay Science*, n. 304, p. 244.
37 Nietzsche, *The Wanderer and His Shadow*, in Walter Kaufmann (ed. and trans.), *The Portable Nietzsche* (New York: Viking Press, 1954), pp. 71–2.
38 Ibid., p. 72.
39 Nietzsche, *The Gay Science*, Book 1, n. 2, pp. 76–7.
40 Nietzsche, *Genealogy of Morals*, Book 2, section 11, p. 75.

Bibliography

Listed here are a few texts about modernity as well as some secondary studies of Hobbes, Rousseau, Hegel and Nietzsche. Each of them helped me to clarify my thinking on the theorists and issues explored in this text either by influencing me affirmatively or by articulating an alternative stance which challenged me.

Is the idea of 'modernity' or 'the modern age' too broad and porous to serve as a medium through which to become more reflective about the parameters within which contemporary debates typically proceed? Since the notion has entered into the consciousness of many moderns, it certainly carries some weight. And it may be that the most dangerous issues facing human life today cannot be engaged unless thought is lifted to the level of modernity itself. Hans Blumenberg in *The Legitimacy of the Modern Age* (Cambridge, Mass.: MIT Press, 1983) claims that the problem of the legitimacy of this age is 'latent in the modern age's claim to carry out a radical break with tradition, and in the incongruity between this claim and the reality of history, which can never begin entirely anew' (p. 116). This is the most ambitious and penetrating study of the self-consciousness of modernity. It claims that the key is to be found in the modern consolidation of the principle of self-assertion, a principle which finds many competing renderings but which also frames contending orientations to nature, self, the past and the future available to modernity. Blumenberg's text is presented as a history of lived ontologies, striving to show how the self-defeat of earlier philosophies established a field for modern theories to 'reoccupy,' and trying to convince us that we should not try to answer questions posed by philosophies which were unable to sustain themselves. His is a rich and fascinating defense of modernity against those doctrines which carry a nostalgia for a world we have lost. And he reveals how and why it is not necessary to date the beginning of the modern age in order to discuss its characteristics once it became consolidated. The text does not, however, explore possible self-defeating tendencies lodged in the trajectory of late-modern states.

Several texts by Michel Foucault rectify (or perhaps over-rectify) this imbalance. *The Order of Things* (London: Tavistock Publications, 1970) is pitched at the same level as Blumenberg's study. Foucault's discussion of the 'Prose of the World,' preceding the modern era, demarcates a field of discourse which did not exhaust the western world prior to modernity; but it does delineate a mode which became disabled by modern terms of discourse as they contended and competed on a different terrain. This early Foucaultian text emphasizes breaks and discontinuities more dramatically than his later work. It also, in 'Man and His Doubles' and 'The Human Sciences,' exposes instabilities and ruptures within modern modes of discourse which disturb every attempt to establish the hegemony of a single theory securely. The 'problem of the subject' is constantly under examination in this text. Foucault's studies of the extremities of the social order and the formations of otherness established there provides another window into modern life. *Madness and Civilization* (New York: Vintage Books, 1965), *Discipline and Punish* (New York: Pantheon, 1970), and *The History of Sexuality*, Vol. I (New York: Vintage Books. 1980) examine the forms of otherness produced and subjugated by the most cherished modern achievements. That Foucault's genealogies seek to define dangerous possibilities in the historical trajectory of modernity is brought out in chapter 5 of *The History of Sexuality* when he asserts that 'a society's "threshold of modernity" has been reached when the life of the species is wagered on its own political strategies. For millennia, man remained what he was for Aristotle: a living animal with the additional capacity for a political existence; modern man is the animal whose politics places his existence as a living being in question' (p. 143). The essay 'What is Enlightenment?' in Paul Rabinow (ed.), *The Foucault Reader* (New York: Pantheon, 1984), continues in this vein, probing the 'attitudes' which express the modern temper.

Foucault's texts on modernity are best read with and against those by Heidegger. The most salient text here is *The Question Concerning Technology* (New York: Harper and Row, 1977). Heidegger's exploration of modern 'enframing' and the conversion of the world into a 'standing reserve' (which both conceals other ways of being and conceals its concealment) is fundamental for later thought on these issues. And 'The Age of the World Picture,' which includes an account of the frame within which the modern debate between individualist and collectivist theories of politics occurs, anticipates a whole series of recent explorations.

Several other texts serve as useful adjuncts or counterpoints here. Charles Taylor, *Philosophical Papers*, Vols I and II (Cambridge: Cambridge University Press, 1985); Jonathan Arac, *Post-Modernism and Politics* (Minneapolis: University of Minnesota Press, 1986); Richard Rorty, *Philosophy and the Mirror of Nature* (Princeton: Princeton University Press, 1979); Tzvetan Todorov, *The Conquest of America* (New York: Harper and Row, 1982) – all of these are pertinent texts. Each responds distinctively to the issue of otherness in modern life. Todorov, for instance, finds that 'at the same time that it was tending to obliterate the strangeness of the eternal other, Western Civilization found an interior other' (p. 248). And he seeks to formulate an orientation which transcends those embodied in the European/American project to conquer or convert every new exterior and interior world it encountered: 'we want equality without its compelling us to accept identity; but also difference without degenerating into superiority/inferiority' (p. 249). My own thoughts about the late-modern condition and appropriate responses to it, inserted into the interludes and the chapter endings of this text, are developed further in *Politics and Ambiguity* (Madison: University of Wisconsin Press, 1987). There I try to show how an ontology of discordance within concordance can illuminate features of the contemporary condition, and I enunciate conceptions of democracy, selfhood, authority and politics congruent with this orientation.

There are innumerable secondary studies of Hobbes. I have profited from John Pocock's 'Time, History, and Eschatology in the Thought of Thomas Hobbes,' in *Politics, Language, and Time* (New York: Atheneum, 1973); Pocock brilliantly examines parallels and divergencies between the first and last Parts of *Leviathan*. Sheldon Wolin's *Politics and Vision* (Boston: Little, Brown and Co., 1960) is a masterful study of political thought, folding a sustained interpretation of the modern condition into a close study of classic texts of political theory. The chapter on Hobbes is a model of this productive ambiguity in political thinking, bringing out the rule-bound character of Hobbesian sovereignty, its fragility and its subjugation of politics, and meditating on the implications of this model of understanding for contemporary politics. Richard Peters (ed.), *Hobbes and Rousseau* (New York: Anchor Books, 1972) contains excellent essays on Hobbes. W. H. Greenleaf summarizes alternative readings of Hobbes; Quentin Skinner examines the context of Hobbes' theory of obligation; K. R. Minogue criticizes and transcends theories which interpret Hobbes to advance a fixed theory of human nature; and R. W. Hepburn examines Hobbes on the 'knowledge of God.' Hepburn concludes that Hobbes's concept of God 'splits into two irreconcilable parts, the one transcendent to the point of sheer incomprehensibility;

and the other involving God too closely with nature, as part of nature itself' (p. 101). A series of essays in Ralph Ross, Herbert W. Schneider and Theodore Waldman (eds), *Thomas Hobbes in His Time* (Minneapolis: University of Minnesota Press, 1974) explores the Hobbesian conceptions of self, nature, God and piety in very helpful ways. Finally, a new text by David Johnston, *The Rhetoric of Leviathan* (Princeton: Princeton University Press, 1986), while it appeared too late to be taken into account in this study, seems to me to coalesce in some ways with the reading given here.

Rousseau is perhaps a paradigm of the thinker who cannot be exhausted by a single interpretation. I have, for example, under-emphasized Rousseau's account of the self-defeating character of commercial development and ignored his attempt to prescribe modest changes in a polity unsuited for a politics of the general will. Bertrand de Jouvenel, in 'Jean Jacques Rousscau,' in Isaac Kramnick (ed.), *Essays in the History of Political Thought* (Englewood Cliffs: Prentice Hall, 1969), fills the first absence in an admirable way. Three essays in *Political Theory* (November, 1985) explore Rousseau's theory of manners and passion in insightful ways. Benjamin Barber in 'How Swiss is Rousseau?' examines the rusticity of 'Rousseau the exile, Rousseau the walker, Rousseau the recluse, Rousseau the botanist, Rousseau the refugee, Rousseau the dreamer (p. 485).' Charles Ellison, in 'Rousseau and the Modern City' explores the conflict between manners in the city and the country as Rousseau understands it, probing his account of how city manners in dress and speech foster corruption of the self. And Mary Nichols, in 'Rousseau's Novel Education in the *Emile*,' examines Rousseau as an educator of the emotions. She rejects any equivalence between the natural religion of the Savoyard Vicar and Rousseau's own position. While this seems right, she goes too far in my view in her minimilization of the role of faith in Rousseau's theory, at least as it applies to the dream of the general will. Roger D. Masters, *The Political Philosophy of Rousseau* (Princeton: Princeton Unversity Press, 1968), provides a thorough and reflective overview of the corpus of Rousseau's work; Judith Shklar, *Men and Citizens: A Study of Rousseau's Social Theory* (Cambridge: Cambridge University Press, 1969), reveals a variety of ambivalent tendencies in Rousseau's thought, refusing to allow it to fall neatly into one of the categories prepared for it in contemporary thought; and Allan Bloom's Introduction to his own translation of *Emile* (New York: Basic Books, 1979), brings out the strategic role sexuality plays in Rousseau's thinking and the subtlety of his understanding of the emotional life. Perhaps Barber's quotation from *The Reveries* best captures the element of ambivalence toward society in Rousseau's texts: 'As soon as I feel the yoke of necessity or of men, I grow rebellious, or rather, I grow recalcitrant (p. 495).' The 'I' here can be generalized to include others who experience disalignment between nature and society without being able to eliminate either from the life of the self; and it expresses a strand in Rousseau's thought which becomes thematized more dramatically in late-twentieth-century French thought.

Hegel: to be American, I suppose, is to read him as a collective enterprise. That has certainly been true in my case; I find myself consulting a variety of secondary texts each time I make a move in my own reading. Charles Taylor's *Hegel* (Cambridge: Cambridge University Press, 1975), serves as a valuable touchstone in many ways. First, it places Hegel in the context of a broader field of reflection at the end of the Enlightenment. Second, it links central themes in Hegel's work to a variety of ethical, political and epistemic issues which have plagued theorists and philosophers in the Anglo-American tradition. Third, it treats the engagement with Hegel as an occasion to think about the contours and prospects of life in late-modernity. Taylor agrees that Hegel went 'seriously wrong in his characterization of the coming age.' And he finds it incredible today to see 'history as the unfolding of spirit' or 'nature as the emanation of spirit' (pp. 543 and 545). But Taylor then tries to resurrect as much of Hegel as possible after the demise of spirit and absolute knowledge. 'We need a notion of a bent in our situation which we can either endorse or reject, re-interpret or distort' (p. 564). Much of my study can be taken as an endorsement of Taylor's reading of Hegel and a contestation of his response to the demise of Hegelianism.

There are several other studies of significance here: Richard Norman, *Hegel's Phenomenology* (London: Sussex University Press, 1976), is more introductory in character. It also mediates between Hegelian language and the terms of analytic philosophy, and its discussion of the dilemma of epistemology is very lucid. Jean Hippolite, *Genesis and Structure of Hegel's Phenomenology of Spirit* (Evanston: Northwestern University Press, 1974) provides a dense and rewarding reading of the text. Quentin Lauer, *Hegel's Concept of God* (Albany: State University of New York Press, 1982) elaborates and defends Hegel's attempt to vindicate a God which humans could have access to, exploring the mediations between finite human beings and an infinite being. George Kelly, *Hegel's Retreat from Eleusis* (Princeton: Princeton University Press, 1978) examines, among other things, the changing relation of Hegel to the Greek ideal of community and Hegel's account of America as the world of 'civil society.' Jane Bennett, *Unthinking Faith and Enlightenment* (New York: New York University Press, 1987), takes Hegel's account of the dialectic of faith and enlightenment as a point of departure to explain a series of contemporary debates. She then develops a 'post-Hegelian perspective' which enables thought to break the impasse prepared for it when it oscillates between these polarities or strives to transcend them in Hegelian terms. Michael Allen Gillespie in *Hegel, Heidegger, and the Ground of History* (Chicago: University of Chicago Press, 1984), provides excellent accounts both of Hegel's reading of absolute knowledge and Heidegger's attempt to reopen the question of being by disturbing each fixed answer to it (including Hegel's) in the history of western metaphysics. Since we have barely scratched Hegel's account of absolute knowledge in this text, I will let Gillespie state the issue: 'The crucial . . . question . . . is whether the absolute as the final synthesis of freedom and nature, of the subjective and the objective, of the noumenal and the phenomenal is itself rational and comprehensible . . . Absolute knowledge, however, rests upon absolute negativity, upon the negation of negation . . . The highest ground thus seems to be a rather mysterious tautology that consequently serves as the first principle or premise of Hegel's thought (pp. 113–14).' In more prosaic terms, the ground of the Hegelian system rests upon faith.

Martin Heidegger has informed my reading of Nietzsche, though I think he often subtracts the 'gentle' dimension from Nietzsche's thought and appropriates it for his own position. The most important volume here is *Nietzsche: Nihilism*, Vol. IV (San Francisco: Harper and Row, 1982). Heidegger accuses Nietzsche of repudiating one dimension of subjectivity (the subject as a unified center of will) and accentuating another (the human as the creator of knowledge and mastery). 'The securing of . . . absolute dominion over the entire earth is the secret goad that prods modern man again and again to new resurgences (p. 99).' Yes, but Nietzsche is a thinker who at once reveals the manifold expressions of this tendency, consummates one of its versions in a dominant tendency of his thought, and inspires a contemporary re-evaluation of it through other dimensions of his thought. Volumes I and II present more appreciative readings of Nietzsche's thought, with *The Will to Power as Art* (San Francisco: Harper and Row, 1982) providing a somewhat different reading of 'The History of an Error' to that presented in this text and *The Eternal Recurrence of the Same* (San Francisco: Harper and Row, 1984) exploring the meaning and status of this most mysterious dimension in Nietzsche's thought. Is eternal recurrence actually a 'doctrine' (contravening Nietzsche's strictures against the possibility of such a total view) or is it a thought which enables those who think it to rethink the status of any metaphysical doctrine which presents itself to be obvious, knowable or necessary?

A few other studies of Nietzsche are particularly relevant to political theory. Tracy Strong in *Friedrich Nietzsche and the Politics of Transfiguration*

(Berkeley: University of California Press, 1975), understood the relevance of Nietzsche to perplexing questions in political theory well before others of his own generation did. He clarifies many dimensions of Nietzsche's work and thinks about a political position which could draw upon it without lapsing into a renewal of aristocraticism. Alexander Nehamas in *Nietzsche; Life as Literature* (Cambridge, Mass.: Harvard University Press, 1985) reads Nietzsche as one who understood that 'every attempt to escape "metaphysics," precisely because of the circle I have been discussing, always runs the risk of being taken as, and therefore of being, a part of metaphysics in its own right' (p. 133). Jacques Derrida in *Spurs/Éperons* (Chicago: University of Chicago Press, 1979) and David Farrell Krell in *Postponements: Women, Sensuality and Death in Nietzsche* (Bloomington: Indiana University Press, 1986) ponder the category 'woman' in Nietzsche's texts and the ambiguous relation Nietzsche himself bears to it. Derrida also offers a criticism of Heidegger's reading of Nietzsche. I had the opportunity to read Mark Warren, *Nietzsche and Political Thought* (Cambridge, Mass.: MIT Press, forthcoming) after this study was completed. It is pertinent to the perspective developed here. Warren argues that the political metaphors which populate Nietzsche's philosophical thought do not translate neatly or necessarily into a political doctrine. He agrees that the philosophical stance creates a space which excludes teleological theories while providing room for several other positions to be defined and debated, and he thinks about alternatives within this space even while acknowledging that some of the possibilities go against Nietzsche's own political intentions. Those who insist that this is impossible might ponder the case of Michel Foucault, who is best and most briefly characterized as a Left-Nietzschean.

Index